MW01503073

A MEANDER IN MENORCA

David M. Addison

Bloomington, IN Milton Keynes, UK

First published by AuthorHouse 2/21/2006

ISBN: 1-4208-9615-6 (sc)

Printed in the United States of America
Bloomington, Indiana

This book is printed on acid-free paper.

By the Same Author

AN ITALIAN JOURNEY

For Fiona the Fair

who is not, in any way, shape or form, the same as
Iona the Irascible.

The lady doth protest too much, methinks.

Shakespeare.
Macbeth Act 3 Scene 2

Table of Contents

1. There May Be Trouble Ahead

Our daughter, Hélène, is driving us to the airport in my old Rover which I gave her when I bought the Jaguar. It's been in the wars since I handed over the keys. Since I saw it last, it's had a close encounter with a tree and then a wall (which both apparently just leapt out at her without warning) but the only water it has seen has been rainwater which has failed to wash off months of accumulated dirt. Gone is that gleaming polished skin and with it, much of its good looks. Now, like a fading beauty, old before her time, her skin has lost its lustre and she looks jaded, past her prime.

The inside isn't looking too good either. Beside me, in the back seat, there's discarded crisp packets and empty Irn Bru and Coke bottles, plus another which is half full, two months past its sell-by date which shows you just how long it's been rattling around in here, and in addition, sweets and chocolate wrappers are carpeting the floor. It is, you might say, a bit untidy, not to say a health hazard but I don't rubbish Hélène's car-keeping skills because I am grateful for the lift.

She can talk all right, can La Belle Hélène, but she gets it less from her mother and more from her maternal grandmother, whom I believe, was single handedly responsible for the vast number of donkeys in Essex (where she was brought up), being reduced from four legs to forelegs since she had talked their hind legs off. Right now she is telling us about her new flat. The problem is that she needs hands to describe it to us which means that she periodically

1

has only one hand on the wheel, and alarmingly, on one occasion, none at all, her narrative thread, unfortunately, having coincided with her threading her way through a narrow passage with cars parked on either side. And still I say nothing.

And there's the slight matter of her skin. She is worried about that all right, even if she doesn't care for the appearance of her car. From my perspective, I can see why she is worried – there is a chain of volcanic activity on her chin. One cone of Etna proportions, capped with a juicy yellow head, is right for the squeezing. La Belle Hélène flips down the visor so she can view the damage. She contemplates bursting it now, splatting its contents against the mirror but decides against it; she'll save it for later. It's tempting now but by the time she gets back from the airport, it may have turned fatter and be much more satisfying to squeeze. Besides, she can devote more loving care and attention to it, nipping it between the nails of the index fingers of each hand.

All that's bad, but it's not the worst. There is some infernal noise coming from the tape deck. When I had this car, it played nice music, like Sounds of the Sixties and violin concertos, Mendelssohn's, Tchaikovsky's and my favourite, Max Bruch's. Now it's playing some hellish cacophony and I can be silent no longer. I may not have screamed at the danger to my life by her driving; I may not have declaimed about the danger to my health from the rubbish in the car; I may not have protested at the puncturing of the plooks – all that have I resisted - but this din! No, I really cannot tolerate it any longer. It's driving me barmy and I can't even think while it is going on and I bet the strange thing is that Hélène isn't even aware that it is on. If there's one thing I really cannot stand, it is people who have an execrable taste in music stuffing it down your ears, particularly when they are shutting it out of their own.

"What a bloody din!"

Not the most tactful way to put it, I have to admit, but I am driven to distraction. Anyway it has the desired effect and Hélène switches it off. Oh, the relief! How wonderful to be able to think again! Oh, that beautiful silence! Only it isn't. La-Belle-Dame-Sans-Merci is taking me to task.

"Stop moaning! It's very nice of Hélène to take us to the airport in the first place."

She may say that, but I bet she is glad that I said it first and she can enjoy Hélène's ceaseless chatter without the background clatter. It's one of my few uses – taking the blame.

Hélène's phone bleeps. Someone has sent her a text. She reads it but does not reply, thank God. In this respect at least, she is sticking to the letter of the law by not sending letters through the ether as she drives.

Without further incident, we come to a roundabout. We need the first exit which will take us on the motorway to Edinburgh, but Hélène is talking so much she misses the turn. I expect she's on autopilot. She used to have a boyfriend who lived in Linlithgow, which is the second exit, and she was probably heading there without thinking about it. Iona and I protest in unison. I know we are both thinking of the nightmare time when we were going to New Zealand and the taxi driver took us on the motorway to Glasgow instead of Edinburgh and consequently we missed our flight.

"I'm sorry! I'm sorry!"

Methinks La Belle Hélène doth protest too much. She sounds stressed. I expect her plooks are getting to her. She's just got a new boyfriend and it's so early in their relationship that I expect she thinks if she doesn't get rid of these spots, he may spot someone else. No good telling her that she's so pretty she'd knock the spots off all the other rivals, even if she can't knock them off her own face. She wouldn't believe me though as everyone says she looks just like me. That worried her as a child, to think that her delicate nose, yet to form its own personality, might end up being spread right across her face, like mine, and even worse, she would end up growing "pristles" as she called them, on those downy cheeks.

It's just a matter of moments to swing round the roundabout once more and we are on our way to the airport at a steady 85mph, except when we are going at 90 and the car is on a steady course too, even although it is being guided for the most part by one hand. I say nothing, but I bet Iona did not include this rate of progress in her calculations. She will have left a safety margin in case of the unforeseen, such as a flat battery which is what happened to us on our last trip, to Skye, but I bet she will not have imagined we would be travelling flat out like a bat out of hell. We have had no hold ups and have left on time, so we are going to be hellish early at the airport and that *is* hell. Two hours before departure is plenty long enough already without adding to it. Iona would rather be dead early for things and doesn't mind hanging about, whilst I prefer the excitement of just getting there on time. It makes life more interesting.

We are there in loads of time right enough. We kiss Hélène good-bye and make our way into the terminal building. What's gone wrong? It is a trouble-free arrival and check-in. Third time lucky. After the flight to New Zealand fiasco, the next time we flew, we were involved in a BA strike, a mere couple of months ago, when we were supposed to be going to Naples and only got there by paying for another flight from another airline. BA did compensate us, I have to hand it to them, but of course, we did not know that at the time. You just don't know what trouble may be ahead when you go on holiday, but I've come to expect it.

In the queue for checking in, there are children to the left of us, children to the right of us, children ahead of us and children behind us. No matter which way you turn, there are bloody kids. That's the snag of being teachers – you *have* to go in the school holidays and so do they, so you never get away from them. It'll be nice when Iona joins the ranks of the retired like me and we can go away when they do not - and stay at home when they go away.

Our luggage, unlike my heart at the sight of all these children, is light – 16 and 15 kilos respectively and we are allowed 20, so that's 9 kilos of weight allowance for bringing back some cheap Spanish gin and brandy. Now, that *does* lighten my heart. That's the one good thing about the EU – the only good thing as far as I can see - you can take back as much cheap booze as you can carry - (and your wife will let you).

Apart from the terminal boredom, the main problem about arriving early at the airport is that it leaves you plenty of time to spend money. Well, I don't, but I know someone who does. First thing on the agenda is coffee. I'm married to a caffeine addict.

I grudge the prices they charge at airports for food and drink. Two mocha coffees and a toasted cheese and ham *panino* - £6:39. We're only having one between us so we still have some money, fortunately, to spend on the rest of the holiday. Iona goes off to find a table whilst I wait to be served. The assistant is a somnambulist, going about his work with the speedy enthusiasm of someone about to attend his own execution. Of course, he may well have been up since the crack of dawn – to me a strange twilight world inhabited by shadowy figures as in some parallel universe, for it is not a time of day of which I normally have much experience. If that's the case, he's quite entitled to be walking as in a dream as he must be near the end of a twelve hour shift.

After I'm served eventually, Iona is nowhere to be seen, and I wander up to the left before I realise that I'm in the smokers' zone before I head back towards the other end.

She might have kept a lookout for me. The *panino* is on the colder side of warm but it has nothing to do with the time wasted looking for Iona; it was cold before I started out. I can't be bothered going to complain. It's only a couple of mouthfuls and I couldn't bear to watch Speedy Gonzales again.

There's still plenty of time to waste, unfortunately, so we gravitate naturally towards the bookshop. They have a special offer – three books for the price of two – but it still comes to £15:98.

"Are you sure you took one off?" I ask the assistant. Iona blushes. She thinks I am being sarcastic and perhaps so does the assistant too as she only gives one of those wan smiles that people do when they're not sure if something is merely extremely humourless and in bad taste or said with deadly serious intent. Well Iona can carry them all the way to Menorca and back, even if I am allowed to pick the "free" book. I suppose they could be useful if it rains, but it's not likely to do that.

On the way through security to the departure lounge, I am stopped whilst a guard frisks me for weapons and bombs, even although I have not made a bleep. My hip flask is in my hand luggage. Maybe that's why they stopped me.

"You must look suspicious," says Iona, who was not stopped and who is waiting for me.

"You may think that," I reply, "but I think he fancies me. Did you see where he put his hands? Unless he thought that was a pistol I had in my Y fronts of course."

"Shut up! People will hear you!" La-Belle-Dame-Sans-Merci is affronted. Knowing perfectly well I wear boxers, I expect that is why she is embarrassed - to think people might think that I am so far behind the fashion that I still wear Y's.

6

At the departure gate, once we get there, once Iona finds where she has put the boarding passes in her bag which has more zips than Johnny Rotten's trousers, we find the place is swarming with kids – not a good sign. I bet they are all going on my plane. And here's another bad sign - the blonde with the black roots and dark lipstick with a chain belt from which are dangling hundreds of charms is in charge of three boisterous boys. Charming I don't think. She doesn't seem to have a man with her – probably a single parent, but she does have something else with her, and this is what worries me – a ghetto blaster.

"I hope she isn't going where we are going," I say to Iona, for, as you may have already gathered, if there is one thing that could be calculated to ruin my holiday, it is listening to other people blasting the air waves with their fiendish brand of "music". We had experienced this on our last holiday in Sorrento. It had made sitting on the balcony having an apéritif or *digestif* impossible. But although I say it, I do not really believe it will happen. It's not that I'm an optimist. I think that's fatal, but statistically speaking, even if she were on our flight, out of all the people in the entire aircraft, the odds are she will not be going to our resort.

From time to time, even in this confined space, the boys hurl themselves at each other like medieval jousters and roll about on the floor, and over people's legs, an activity which seems to escape the attention of the fond mother completely, however. God preserve us! I sincerely hope they are not going where we're going. Of all the kids milling about here, these look the wildest.

It's time to board. To my disappointment, I see that Ghetto Blaster Woman and The Wild Bunch are also going to Menorca. Still, it's quite a big place, relatively speaking, and at least the kids won't be able to charge about the plane as if they were re-enacting *The Charge of the Light Brigade*.

We're with a Spanish airline which I've never heard of before. Our seats are near the back. As usual, I have the window seat so I can look out, but more importantly, so I can use my hip flask with less fear of detection. The prices of the mixers are bad enough without paying for the alcohol as well.

We're hardly installed in our confined space, when Iona wrinkles up her nose. I can't smell anything, the result I believe, of having spent too many hours in a sauna on a mini cruise from Newcastle to Esbjerg.

"It smells like a toilet!" she says under her breath.

If that's the case, I'm glad I can't smell it. I hope she doesn't think it's me.

"*Dos tonicas, por favor.*" I am showing off to the steward as he comes round with the drinks trolley. I don't even know if it's proper Spanish. I have been so used to speaking pidgin Italian recently, it certainly sounds strange to me, so God knows what it sounds like to the steward.

He asks me something and I am hoist with my own petard.

"*Que?*" is all I can think to say, like Manuel out of *Fawlty Towers.*

Iona, who has got Standard Grade Spanish, comes to the rescue. "*Sin azúcar, si. Si, con limone.*"

Ah, so that was what it was about – slim line and lemon. That'll teach me to show off like that. He asks me in English if I want to pay in euros or pounds. £1:60! Unbelievable! For those little tins! You can get a litre bottle for less than that in the supermarket. God knows what it would have cost if I had been buying the bloody gin as well.

I have to wait until the stewards have disappeared down the aisle a safe distance before I can fish out the gin but they are taking ages and it looks suspicious just sitting there with the unopened cans on the tray, so in the end I pour the tonic in first. Perhaps there was an air bubble in the hip flask but anyway the gin came out with a rush and to my horror, I am powerless to do anything but watch as it overflows the plastic glass, slops out onto the table and drains onto my trousers where it leaves a spreading dark stain which fortunately no one can see at the moment and which I hope will have dried in before I have to stand up, but it has released the pungent scent of juniper berries and it seems to me, the whole cabin is so redolent of it that at any moment now the cabin stewards must come to investigate.

But they don't and my crime remains undiscovered, and the only stain is that on my trousers, not on my character and at least it does cover up the toilet smell and should anyone see it, they are unlikely to connect the two, though perhaps on reflection, I might prefer it if they did discover the stain was gin.

The meal is turkey salad with *fusilli*. There is some meat in there somewhere and I'm not fussy about *fusilli*. Neither is Iona's neighbour apparently, for he has left most of his, though he and I both have second cups of coffee, even if the milk is powdered, out of bendy cups which challenge you not to spill the contents on your lap and provide the dry cleaners with a challenging mixture of stains. He's very friendly, the neighbour, chatting to Iona as if they had known each other for years, but when he breaks off the conversation to do a bit of reading, Iona looks over to me and makes a face. She's staring fixedly at my oxters then like a cuckoo clock, making her eyes go to the right, indicating that it is the neighbour's, not mine, to which she's referring. Well thank God for that! But could this really be the cause of the toilet smell?

A few minutes later, she screws up her face and turns it towards me as if she were experiencing an excruciating pain. I look past her to her friendly fellow passenger on her right, who puzzled by some conundrum in his crossword, is scratching his head and thus allowing the noxious fumes to escape the confines of his pits. Poor Iona! Fortunately for her, she has acquired the skill of blocking off her nose, but still retaining the capacity to breathe. I imagine she has gone into that mode now.

Nor is that the end of her troubles. There's a small kid behind her, squirming around, whose little legs must be sticking straight out and are pressing against the back of her seat, giving her a kick in the back with irritating irregularity. The joys of air travel. If you're not being gassed to death first, you're being kicked to death. It brings a whole new meaning to Christ's dictum to *suffer the little children.*

Ghetto Blaster Woman's youngest child, about 5 or 6, and five or six rows in front of us, is standing on the seat and pinging the button to summon the stewardess. The mother's solution is to raise a languid arm and switch it off again… and off again…and off again…It's good to see that she may be a single parent but she can single-handedly cope with keeping him under control.

Iona's neighbour sneezes, and there is a strange unpleasant smell coming, I would say from the seat in front. Bloody hell! Flying really *is* dangerous. The way that they recycle the air in these planes, you have every chance of picking up something which is hazardous to your health.

At last, not before time, we are beginning our descent. It is 9:15, 10:15 Spanish time and those lights below I take to be the lights of Barcelona. It would be nice if they told you these things when you are flying over sites of geographical interest, even if you can't see them, and let's face it, most people can't. But it would still be nice to know. I like those planes where they have a little plane showing you the flight path, and where you are, though some of the names are obscure. Well they are to me, where there are as many as seven seas I've never heard of before.

As we fly even lower, kids start screaming, presumably at the change in motion. Maybe they think we are about to crash as flying is not an experience I imagine they are familiar with and having said that, it's not the smoothest landing I've ever had. The plane bounces. Iona and I look at each other possibly for the last time. It bounces again; the kids scream even louder and as we begin to slow down and stop bouncing, some people break into spontaneous applause. I think that's a mistake: *Don't do that for God's sake, he'll think you'll like it or that he's good at it!*

Because we are at the back of the plane and they have opened both front and rear exits, we are amongst the first off the plane. If death is the Great Leveller, airports are the great levellers of life. We have to wait in the transfer bus which takes us to the terminal building until it is full. At least we can get a seat - as if we had not had enough of sitting down in one place for hours already, but it's better than the sardine crush which the standing people have to endure, though not for long, for less than a minute in the bus at a walking pace and we are there. Why we couldn't just walk instead I don't know, but we could have been there before the bus if we'd been allowed to go under our own steam, but it doesn't matter as that's what a package tour means. You and your fellow travellers are forced into an unnaturally symbiotic relationship and no one goes anywhere until you all go.

In the entrance hall, I see a native from my own home town. It's amazing how small the world is. You come to Menorca and the first person you see practically, is someone you know, though it would be more remarkable if this happened at a concert in Katmandu. He's quite famous, or used to be in the days when he introduced a sports programme on the telly. He knows me slightly too, from the days when I used to be a thespian and he was an adjudicator but he's not focused on me. He has a haunted, stressed sort of look in his eyes. Airports are good at doing that to people too. Presumably we have been on the same flight and he'll never know that I was on it too. Well, I never! Isn't that remarkable!

I leave Iona to watch for the luggage on the conveyer, that other great leveller of those that would be first to leave the airport and begin the holiday. The gods often play tricks on you by sending up one bag early and you think you'll soon be on your way, but the other one never comes till the belt is practically empty. I am off to the pabby, (which is my childhood word for the toilet and which I'm trying to introduce into the language). I had not gone on the flight, preferring not to use aircraft toilets but I was afraid mainly, after my accident with the gin, that on this plane from Spain, it would be on the stain that the looks would rain, as Eliza Dolittle might have said.

I like to go into the cubicles for privacy. Sometimes standing next to other men puts me off and I can't go, even if I need to. I think I'm nervous that my neighbour will look across and down at me and start to laugh. Also, if you are in a cubicle, you can mop up any nasty drips with pabby paper, which I think is more efficient than the shake-the-last-drip-off method favoured by most of my sex, who fortunately don't agree with me or we'd be in the same situation as women and having to queue endlessly to pee. Besides it's much more hygienic as the gods have always got one more drip up their sleeve when you think you've shaken the last one off.

There is a little voice coming from the cubicle next door.

"I did a very big one daddy!"

"Yes, that was a very good little girl!"

My God! A female intruder in the men's toilets! Are there no jobs from which modern fathers are immune?

To my surprise, when I rejoin the throng in the baggage reclaim, Iona is all packed up on the trolley and we are ready to roll. The rep tells us where to go. We have to look for bus T 28. I can't help noticing hers. It looks more like a 38 D to me.

We find it easily enough. The bus driver checks us off on a list and tells us to put our luggage in the right hand side of the hold.

I am surprised to see there are two young women on the bus already, sitting at the front, as we had been out of the baggage reclaim in record time and hadn't seen these two ahead of us. Not only that, but they are sitting there as if they'd been sitting there for some time. We sit at the other side of the passage in the second row of seats as there is a pile of envelopes occupying it. That will be the rep's seat. All we can do now is sit and wait. It does not matter if you're the first or the last; we all leave at the same time.

Damn, here comes Ghetto Blaster Woman and The Wild Bunch. Well, the options are certainly narrowing down. The next test will be to see if their luggage goes into the right or the left... I knew it! The right, and I am left feeling afraid, very afraid.

She sits down on the pavement to have a fag. It's probably not her first since we landed. The kids have spotted a drinks vending machine and pester her for money, before oblivious of all vehicular and pedestrian traffic, they run, whooping, over to it as if their lives depended on it. They will be suffering from E-factor deficiency. This should soon get them hyper again but they are experiencing some difficulty it seems, as the two youngest are banging it with their fists whilst the oldest is giving it a good kicking. At last they get it to cough up whilst mother, on the kerb, has a good cough herself.

The bus is gradually filling up now. A woman comes on board and spots the pile of envelopes. "It's got our name on it," she remarks to her husband who is behind her, and she lifts the whole pile of envelopes and moves on down the passage. Iona and I look at each other aghast. So do the young women across the passage. They begin a consultation then the one on the outside seat gets up and follows her.

"Could I have those back, please? They are the instructions for everybody's accommodation."

The woman is flustered. "I thought it was mine."

She must be feeling a right idiot. I should think just about everybody can hear.

"And could I have that back as well." It's not a question. "The rep will want to hand it to you personally and check you off his list."

I imagine the woman wishes the ground would open up and swallow her.

The rep, a young bloke who looks as if he just left school yesterday, takes his place in the bus. Seeing him arrive, Ghetto Blaster Woman and The Wild Bunch follow him on board.

"Drinking is not allowed on the coach," he tells her.

"I'll take them off them when the bus starts."

"Open cans are not allowed on the bus."

"I'll make sure they don't spill them."

"Oh, all right then, as long as they don't spill them."

He capitulates as easily as that. I don't fancy my chances much if I have to ask her to turn her bloody noise down. If she can argue the point like this I can't imagine her seeing my point of view about rejecting her generosity in her sharing her "music" with me. Of course I know what's really motivating her - she's scared her kids will create a riot if she has to take the cans from them - which they certainly would and which is why I know she has not the slightest intention of relieving them of them. After all, there are three cans and she is single-handedly bringing these boys up, so how could she possibly carry the can for two boys, let alone three?

The rep hands out the envelopes and we're ready to go. Reps have to be cheery. It comes with the territory, regardless of which country, which resort they're in. That's what bugs me about them – this forced gaiety and jollity. He asks us if we're happy to be here. There's a muted response. Some of us grudgingly admit we are happy to be here.

"Come on, you can do better than that! Are you happy to be here?"

The response is hardly more enthusiastic. In the main, we're not a young crowd, certainly not an 18-30's group, the sort that is determined to get into the spirit of the thing, right from the word go. We would prefer to go to sleep. It's late, for God's sake. We've been travelling for hours and it's as dark as pitch outside and it looks like the middle of the night although it's still not yet midnight.

The rep must be disappointed in our effort but realises the futility of pursuing the matter.

"Right then, my name's Alan and I'm your tour rep - for my sins." Pause for laughter, but when none comes, he resumes. "Just some points of safety I have to point out." No laughter at the pun. "Don't eat, don't drink, (are you listening Ghetto Blaster Woman and Brats?) don't stand, and don't put your arm rest up. You can do anything else you want – if there's anything left, that is." Weak laughter. (Don't say that, for God's sake, The Wild Bunch could do anything).

"Maybe I should rip your knickers off," I whisper to Iona. We've never been to Menorca before. Mallorca twice, but we fancied a change and Iona must consummate each new location. It's one of her foibles, a sort of occasional hobby. Although I am only joking of course, it would be good to get it out of the way and we could concentrate on getting on with the holiday. It tends to hang over me like the sword of Damocles.

"Don't be so crude!"

That's the trouble with me. I have no sense of timing. I'm crude and I'm lewd and I'm sure I'm a boor because La-Belle-Dame-Sans-Merci tells me so.

Reps, on the other hand, normally tell you about what a wonderful island you've come to and how great the weather has been and how it is going to be even better, but Alan has obviously given us up as a waste of time. He tells us that he's going to shut up now and let us sleep. Silent heartfelt thanks. He starts chatting up the girls on his left. I'm not deliberately eavesdropping; I can't help but hear and it does relieve the monotony of the journey as the headlights of the bus slice into the darkness.

It turns out that the girls are not really reps in the true sense of the word. That job's bad enough, but their job is even worse, in my opinion. What's worse than being a holiday rep? Being a child minder for happy holiday-makers of course. They're feeling a bit under the weather. Apparently someone went home yesterday and they had had a farewell party which had lasted well into the small hours, and from which they are still not recovered. I can quite believe they would have had some party, alcohol being the price it is in Spain.

After we've been going a while, a van passes and pulls in front of the bus. A young man leans out of the front passenger window till half his torso is hanging out and leaning back, he waves excitedly at Alan, presumably. Alan leaps to his feet and gesticulates wildly back, though it's difficult to imagine that the youth in the van can see him, illuminated as he is by the bus headlights acting like spotlights whilst we, like an audience in the theatre, remain in the dark.

However we are not kept in the dark for long as to who this person is. This is Dave, a former rep, back for another spell of duty, Alan informs the girls. Well, he must like it all right. It may not be my cup of tea, but they seem to lap it up all right. Except it won't be tea they're lapping up most nights. Of course they are only half my age and at that age, perhaps I would have liked that job too. Perhaps. Maybe.

It has taken only 40 minutes to cross the island, and that in a bus. In my hire car, I should be able to do it in less than that, if I wanted. Nice and small. We should get round it and see everything it has to offer in a week, no problem. Passengers are beginning to be dropped off. We are to be the second last. The bus thins out and still Ghetto Blaster Woman is there with The Wild Bunch. I don't like the look of this.

As we pull up at our apartments, for some obscure reason known as The Columbia, the whole place is in darkness. And darkness descends on my soul when the only other passengers to alight, apart from us, is Them. Out of all the people on that flight, she is the only one with a ghetto blaster and the most unruly kids! Of all the resorts in Menorca, she has to come to the same one as me! Of all the holiday apartments in this resort, she has to come to mine. Well, ye gods, I hope you are satisfied. I hope you are having a really good laugh.

In fact, I am sure I can hear them now. It surely wasn't the sound of distant thunder was it? Impossible. The stars are sparkling. Mars is glowing orangey-red like my eyes when I have a hangover. That's where the gods are watching from, enjoying their joke, waiting for the climax, as we end up neighbours and no doubt, they hope, warring partners. The ghetto blaster is bad enough, but the thought of those kids running rampage gives me a horrible feeling in the pit of my stomach. I am beginning to wish I had never come here. This is what happens when you book a cheap package holiday.

Alan jumps down from the bus, showing his youth and energy by swinging himself to the ground like Tarzan by holding on to one of the huge hinges of the pneumatic door. He can tell right away by the sensation on his palm that something nasty has happened. He, and we can see also, that his palm is black with grease. He is looking at it incredulously - as if tar's on his hand.

But I've got to hand it to him, he doesn't panic or instinctively wipe his hand on his trousers. "Just stay there," he says to Ghetto Blaster Woman. "I'll come back for you in a minute." And to us, "Follow me." Can it really be true – we are not actually going to be cheek by jowl after all? I may not hear her "music" after all.

We have a ground floor apartment. The door was unlocked, with the key in the lock, (one of those credit card types) and Alan slips it into a slot behind the door and the place is instantly bathed in light. They don't appear to be worried about intruders or thieves apparently. He explains that it an open key policy. He also tells us that we have to pay an eco tax of 50 cents per person per day, that's towards all the water and resources we are going to use on our stay. Not a bad idea really. I really don't mind paying that, especially as it is not very much. We have to hand our passports into reception tomorrow where they will hold them. (No chance of escaping without paying the eco tax then). Finally he tells us that our rep's meeting is at 10 am tomorrow - not him, Jane. An appropriate name for his colleague, given his style for descending from buses.

I invite Alan to wash his hands, but there is no soap in the pabby and not even any dishwashing liquid in the kitchen area. Fortunately, I have brought my own little packets of guest soaps from Italy but they're in the case. However, Iona has a packet of wipes in the bag with many zips which removes most of the grease. Alan thanks us and removes himself to deal with Ghetto Blaster Woman. What must she be thinking, standing at the corner in the darkness with only her cases and her devilish brood for company? It's like the setting for a horror movie, except they won't be scared; they *are* the main protagonists; they are the horrors.

The apartment seems quite nice, at first glance. There is a big dark oak Spanish dresser, a round table and four chairs, a settee which probably makes into a bed, and a sink and cupboards at the far end before a short corridor leads to the bathroom and bedroom. There's no TV but that's not a blow. I'll just have to do without the news for a while, for a week, to be precise. That's no bad thing when you are on holiday, on escape from reality.

In the bedroom there are twin beds and we can go out from there onto a terrace at the back which looks on to a piece of waste ground. Like the one at the front, both terraces have flat roofs so I'm not going to be able to do any sunbathing here, not unless I sit out beyond the roof, or the sun is very low.

Right, that's enough exploration for the moment, but I must find out where Ghetto Blaster Woman's apartment is. She may not be beside me, but I fear she will be *above* me. I know how sounds travel through these tiled floors and with the minimum of soft fabrics, no noise is muted. You hear every scrape of a chair, each knife that clatters to the floor, each footstep of wooden sandals sounding like a troupe of Morris dancers doing a clog dance. That's just inside. If she is above us and sits out on her balcony, we're going to hear her "music", just as if she were right next to us.

"Don't be so paranoid," says La-Belle-Dame-Sans-Merci, beginning to unpack. "I want to get to my bed." By which she means I must get to mine as she cannot settle until I have retired. It's got nothing to do with the consummation of the island. Plenty of time for that. She's merely tired.

But I have to know. It's well after midnight but it's still warm. The cicadas are making melody in some near but undisclosed location. Iona and I call them nightingales because in Athens, many years ago, our guidebook told us that Klafthmonos Square is famous for its nightingales. But all we could hear were the cicadas, so that's why we call

19

them nightingales. To me, they have a sound just as sweet, redolent of warm summer evenings, as inseparable a part of a continental holiday as a muezzin to a mosque, that other sound, in other parts, which evokes in me that delicious sense of foreignness. But then I don't live in Bradford.

There's no sign of the enemy. The place is as silent as the grave and almost as dark. The bus, with Alan and remaining tourists, has already gone, leaving the darkness and all other signs of life to the nightingales and to us. But what's that smell? Now that I've dealt with the sights and sounds of my new surroundings, the sense of smell has just impinged itself on my consciousness. It smells like tomcats. Phew!

It's a funny thing, but now that I'm here, I've lost my tiredness. It's true, I waken up at night, am a bit of a night bird – my mother always said I should have been a night watchman. I could watch for nightingales and have a nightcap out of my hip flask, but I know I'd never be allowed to and anyway, neat gin is not entirely to my taste. No, I'll have a quick reconnoitre first, see what sort of a resort we have come too and quite possibly I'll be able to hunt down the lair of Ghetto Blaster Woman.

I turn up to my left and come across reception at the corner, then turn left again and come across the bar and swimming pool. Yep! That looks all right. The road running alongside has not been made up. Perhaps the complex has not been in existence all that long, or maybe it takes decades after their construction for these things to be done. After all, the road behind my house has not been finished yet and we've been there nearly twenty years.

There's a flight of steps which lead down to the pool and up to the first floor apartments. I climb them. This takes me onto a broad terrace which runs round the entire block like the brim of a hat, and forms in fact, the roof of our terrace. Ghetto Blaster Woman has to be up here somewhere.

They are easy to locate. Nothing but silence from the sleeping interiors of the other apartments, nor even a snore. But from this apartment, the sounds of children yelling at each other and the scraping of furniture across the floor. I pity the poor people below whom, I'm sure, must be awake by now, unless they have not yet retired or - God forbid - it is us. I cannot hear the ghetto blaster at least, so it's not Music and Movement as the radio programme was called from which we obtained our PE instruction when I was in primary school, but merely movement.

Coming back down, I identify the back of our apartment by the only light burning along the entire length of the block, just like the residence of the eponymous Pedestrian in Ray Bradbury's chilling short story. At first glance, all the apartments seem the same but up above, while we have just the one window, they have two. So all the double apartments must be up there which explains why we and Ghetto Blaster Woman have been separated. To my relief, she is not directly above us but she's only two along, not far enough out of range for my liking, but on the other hand, the terrace doesn't look the sort of place where you would sit outside and inflict your din upon the neighbourhood. No, I think the real sufferers will be the neighbours on either side and the people immediately below her. Poor devils.

"Where, the hell have you been?" La-Belle-Dame-Sans-Merci is already in bed. Although I can't see her face, I know she will be my Chinese wife Scow Ling which is one degree worse than my usual wife, Frau Ning, who of course, is German. She has made a sandwich of her head, with one pillow above and one below, another of her little idiosyncrasies. She's an incredibly light sleeper, the result of her mother tiptoeing about her when she was a baby. I've been tiptoeing about her ever since, scared to put a foot wrong.

"Just having a look around, to see what's it's like and where the pool is." I know better than to say I've been tracking down where Ghetto Blaster Woman is as well.

"What do you want to do that for? It's pitch black for God's sake and surely to God you're not going for a swim at this time! Will you just get your clothes off and get to bed!"

I unpack only the necessities from my case, chief amongst which is my life-support system as I call it, that is to say my Walkman. I am an insomniac and listen to plays I've recorded from Radio 4 during the night. I couldn't possibly get to sleep without it.

Eventually I climb into bed, well satisfied with my little survey. Of course, we have not met our neighbours yet. There's no way of telling what they'll be like. Time and tomorrow will probably tell.

2. Neighbourhood Watch.

I am second into the shower. I always let Iona go first. I'm a bit of a gentleman that way but she thinks it's so I can lie in bed a bit longer, getting up in the morning being another of the skills in which I am severely lacking.

By the time I do make it in there, the floor is awash. Having performed my ablutions, as I shave, I can see what the problem is. The wash-hand basin butts onto the side of the shower and water is running freely from that joint on to the floor. It's like being in a paddling pool.

That's the first setback of the day for me, but Iona has already discovered an earlier, and for her, more major one – we, I mean me, of course, has apparently forgotten to pack the adapter. If it's bad for Iona, who cannot dry her hair and will look as if she has been dragged through a hedge backwards, it's a tragedy for me, for once the batteries in my personal stereo are flat, what am I going to do? How will I get through the night without being able to listen to my plays?

"Huh! What are you worried about? Just look at my hair!"

I think it's quite attractive in a woolly, Wild-Woman-of-Borneo sort of way, but I wouldn't dare say so. She would just say I was trying to mitigate my sin of omission or more likely, trying to crawl out of the hole I had dug for myself.

"You can always buy batteries, can't you?"

Ah! I hadn't thought of that! The world doesn't seem to be such a dismal place after all.

"And I'll tell you another thing!" La-Belle-Dame-Sans-Merci is just getting into her stride. "There is nothing to make a cup of coffee with!"

Ah! That's it! She's missing her drug. Neither of us has slept well in spite of being tired from the journey. What sleep we did get in the end was curtailed early by the sound of a kid above us running amok and the scraping of furniture on the tiles. I suffer the little children all right, that's for sure.

"And," continues the trouble and strife, well and truly mounted on her high horse by now, "there's no washing-up liquid, no kitchen towel, nor a dish towel. How is anyone supposed to be self catering without that, pray?"

"Erm." There's not much of an answer to that, but it's scarcely *my* fault although she is talking to me as if it were. I don't see them as much in the way of problems anyway. I drink instant coffee, I'd let the dishes drain, in fact, a good excuse to do that, and if we need kitchen towel, for whatever inconceivable reason, I'd use toilet paper. The washing up liquid is a slight problem, I do concede, but I don't suppose we'll be eating in here much at all. But it's not the time to voice an opinion. It's the time to hold my peace, not fan the embers of smouldering resentment into a conflagration.

We have the rep's meeting at 10 am. It's held in the café by the pool and it's a chance to meet our fellow holiday makers. There's no sign of Ghetto Blaster Woman. In fact, the meeting is quite sparsely attended and there's no real reason why we should attend, since we have no intention of joining any of the arranged tours or entertainment evenings, but we might pick up some useful tips, you never know.

Our rep is Jane, all red-hair and freckles and by her vowels, a Scouser. The first thing she gets us to do is put our left arm in the air, (confusion from those who don't know their lefts from their rights, all women,) then our right arm, so it doesn't really matter anyway, then we have to bring them together and pull them apart, then bring them together again. It takes me only a couple of moments before I realise that I am giving Jane a sort of sitting ovation, which she receives graciously. It's all designed to get us in a happy, clappy sort of mood, like Christians. The tricks these reps resort to!

I'm most definitely not a happy clappy sort of person, especially in the morning, (though by ten I am generally beginning to come to) and especially if anyone should insist that I should be full of the joys. In fact, nothing is more calculated to make me take the perverse view and be the most miserable, morose microbe under the sun. And then I look at Jane and I think how plain she is and then I think what if her boyfriend dumped her last night and here she would have to be, merry regardless, having to act as if nothing had happened, trying to make us feel as happy as Larry whilst all the time, as G K Chesterton put it: *The folk that live in Liverpool, their heart is in their boots.*

I start clapping merrily to please plain Jane. It's totally irrational. I've absolutely no reason to suppose she's feeling down in the mouth. In fact, she might be feeling really happy because Dave's back and maybe he's the love of her life and they are going to pick up from where they left off and that's why she really *is* so happy this morning. But somehow I don't think so. In my experience, Daves tend to be handsome devils and Davids just a little less so, or at least passable, as my friend Bruce once gave that ringing endorsement of me to a divorced friend of his who wanted to know what I looked like when she heard I was coming to stay with him in Nice. Bruce didn't say who it was and if I ever met her, I mustn't have got through quality control because she never made a pass at me. Which just goes to show you that Bruce was right after all. I am passable.

No, as Shakespeare pointed out, with reference to a rose, her name's Jane and it doesn't matter if you spell it Jayne, it doesn't change a thing: you're still plain. My own mother was a Jane, but she had to be known by her middle name of Elizabeth, as when she grew up, she turned out far too good looking for her first name. People say I look like her. I am happy about that. If I'd looked more like my father, I'd have to have been called George. Even so, some people mistake me for a George: George W. Bush in fact. I'm not happy about that, as you can imagine.

Now we have to shake hands with the people next to us and wish them a happy holiday, in our case a tall thin man with dark hair who looks as if he's been stretched like an elastic band, and his short, dumpy, "blonde" wife who looks as if she's been compressed, and their two children. It's amazing how opposites attract. In the background, glasses are being clinked as the barman prepares some sangria to sustain us through Jane's exposition.

She tells us where the shops are, just up to the main road, turn left and we'll come to a *Spar*. It's also where we can catch the bus into Ciutadella. If we want a longer walk, we can walk past the swimming pool and we'll come to the coast and if we follow that road round, we'll eventually come to the Commercial Centre where we'll find a choice of restaurants, though of course, we don't need to stray further than from here because the food here, at Barry's Bar is excellent, really excellent. We had looked at the menu when we came in and it looked like ordinary fare to us, like chicken and chips – in fact, chips with everything. I don't think we'll be eating here somehow. The name seems to say it all. You can always tell by the name.

Jane tells us about the two tours we can do of the island and the rep's show which is really great entertainment, a great laugh and if that were not enough, we can have all the sangria we can drink at it. No doubt that would predispose the clientèle to appreciate the entertainment on offer more kindly, but it sounds more like a bribe to me. Not for us either.

She says we might like to hire a car and she can arrange it for us and there's a really good deal on just now – we can get an extra day's car hire – four days for the price of three. This is bad news. I had arranged my car hire before we left and only took it for three days as I thought that would be long enough for such a small island, but another day could have been useful. You never know what you might come across. Not only that, but if anything went wrong, Jane would be on the spot to help sort things out. As it happens, I'm not even convinced that the car is going to come. All I have is a flimsy piece of paper and a telephone number. I have to phone up the day before. It looks as if I'd probably have got a better deal here, but how was I to know they'd have a bargain offer? If we want to do that, we have to see her at the end of the meeting.

It's a kind of masochism, but I hang about earwigging as the family at our table are first in line to sign up for the car, all the time pretending to be deeply interested in the décor of the bar. I'm desperate to find out how much it costs, but Jane is spending ages being jolly and friendly before she begins the paperwork and it exercises all my ingenuity to look interested in the bottles behind the bar and the bodies by the poolside. At last all is revealed. €96 for the four days. Just about the same price as I had paid, but they've got the extra day. Damn! I shouldn't have listened. Once you've made a purchase, you should just say that's your decision made and not go looking anywhere else, as Iona says. But if you don't, how else do you know if you've got a really good bargain?

The first thing we have to do is go to the *Spar*. It's quite a pleasant walk by oleander hedges, bordering villas of various sizes and designs, but each with a swimming pool. Probably rented to tourists. Indeed, English voices are carrying from beyond this hedge and this elderly couple, by the pallor of their skin, could only be British.

We make some essential purchases. Beer and wine. We also get some other incidental things like kitchen towel and washing up liquid and some bread and cheese and tomatoes for our lunch. I don't bother with the gin and tonic just yet. This is a small shop with probably big prices, so I'll just wait and see what the prices are like at the Commercial Centre.

"What about a corkscrew?" I ask. I don't recall seeing one at the apartment and it's hardly the best equipped apartment on the planet. If we don't even have washing-up liquid, for God's sake, how can we reasonably expect to have something like a corkscrew which is probably classed as an unessential item by the moron who stocked our place?

"It's all right. We've got one."

"Are you sure?"

"Yes."

Reception is open when we return – just an office big enough to hold a desk and a couple of chairs and we call in to pay our eco tax and to leave our passports. Jane had told us that we'd be able to borrow an adapter and right enough, there's a pile of them in a plate at the end of the desk. Not having to buy that is going to pay for our eco tax twice over. Things are looking up.

But as we go back to the apartment, the smell of tomcat I smelled last night is decidedly back. It *must* be bad if I can smell it – my sense of smell is very poor, as I said already, if you remember. Neither of us can place where it's coming from though.

It's lunch time. We're going to sit outside at the front and have the cheese. If I manoeuvre my plastic chair just so, I can catch a wedge of sunshine. There's a palm tree shading most of our patio area and the base of the tree and the ground is thick with little black seeds like peppercorns.

Plop! Plop! Plop! They fall at regular intervals like insoluble dirty raindrops.

"What are you looking for?" Iona wants to know as I rake through all the drawers in the kitchen.

"Bloody corkscrew! Where did you say you'd seen it?"

"In one of the drawers." Iona is busy preparing the lunch. "Would you just look at this! This cheese is a month past its sell-by date."

She's right! Oh well, too bad, I don't have much time for sticking rigidly to sell-by dates, like some people I know who actually throw good food out, just because it's a day over the limit, never mind a week. I regularly eat things well past their limits and I don't mean days or even months, but sometimes even years and I've never been ill with them yet. I'm well past my own sell-by date and I'm still not past it, good for quite a number of years yet, I hope. A month is nothing as far as cheese is concerned. I've even had a malt whisky which was as much as 12 years old and that never did me any harm, though La-Belle-Dame-Sans-Merci says that in the quantities I drink it, it should. She may nag me about it but at least she's not like the newly bereaved widow I heard about who, stumbling across her late lamented's secret store of malts, poured the lot down the sink because they must surely have been off since they were all at least 10 years old.

But where the hell is that bloody corkscrew so we can have some wine with the out-of-date cheese?

It exasperates Iona how I can't find things. I hunt and hunt for things then she just comes along and puts her hand straight upon it in a place where I have already looked: *You've got to move things,* she says. *But I did,* I say. It's a waste of time me looking – I don't know why I don't just get her to look for them in the first place. Actually I do. It's because she insists on making me go through this charade first. I just can't get her to see that it would save a lot of time and hassle if she just found them in the first place, but she thinks she is training me to be more self-reliant. I don't know why. Statistically speaking, I am much more likely to go to heaven before her.

"Oh, out of my way," she snaps impatiently. But it's no good, rummage as she might, there's no sign of the corkscrew. It's not as if there's a million kitchen implements for it to get lost amongst. It's no consolation either that she can't find it, nor to be proved for once at least, that I'm not the complete idiot.

"That's funny! I could have sworn that I'd seen one. Anyway, you don't need it just now. It's not good for you to drink at lunch time."

I had hoped to have a glass as an antidote to whatever bugs might have been lurking in the cheese, especially as I won't be able to when I have the car, but I'm not going to now either, evidently. Life's full of disappointments like this and the secret of a happy life is never to look forward with keen anticipation to something too much because somehow the gods get wind of it and, determined to show you who's boss, screw you up. I'm a bit cheesed off, I have to admit to myself, but I'm not going to let the gods see it, so I say nothing and instead we sit and inhale the smell of tomcat and look across the road at the private houses, the owners of whom I bet were over the moon when these apartments were built opposite their villas, blocking their view of the Waste Land, now repulsed to outside our back door, and thus losing all of the empathetic ambience as they read their T.S. Eliot.

They've got very attractive five barred gates, made of olive wood I presume, not straight like ours, but bowed. In the villa to our right, there is a dog whining. I wish somebody would come out and see what it wants or tell it to shut up. It's bad enough smelling cats without hearing dogs. At least it's not raining them, that's something I suppose, for apart from that and the plop of seeds dropping onto our plates, it's silent and the sun is shining. Not a ghetto blaster within earshot. I'm glad I came now. But a glass of wine would be nice. It's not fair that dog is allowed a whine and I am not.

I'd like to go to the pool now but Iona thinks it's far too early; she's not a sitting-by-the-pool sort of a person, so we walk to the Commercial Centre instead, taking the path along by the sea which is crashing into caves and inlets carved out through millennia. Over to the left, far in the distance, we think we can just make out the peaks of the east coast of Mallorca. According to Jane, it is one of the things to do at sunset, to go to the cliffs in front of the Commercial Centre at sunset and sit on a bench and watch the sun set over Mallorca. You and half the rest of Menorca, I should imagine. It would be quieter here, but there are no benches and the rocks are too sharp to sit down on so there's not much point, or rather far too many of them, to be precise.

The rest of the walk is through leafy lanes where sleepy villas are snoozing the siesta away behind secluded and secretive shutters. Sssh! Even the guard dogs are asleep. It seems no one else is awake or out and about but us and the invisible cicadas chirruping their incessant lullabies.

There are some people in the Commercial Centre at least. It's a broad, paved pedestrian precinct fringed with plenty of bars with tables on the outside as well as the inside. At the bottom of the street there is an obligatory Irish Bar as quintessential as tattoos on men with shaved heads with rings in their ears. There's a posh restaurant which we'll probably not go to, not on the grounds that it's really expensive, but because we're just not posh enough to be let into a place like that, and a couple of others with big screens, one showing some football match or other, and the other a Grand Prix. We'll not be going to them either. There's also a Chinese

Restaurant and another place which looks a possibility, so we'll not be stuck.

In the meantime, there is a supermarket, a bit bigger than the *Spar* with the wines and spirits in a phalanx along the whole frontage. Now, that's my idea of shopping. It also looks what I would call a temptation to smash and grab. I buy some Menorcan gin called Xoriguer with a picture of a windmill in full sail on the label. That's enough to make me want to buy it, but I would have anyway, as it's the local produce. It's made in Mahón, or Maó, in Menorquin, which is the dialect of Catalan spoken in Menorca. According to our guidebook, you can visit the distillery. I should imagine we *will* be doing that when we get the car.

Meanwhile we lug the gin and the *tonica* back through the quiet streets to the apartment. Iona has also bought some *Turrón de Jigona* or *Torro de Xixona* in Menorquin. I've got to lug that as well. It's not the weight it is to carry, that I object to, it's more the weight I'll have to carry when I help her to eat it. I prefer my calories in liquid form as I'm not really a sweet person, but I have to help her keep hers down.

At last we can go to the pool. There's quite a lot of sunbeds to choose from. Near the bar, a maid is giving one a good soaping and washing it down with a hose. There are some beds near her but it seems a bit rude for us to be lounging about whilst she works, so we move away a discreet distance, unlike Jerome K Jerome who famously said: *I like work: it fascinates me. I can sit and look at it for hours.*

"I think these'll do, don't you?" It's far enough away not to hear the piped "music" from Barry's Bar clearly. It's there in the background, but it's not so intrusive that I can't shut it out.

"Huh!" says La-Belle-Dame-Sans-Merci, dumping her towel on the sunbed nearest to her.

"What have I done wrong now?"

By way of an answer, she glowers beyond me to the pair of sunbeds next to us. Somehow, amongst all the spare beds around the pool, we have ended up next to a pair of slim, and as it happens, topless young ladies, their bodies brown as toast, glistening with sun oil all over, at least on the more interesting side which they are presenting for my vision, (now I happen to notice it) and which suggests to me that they make a habit of this exposure, for this tan, like Rome, wasn't built in a day.

As far as I can see, now that I take the trouble to let my eyes roam, there don't appear to be any other bare ladies around the entire pool. Isn't that a remarkable thing, that we should have just happened to have ended up beside this pair or should I say, this couple of pears? But plainly La-Belle-Dame-Sans-Merci thinks it was no accident. It's no good trying to explain that it was only in deference to the maid and to escape from the "music" that I chose these beds to lie on – she would just call me a liar, so I say nothing, spread my towel on my sunbed, and averting my eyes from my companions to my right, lie down and look straight ahead at the pool.

Children are the only people in the pool, splashing and laughing. I recklessly try an exploratory foot, never mind toe, in the water and snatch it out again as if an alligator had bitten it. No wonder the kids are the only ones in the pool - it's absolutely freezing. They're having so much fun and constantly moving about that they don't notice the cold.

Not for much longer. Here comes Ghetto Blaster Woman with The Wild Bunch. She's in a bikini with some sort of dangly chain dangling from her belly button. But that is incidental. They are lugging an enormous inflatable boat amongst them, complete with oars. It looks the sort of thing you would use on a loch, if not to go out to sea.

They go round to the other side of the pool and prepare to launch their vessel. The kids in the pool stop their splashing to look, awestruck. Talking about making an entrance! The whole poolside assembly has stopped whatever they were doing to watch. They can't believe their eyes but one thing is for sure; when that boat goes in, the kids will have to get out. There's certainly not room for them all.

And indeed, that's in fact what they do and stand wrapped in towels as The Wild Bunch row up and down the pool. Why don't the parents say anything? It's none of my business. It doesn't affect me. I don't want to go into the pool anyway. What's the matter with them? Are they sacred of Ghetto Blaster Woman or something? But no one says anything to the lady in question who has lit a fag, is reading a mag and is nonchalantly puffing away, not even watching them and is seemingly totally unaware of possibly having caused any offence by her invasion and complete takeover of the pool.

Splash! I'm too late to see what's happened but one of the trio is in the water now and is trying to capsize it, trying to tip the other two out. That's more like it! This is what the boat is really for: being pushed out of, trying to climb back in and being pushed back in to the pool. But even that begins to pall after a while; they haul out the boat, the other kids re-occupy the pool and normal poolside activity is resumed.

Except activity is hardly the right word for what happens at a pool. It may be very pleasant for a while but I could not do this all day, which is to say do nothing apart from turning over on the sunbed and turning the pages of a book, and certainly not every day for a week, though in the view of some people, that's exactly what constitutes a good holiday. This afternoon I have a football match to watch – Scotland v Holland. It's the first leg of a two-leg play-off to qualify for the European Cup as we have not earned the right to go through after the group stages, although we played the likes of the lowly Faroes. There's a surprise! So now it's us against the once mighty Holland. I'm more masochistic than optimistic. The irony is that if I'd been at home, I wouldn't have seen it as it's not on terrestial TV.

There's a big screen in the bar. I buy a pint of *San Miguel* and try to get the best of both worlds by sitting in the sun and watching the screen. It's no good though. I can't see the screen properly if I do that - there's too much light on it. I try it with my head in the shade and my legs in the sun. That's better but still not good enough. I'll have to come right inside if I want to see the game properly. But do I? Perhaps it'll not be so bad on a screen which I can't see properly for the sunlight and we'll be let off with a light thrashing.

It's mainly men and Scots in the bar. Iona has gone back to the apartment. I sit at a table with a woman and a man who speaks like, but does not look like, Sean Connery. It's hard going - not the match, as surprisingly, Scotland doesn't look that bad, or maybe it's just Holland isn't playing very well - no it's hard work making the beer last as I have decided that I'll ration myself to two pints, one for each half.

It's unbelievable! We've actually scored! The bar erupts. I do one of my whooping noises of delight. Now all we've got to do is hang on. I am so happy I take a huge swig of San Miguel to celebrate. Maybe I'll buy another one as well. Hang on a minute! Let's not get carried away. There's still 15 minutes to go till half time, to say nothing of the whole of the second half. It is, as the commentators never tire of reminding us, *a game of two halfs* (sic).

What if Holland scores again, twice even! I've not followed Scotland all these years and not learned a thing or two. Forty five minutes is a long time to make a pint last and I am glad when it's half time and I can go outside and get some rays and work up a thirst for my next pint. I'm not interested in the half-time analysis.

When I come back, my place at the table with Sean and his wife is taken by a thin, hippy-looking man with a T shirt cut away at the shoulders. He won't feel the draught though as his pepper and salt stringy hair covers them up. Unfortunately it doesn't cover up his tattoos. He'd need a hair suit to do that and he's not that hirsute, for he's thinning on the top. Well he might. He must be well into his fifties. Unfortunately it soon becomes apparent he also is a chain smoker, but maybe it's just his nerves as Scotland look as if they may even win this, like that memorable time in the World Cup of 1978 when we lost to Peru whom we were supposed to beat, drew with Iran, and in our last game, when we'd already booked our return tickets, beat Holland 3-2 who went on to end up as runners up to Argentina in the final.

It's a sobering thought that that was a quarter of a century ago, only I don't need sobering as I am making my way slowly down my second pint, perched on a stool at the bar like a sparrow with a bird's eye view of tattooed T Shirt Man's bald spot.

At last the nerve-tingling moments are over and we have actually won! I give another of my whoops, like Tarzan. I know it is only to fight another day. There is still the return leg to face and I doubt if Holland could be as mediocre again, on their home territory. Anyway, let's enjoy the moment. My beer is long since finished, but my six-pack in the fridge will be cool by now, so I leave straight away. I can't be doing with post-match analysis from the pundits who can be so wise after the result, who predicted this win all along, or chewing the fat with thin-as-a-rake tattooed T Shirt Man or Sean and the others and having to buy *San Miguels* all round. Better hurry back and tell Iona the result, who will be in a lather of sublime indifference.

"So you won then?" she says before I can open my mouth. She's apparently spent two happy hours reading and cross-stitching inside, wasting the sunshine – you'd think it were an everyday Scottish phenomenon, (unlike the national team winning a football match) that you could treat it with such supreme contempt - though the sliding glass door which is our front door is open, so at least she is letting in some fresh tomcat air.

I am amazed. Why didn't she say, as usual: *So you lost again?*

"Yes! How did you know?"

"I heard you."

"What, us, all the way here, from the bar?" I didn't think we'd been that riotous.

"No, not them – just you. I could pick out your voice."

"Bloody hell!" I had no idea I possessed this skill, but I'm not going to broadcast it.

It's time for an apéritif. We are at the back door. It may not have such a scenic view, not that the front door is exactly scenic either but it does have some trees and a very nice gate directly opposite, but we're a bit cramped for space and there's no sun at either door, so we may as well be out the back. It's quieter there though there's not a peep from the people to our right. They are really good neighbours. We've seen neither hide nor hair of them since we came. We can hear the family from next door to our left, but it's only normal family intercourse. By the sound of it a couple and two small girls. Meanwhile, up above, the family are banging about preparing the family meal. It's an omelette and by the sound of it, it's made from an ostrich egg. How long does it take to make an omelette for God's sake?

But at the back, it's so quiet that we could be the only people in the whole complex. Ah, give me the simple life!

This Menorcan gin is very nice. It's got a delicious bouquet and tastes quite different from any gin I've had before. Not exactly surprising as I've never seen it before. Forget the supermarkets at home, I've never seen it in

Mallorca even. Maybe it's so good they want to keep it for themselves. Maybe it's inter-island rivalry: *We're not selling your bloody poison over here; we've got a tourist industry, even if you don't have.* Maybe I just didn't notice it, but I don't think so somehow. Maybe I could start importing it, start up an export-import business. No good exporting whisky – there's whiskies in the supermarket I've never heard of before with improbable sounding names all beginning with Glen – at least they know that much – Glen Affro, Glen Disiac, but I wonder if they know they are most efficacious when taken together.

No, that market has been cornered. I don't know what I could export that the Menorcans would like. I can't see haggis or kilts or bagpipes catching on somehow. I think I'll just have to stick to the import business. All you need are some empty bottles which contained a fizzy drink of some sort because they're light and they've got more strength than non-fizzy drinks and thanks to our membership of the EU, you can take back as much as you are able to carry and they don't break when baggage handlers throw your bags around.

It's time for another gin. A small one for Iona and a larger one for me as I am the lion and should get the lion's share. Actually, I'm lying. We should have fair shares but the truth is that I have twice as much as Iona and the good thing about gin and T is that they look the same, so Iona doesn't know – I just have to be careful not to mix them up or I'll end up with a tearful wife getting maudlin about how she bosses me about so much. Left and right, hers and mine, that's right.

Ghetto Blaster Woman and The Wild Bunch struggle past with their inflatable boat, so wide there is no room for them and the boat on the pavement. It's going back to harbour apparently and I wonder how many people she's left at the pool harbouring resentment at her and her brood for her thoughtless behaviour.

A little later, the two topless ladies, our neighbours on the sunbeds, pass by and, surprisingly enough, I recognise them as I had scarcely given them a glance all the time we had been lying side by side.

I've got the gin mixes right apparently. Iona is still able to thread her needle and I have not needled her by passing negative or positive comments about the passers by. It's time to go out for our meal and by the time we get there, I might even be hungry.

It looks very ambient by night, the Commercial Centre, with its avenue of orange trees and on both sides of the pedestrian precinct, the alfresco restaurants all lit up, their tables laid in a rainbow of crisp napery set amidst diminutive palms, whilst overhead, the neon lights competing for our patronage, find their message reflected in the polished paving stones. And the message, I reflect, is that we might as well be at home, except for the deliciously warm temperature, for we can choose to dine at Tim's Bar or Liam's Bar or, just for a change, at the Irish Bar at the bottom of the precinct, the one with the illuminated Guinness sign. Or, for something a little bit more exotic, what about the regulatory Chinese Restaurant whose bright-red, three-foot high neon sign originally proclaiming THE YANGTSE outshines and dominates all the others? In spite of that though, it remains pathetically empty. Maybe if we go there, others will follow. All they need is someone to get it started. It seems ridiculous to come all the way to Menorca, just to eat Chinese, but when we have the car we'll be able to spread our wings and explore the restaurants in Ciutadella. At least, if we choose this, the service should be fast.

Across the street is what appears to be a very tempting offer:

STARTERS
TOMATOE SOUP
CANELONIS MEAT
SPAGHETTI BOLOGNESE
ASPARRAGUS SOUP
MAIL
PORK KEBBABS
1/2 ROAST CHILLEN
GRILL PORK LION
GRILL SOLE
HARE IN BATTER
SWEET
ICE CREAM
DRINK
WINE AND BREAD.

And in big black letters beneath: **5: 75 €**

What!!! That's not even £4! For all that! There's something wrong here somewhere. If it looks too good to be true, then it probably isn't. Maybe it isn't loin after all, perhaps it really *is* lion; perhaps it *is* hare, not hake – it's not a mistake. There must be a catch and it wasn't hake they caught. Perhaps they really do mail the main course to you. I can understand how they made most of these rather entertaining spelling mistakes, but for the life of me I can't understand how they got *chillen* from children. It surely can't be the neighbourhood children can it? If it is, quite right to sell them only in half portions. I could never eat a whole one.

Just to work up an appetite, and still undecided, we walk up the street to the posh restaurant. Talk about extremes! It is closed today anyway, so regrettably we cannot go there to enjoy the fare where they really do have hare and quail and partridge and other rare birds such as Bombay duck too – (that was a joke, by the way). I'm glad to duck out of this one though as they have fancy prices to match the fancy food. The cheapest starter is dearer than a whole meal at the other place. At those prices, I'd rather have the hare in batter at the cheap place.

Fortunately, there's a more moderately priced place too. *Es Choix*. Mmm. Well, that looks a possibility, could be our choice, but a curious choice of name. Perhaps it's a mixture of French and Spanish food. Unfortunately, there is a hell of a noise coming from the adjacent Irish bar which is destroying the ambience with its big-screen sports coverage which it's difficult not to ignore from here, not unless we want to eat inside - which we don't. We eat inside all year. The idea of coming to the continent is to eat outside. Not our choice tonight then, perhaps tomorrow.

So, in the end, we decide to go to *The Yangtse*. The British/Irish bars are non-starters. Apart from the unremarkable menus, they either are blasting out more unappealing music, the sort which I imagine might appeal to Ghetto Blaster Woman or, like the one next to *Es Choix*, they all have huge screens which seem to offer a variety of sporting fare – here a football match, motor racing over there or athletics down there. On the banks of *The Yangtse*, we can eat outside, and it's far enough from the big screens that we can't see them unless we crane our necks like - well – cranes and too far away to pick up the musical renditions also.

We give our order to a little middle-aged Chinese waitress who materialises from somewhere inside and we decide that a rosé would be an appropriate compromise as far as the wine is concerned. I choose the house wine – Viña del Mar from Cataluña. It's only 11.5% but it's nicely chilled and you don't taste it much after the food hits your palate anyway.

Some potential customers stop and look at the menu for a moment, then pass on. Maybe they don't like the look of the menu or maybe they don't like the look of us. Maybe we don't look romantic enough – just about everyone is holding hands like they were in love or something, even wrinklies like me who should know better. Maybe it's the holiday spirit coming out or the effect of the climate. I can't imagine them doing that in Bradford or Barnsley or wherever they come from. They'd be in too much of a hurry to get out of the rain.

"Listen!"

Iona, who has ears like a hawk, says that she can hear the microwave whirring. I strain to hear the ping! which I should hear if she's right. And she is! So that's how they do it, how they manage to have a hundred and one choices on the menu. For all that, the food is good, so good in fact that I run my finger round the bowl to scoop up what's left of the black bean sauce.

"Will you stop that!" says La-Belle-Dame-Sans-Merci. "For God's sake, show some manners!"

"I'm only trying to help the restaurant by showing how good the food is. And how are you supposed to get this sauce up with chopsticks anyway? Anyway, there's no one to see."

It's true. Throughout the meal, no one has followed our example and dined either within or without *The Yangtse*. The waitress has retreated to somewhere behind us and our only companion has been a ginger and white cat with whiskers like a walrus. It was begging to begin with but gave up when it got no response and now it has moved off a little distance and in an insulting riposte to us, is showing us its bum, one leg swung effortlessly over its shoulder, a study in indifference: *Didn't want any of your poxy food anyway.*

If I were you, Tom, I'd be careful what I said. You know what they say about Chinese restaurants. If business doesn't improve, *you* could be on the menu next!

3. Ciutadella Suits Me

Today it's a bit cloudy, but the real cloud which is hanging over me is I have to phone about the car as we are supposed to be getting it tomorrow. I have a bad feeling about it. Part of it is my lack of Spanish and unfamiliarity with the Spanish telephone system. It makes getting up, which is difficult at the best of times, even harder, but the purposeful slap slap of La-Belle-Dame-Sans-Merci's feet on the tiles as she comes through the living area from the front door where's she's having breakfast, galvanises me into action.

Half an hour or so later, I have my flimsy with the telephone number and a pocketful of change and am studying the phone by the bar with dismay. How much do I need? Which numbers do I need? Do I need them all? What if the person at the other end of the line doesn't speak English?

The boss's wife is sitting further along the bar with a pile of papers and a cigarette between her yellow fingers, the smoke spiralling lazily upwards. She looks a bit stressed now and a bit scary at the best of times. She has died yellow hair with black roots and aquiline features and glasses. Her skin is walnut in colour and texture. I think she must be called Prunella. I've seen her going into a villa at the far end of the swimming pool where she presumably lives with her husband and a gorgeous girl in her late teens whom I take to be their daughter. Obviously adopted, unless her mother was less frightful eighteen years ago than she is now or she gets her looks from her father whom I've seen about the place, snappily dressed in a blue and white striped shirt, three buttons open at the neck to show his manly hairy

43

chest and gold necklace, and sleeves unbuttoned to reveal tendrils of black hair on his tanned forearms. I don't know if his wife still fancies him or not, but it doesn't matter as he fancies himself anyway. He looks a lot younger than her but perhaps he's just better preserved or he's got a better taste in hair dye.

Prunella doesn't look as if she wants to be interrupted but I screw my courage to the sticking point and approach tentatively.

"*Scuso.*" I don't even know it's a proper word but I know it's *scusi* in Italian and I hope it's close. I show her the flimsy and point to the number and show her my fistful of coins and put a questioning look on my face. She picks out a 20 cents coin and her nicotine-stained finger indicates that I don't need the first three numbers.

As I feed the money into the machine, I wonder why did I do that? Why did I just not speak English? She can probably speak it like a native of Birmingham and Yorkshire and everywhere else in the British Isles they flock to from to here. And as for her, why did she just not explain it to me in English? She must think I'm a moron. Or maybe she just couldn't be bothered. I'd interrupted her engrossing paper work after all and judging by her expression, it's not happy reading. Maybe she's been over-charged for the essence of tomcat that they seem to spray the air with here.

The telephone is dead. I can't hear anything. Have I done it right? I look at Prunella but she's either pretending not to notice me or is really wrapped up in her work. Anyway I don't dare ask her. Besides, I'd only confirm my idiocy. Then I notice that the 20 cents has gone right through the machine and has been returned to me. I try again, this time making sure that it stays in and redial. It's so faint I can't be sure it's ringing but then I hear: *Hola!*

I could *Hola!* her back, but I don't want her to think I can speak Spanish and be carried away with a torrent of it, so I say hello and tell her that I am ringing up to confirm the booking for the car tomorrow. I give her the reference number.

"Just a moment." There is a rustling and then there is silence. I don't like the sound of this. I knew I was right to have a presentiment about it. Meanwhile my money is running out. Should I feed in another one or will there be a *feed me, feed me* tone like we have back home? Although it is early in the morning and the sun is only intermittently shining, I notice that I'm sweating and my palms are clammy.

"Hola!" She's back again. "I can't find your reservation. What is your name?" I've had this sort of problem before. They think I am saying *Anderson* or *Adamson* or even *Allison*. I even sound like an Alison as I am often mistaken for a woman on the phone. It can be embarrassing sometimes but at other times quite useful for beating the Data Protection Act when I am pretending to be Iona when I am sorting out one of her crashes with her insurance company. She could drive before I met her but I think it must have been a crash course. She passed first time too which shows she must have been good at it as later events seem to bear witness.

"A-D-D-I-S-O-N," I spell out. There is more rustling. For God's sake woman, hurry up!

"No, there is no sign of anyone with that name."

Bloody hell! I knew it! I knew I should just have got the hire car when I was here, but I had to be smart and try to save money. Well, now I am paying the price.

"Where is your accommodation? I'll send a car round for you. What time would you like the car?"

"Er...erm...ten o' clock." I give her our address. I am glad to get off the phone and glad to have arranged the car but as soon as I hang up, I think: *But I've already paid. This sounds like a new contract. Why oh why, didn't I just wait till I got here?*

I go back to tell Iona what has happened. By then I realise that I haven't said what class of car I want – the smallest and the cheapest for this little island. There's nothing we can do about it now – we'll just have to wait and see what tomorrow brings and hope we can sort it out. It's too cloudy for sunbathing, too early, too boring and besides I want to do something to take my mind off the car business.

We decide to get the bus to Ciutadella. There's a bus timetable attached to the window in the cubby hole which serves as an office. As Iona is busy doing her Madame Defarge stitching, I volunteer to go and check the times.

The next one is in forty minutes. I may as well have a walk about. In spite of the spasmodic sunshine, there's a scattering of hopeful sunbathers at the pool. I decide to take a stroll round the block, the long way round to waste some time. I am noiseless in my sock-less sandals. This must be the kitchens and oops! – here is the boss and the maid I saw washing the sunbeds earlier, engaged in a passionate embrace. He has his back to me so it is she who sees me first. She pushes him away, looking flustered. I don't see how he reacts as I have already passed on. I'd like to look back but instead, for some reason, probably to cover up my own embarrassment, I pretend that I haven't recognised what I've seen. Hmm! How interesting. Maybe his wife already knows or suspects something, which perhaps explains why she doesn't exactly look the happiest person in Menorca. Maybe it wasn't the paperwork at all which was bothering her. Maybe she was thinking: *Where's the philandering bastard now?* Well, I could tell her but of course, I'm not going to. I don't even tell Iona when I get back.

Later, as we pass the restaurant on the way to the bus, the boss, whom I imagine must be called Phil, is having a hearty lunch with the rest of the staff, apart from the sunbed scrubber. Apparently his sexual appetite is not the only one he has to satisfy. Prunella is behind the bar, looking as if behind bars is where she'd like to keep *him*.

Although we had left in good time for the bus, we have to sprint to catch it. It's early and in half an hour or so, it disgorges us in the Plaça d'es Pins, a fine square, and as the name suggests, filled with pine trees. However it's not the main square which is just off to our right - the Plaça d'es Born. It's a born again square. During Franco's time it was modestly renamed after the great dictator but everyone obstinately persisted with *es Born* and now it's officially back to the original again. *Born* means parade ground. In medieval times it was the jousting arena; now they have an equestrian parade in June, which just goes to show you how things change but remain the same.

It's a very pleasant, surprisingly large and open area with a rectangle of trees at its core, in the centre of which an obelisk commands attention. I have to go and see what that's about first. It seems to be in memory of the citizens of Ciutadella who were killed or enslaved by the Turks in 1558.

Dominating the square is the Ajuntament or Town Hall. I love it. If it weren't for the arcades below and the clock on top and the large, Moorish style windows which would make a defender an easy target, not to mention an easy access for an attacker, it would look more like a toy fort than a municipal building with its crenellated battlements, or it could be something out of *Beau Geste* with the palm trees along the façade, standing like a row of soldiers guarding the entrance. I suppose, on reflection, it's not really like a fort at all, but someone had fun designing it and it's a million times better than the cereal packet on its side that we've got for a Town Hall back home.

If that was good, the view from the square down below to the port is stupendous. The sea comes in in a great jagged arm, ending limp-wristedly with a pointed forefinger, not far to our right, while to our left, small pleasure craft, as well as fishing boats, are held captive, prows pointing towards the promenade where the canopies of open air restaurants hug the cliff and where the massive trapezoidal walls of the city walls rise apparently impenetrable, yet not actually invincible, as the monument we have just seen testifies, up to the Plaça d'es Born.

Facing the Ajuntament and occupying the whole side of the square, are three 19th century palaces, the plainest and most ordinary buildings on the Plaça, apart from the Post Office, which occupies the fourth side. They're impressive enough in their own way I suppose, if not for their symmetry, at least for their sheer size; it's just that everything else I've seen so far has been so much more interesting - captivating even.

The palaces are bisected by the Carrer Major d'es Born and this is the route we now take as it leads us to the Cathedral. It's impressively huge, as cathedrals should be, but this is half battleship-fortress with towering windowless walls, and half religious edifice, marooned in a square of grey flagstones polished as smooth as a skating rink. It's constructed of a warm, honey-coloured stone and pleasantly devoid of ostentatious ornamentation like some I could mention in Italy. In former times it was a mosque, evidence of which can be seen by a minaret transformed into a belfry.

"There they go, ringing the changes again," I remark to Iona.

She gives me one of the smiles which looks as if she'd got toothache.

It's Sunday and unfortunately the congregation is filing out of the massive doors. Unfortunately, because now the streets are going to be swarming with people. These Catholic services are too damned short. In fact, it appears that some have been released some time already; maybe they slipped out before the collection, because smartly dressed men are carrying mysterious octagonal cardboard boxes, as many as half a dozen at a time, piled on top of each other so they look as if they were carrying hat boxes. As if to show they are manly and would not dream of carrying, let alone wearing, a hat, their burdens dangle from a nonchalant forefinger. Iona senses food, a speciality of the region and an area in which she has a special interest.

"Wonder what those are? Must find out and get one.'

"We certainly must."

If the congregation is going out, it is safe for us to go in, just for a moment, to see what it is like. A short flight of steps fan out from a porticoed entrance below a rose window high above us. One of the Corinthian columns on the left is so badly worn that it's practically eaten all the way through, like a bone with osteoporosis, so it's hard to see what supporting role it could possibly perform. Indeed it looks in imminent danger of collapse altogether, having more holes than stone.

"Perhaps they've left it like that, a symbol that you're about to enter a holy building, in case you thought it was a fort," I helpfully suggest to Iona.

"Look, are you going to keep that up all day?"

"What?"

"These pathetic jokes."

"Don't know. Just depends."

"Well, I'd appreciate it, if the next time you think of something extremely witty to say, you just keep it to yourself."

"Fair enough." I'm not hurt. If she wants to miss out on the wit and the wisdom, well, that's up to her. She used to like my jokes once but familiarity means she generally treats them with contempt nowadays.

Inside, I'm not disappointed to discover the plainness of the exterior has been carried into the interior. It's large and open and very modern looking, perhaps mainly due to the apse which is especially pleasing, consisting of five long and elegant stained-glass windows. In fact, I think the stained-glass windows of the Cathedral its best feature, especially the turquoise one in one of the chapels, as it's my favourite colour.

As we wander round, we discover that essentially the interior of the cathedral is in fact, modern, as it was badly looted and destroyed in the Civil War. There's a photograph to show how bad it was. It is in such a mess that it's hard to imagine what it was like before, but the restorers have done a really good job and possibly even improved on what it was like originally.

When we come out, we take an intriguing-looking lane to our right and presently come to a shop outside of which there is an easel displaying three of the mysterious octagonal boxes. Sure enough, there is a queue of ex-churchgoers lined up to make their bulk purchase of sugar-dusted pastries, for indeed that's what they are, as we can see them now being packed into the boxes.

"Do you want to get them now?" I ask. "Or do you want to carry them about for the rest of the day?" It's not that they would be too heavy for her to carry; I'm thinking of the nuisance they would be as she's already carrying the guidebook. I have her best interests at heart, as usual.

"Hmm. Perhaps not. But maybe we should get them whilst we see them. It is Sunday after all and they might close."

"It'll be all right. We'll get them later on when we're ready to go back." It's not a big gamble for me if they do close, as I am not a sweet person as I already told you or you may have worked out for yourself by now.

"Hmm. I hope you're right."

There is a maze of interesting narrow, winding streets to explore in Ciutadella, with honey-coloured or whitewashed houses with green shutters or ironwork balconies and carriage-style street lamps which add a certain old world sort of ambience, and altogether much more modern black electricity cables which don't, and the best thing is, that in spite of the Cathedral having spilled its congregation upon them, the streets remain relatively empty, so that if we are patient, we can wait until the other pedestrians amble off and we can have the street to ourselves for a photo opportunity.

We come across a house, conspicuous by its striking yellow-ochre paint. This is the Museu del Pintor Torrent, Menorca's most famous painter. Perhaps he is famous in Menorca, perhaps further afield than that amongst people who know something about painting. I don't know much about art as the saying goes, but I know what I like and he's called the Menorcan van Gogh and I like van Gogh, so we'll probably come back here another day when it's open.

Taking a street down to the right, we have another fine view of the port with the boats packed like sardines at right angles to the shore to our left and to our right, where it looks as if the sea should be, there is a car park. If I can find how to get there, it should be a very handy place to park. Across from us, white houses with terraced gardens spill down to what I'm sure in past times, because of its irregular shape, must have been under water once but which is now merely a sandy floor tapering away to an invisible point.

You can hardly miss the building further over to our right though, the 17th century Bastió de Sa Font, its towering trapezoidal walls dominating the narrow end of the inlet and we head off in that direction. There's a coat of arms on the corner and a flight of steps running up the side to the entrance. It's now the municipal museum. I expect we'll go there too, when it's open. It's quite a good idea this, to come in on a Sunday when the traffic is lighter and to orientate ourselves.

Opposite the fort is an attractive wide, carob-lined avenue, but however appealing it may be, our guidebook directs us down the Carrer Portal de Sa Font, much narrower and much less attractive but boasting one or two bay windows which protrude rather oddly, like paunches, over the flat façade of the street. Bay windows were what the British did for the Menorcans, who, if they did not adopt them into their own architecture exactly, at least adopted them into their language, calling them *boinders*. They called the British gentry *milord* and their wives, *miledi* but it was also a term meaning an ugly (English) lady, so you could smile and be polite and say: *yes, miledi* and *no, miledi* and they might give you a sharp look but couldn't be sure, if you kept a straight face, and kept your tongue in your cheek, if you were speaking with forked tongue or not.

This brings us to the convent of Santa Clara. It's a working convent so you can't visit it, but you can visit the church. It's a modern structure, dating from only 1945, having suffered even worse damage during the Civil War than the Cathedral and that is saying something. I wouldn't normally bother with it, but the entrance looks incredibly appealing. It's through an arched recess, reminiscent of a small inner courtyard, the sort that you catch a glimpse of as you pass ancient grand villas, whitewashed and lined with greenery in terracotta pots. There's a heavy door in the centre, which I bet is locked and leads to the convent, conveniently located, I suppose, so the nuns can go out without going through the church - if they are allowed to go out. Above the door there is an eye-catching image of the Virgin in ceramic tiles, against a bright yellow background.

The door into the church is on the right and the effect as you enter is electrifying. It's just a small chapel, but immediately in front of you as you enter, there is a stained-glass window of vivid red and blue and yellow which transfixes and mesmerises you with a Cyclops eye. No sooner have you recovered from that however, than the gaze is drawn to a painting above the altar, executed in the most vivid rich deep blues and purples and greens.

But there is something even more striking. Near the top of the painting, in a central position, just below a piece which is raised above the main frame of the picture like the board which was nailed above Christ's cross and which I'm sure is the intention here - is a pair of haunting eyes from which the light of the whole picture seems to emanate. I can't say to whom the eyes belong – they look like neither a man's nor a woman's, but they hypnotise, fascinate, unnerve me even. I can safely say it's the most striking religious picture I have ever seen apart from Salvador Dali's *Crucifixion* and I have seen Giotto's frescoes and a lot of Italy's greatest Renaissance art besides. But who painted this masterpiece? I wish I knew, but there is absolutely nothing to tell me.

There is a nun over to our left, behind a screen, reading a good book apparently, no doubt something improving, if not the Good Book itself, but probably multi-tasking, watching us as well, in case we do anything wrong, which I find almost as unnerving as the eyes on the painting. If it weren't for the screen I might have asked her who the artist was, but even if it weren't there, I doubt if I would have asked her. It's not just that it would seem an invasion of privacy, an intrusion on her contemplations, but the truth is, I am just a little bit frightened of nuns.

It dates from the time, when as a boy, I was exposed for the first time to the species when we played football in the Keith and District Primary Schools League, against a Catholic school, and to me the nuns seemed exotic creatures from some alien culture, objects of curiosity - and fear, when I was told by a local savant, a year older than me and in whom I had complete and utter trust, that that thick leather belt round their waist was used to belt their pupils daily and that if they lost this game, they would all be thrashed. I didn't see any reason not to believe it. After all, were we not subject to the same punishment, though what we were belted with was a purpose built tawse consisting of either two or three fingers, in various thicknesses and lovingly crafted in Lochgelly in Fife and sent out from thence the length and breadth of Scotland for the discipline of the young. And the nuns, sinister in their black robes with their wide belts which hardly looked as if they were functional in any other terms – what could they possibly be holding up after all? Didn't nuns have elastic in their knickers just like the rest of us? Well - it all looked entirely believable to me and made feel less inclined to try to win the match, out of sympathy.

Therefore, I creep out as quiet as any nun might, glad that I had been tempted into this little gem of a place, the interior of which our guidebook does not even mention, let alone that mystical and hypnotic painting. However, it does relate an interesting story which happened in 1749.

It seems three young ladies being educated in the convent school had had enough of education (well, I never! Isn't that an amazing thing!) and hopped over the convent wall and put themselves at the mercy of their boyfriends who were soldiers in the local garrison. How they managed to meet them, let alone get to know them well enough to fall in love, God alone knows. Anyway the Governor, General Blakeney, in the unlikely rôle of Cupid, would listen to none of the arguments to return the girls, refusing all demands to hand them back to the convent, but as a sort of concession, had the room in which the girls were sleeping sealed up by a priest each night, thus tacitly setting his seal of approval on the whole affair, but on the other hand, also ensuring there was no sex which was a very British thing to do, I'm pleased to say. Eventually however, the girls said yes and were married and horror of horrors - no, not had sex - turned Protestant.

Strangely enough, the next point of interest is a little street, almost straight across from the church, the Carrer Qui

No Passa. Ah, ha! I think, I bet this is where the girls were sealed up by the priest. No way through for the boyfriends all right. What good luck to stumble upon it, just after we've been reading about it! I wonder how many people pass this narrow little opening and never give it a glance, or realise the fascinating story behind its name?

It begins as a vaulted area of honey-coloured stone and brick, like a small cellar, then broadens out, though still an incredibly narrow corridor, flanked by houses with gleaming white walls and dark green shutters, with a big green arched door with a tall and shuttered window at the end. The curious thing is that although this little street goes nowhere, apart from to the green door at the end which looks more like a cellar door than a house door, there is a car coming up it with both its wing mirrors folded in. Why would you take a car down there, for God's sake? The street is so narrow, you couldn't open the car door unless you lined it up with the door of the house and someone opened that for you and you just stepped straight out of the car into the house. The height of laziness, except the amount of concentration required to avoid scraping the car would require much more effort than simply to walk down it.

Now out of the Carrer Qui No Passa, the driver does a curious thing. Instead of turning to his right and driving down the street, the Dormidor de les Monges, with a squealing of   protesting rubber on the polished, smooth as glass flags, which sets my teeth on edge, he *reverses* down it instead. Why? Easy after having negotiated the Qui No Passa, but all the same why, unless he just likes to do things the hard way? I expect he has sex standing up in a hammock. And then I realise that, if he came out of the Qui No Passa facing the right way, he must have reversed in to begin with. Bloody hell! What does it mean? I don't suppose I'll ever find out. Maybe the man's an idiot, or perhaps he's merely backward.

Iona finds the street in the guidebook. To my disappointment, it's got nothing to do with the ex-convent girls at all. Apparently it cuts through what was the city wall and didn't lead anywhere once upon a time, but now it does. It takes a dogleg and joins the Carrer Sant Antoni which leads out of the Plaça Nova. I have to see it on the map for myself before I believe it; it certainly looks as if it ends in a dead end.

At least it helps explain part of the driver's manoeuvres; presumably he came up the Carrer Sant Antoni but why he should take such a difficult route, God alone knows, nor why he should reverse down the Dormidor either. I reckon I was right the first time: he just likes doing things the difficult way. Like him, we head for the Plaça Nova ourselves. Much more easy, even by foot, if you just go down Santa Clara which is comparatively broad and straight, onto Sant Antoni and then the square.

It's a charming little square, the centre filled with tables under canvas canopies which annoy me, as I like to sit out in the sun, but it's not the open air restaurants which gives the Plaça Nova its appeal, it's the Moorish arches which border it on the eastern side, the Carrer de Sa Carnisseria and Ses Voltes, also known as Carrer J M Quadrado. I don't know who he was but his name sounds fitting enough for a road which leads to a square. I look him up in the guidebook and discover that he was a politician and reactionary. So he was a bit of an old square right enough. I'd like to point this out to Iona, but I'm banned. Oh, well, that's her loss.

This is the street which we follow, underneath the pointed white arches. This place just gets better and better. I've not been so impressed by a city before since Siena and I'm in love with Siena. What other delights does Ciutadella have in store I wonder?

It doesn't take long to find out. When the arches stop, we find we are practically at the back of the Cathedral. In a sort of mini-square, there is a sheep mounted on a pillar with a flag tilted over its right shoulder. It looks as if it is marching off jauntily to war. But a sheep going to war? What can it mean? Iona has the answer, or at least she finds it in the guidebook. The sheep is actually the Lamb of God (silly me, of course!) and the standard bears the cross of St John the Baptist. His festival is held on June 23rd to the 25th apparently, and is the biggest festival in the entire Balearics, which I imagine pleases him quite a bit, except I bet he wishes they could get his name right. They call it the festival of San Joan for some reason.

At the street called Seminari, we look down to our left and spot the unmistakable bell tower of the Diocesan Museum, looking like a bathysphere with its four bulging porthole windows or a pair of trout with overactive thyroids. But before we come to it, there's the Palau Torre Saura which now seems to be an exhibition centre of some kind. The façade looks very tired and eroded, especially the lower half, but look up and the top storey consists of a row of arched windows with a projecting roof on the underside of which are carved in the most exquisite detail, rosettes with a branch of leaves in between, a detail which is carried round the side of the building.

The Diocesan Museum, on the other hand, on its right hand side in fact, is nothing to write home about, except that over the triple door, there is an intriguing sculpture of the fattest Virgin Mary I have ever seen, with a pair of bosoms so bulging, they seem to be coming out in sympathy with the trouts' eyes on the bell tower. The infant Christ, cradled in her left arm, is certainly also the best nourished I have ever seen. All this would be interesting enough, but what is especially remarkable is that in her other hand Mary wields a studded club and is wearing a very determined look on her face: *Ah ken Ah'm a virgin but he's still ma wean an' you're no takin' him aff me, so back aff or Ah'll bash yir brains in!*

We turn right at the bottom of the street and then right again which brings us to the Església del Roser. There's another sculpture of the Virgin here too at the top of the façade, a much leaner Virgin, with a commensurately skinnier infant. She's so high up it's difficult to see clearly, but she looks rather mannish and I can't make out what she is holding in her right hand. It looks as long as a club but she seems to be holding it in the middle and the curious thing is that she is standing on someone's head, so maybe it is a club right enough. But one thing's for sure - neither of these are like the meek and mild Mary I'm used to.

This street, the Carrer Roser, called logically enough after the church, brings us to the side door of the Cathedral which, illogically, is bigger in every respect than the main door. And at the side of the door, there is a notice advertising an organ recital which Iona makes a note of. She's not particularly a fan of the organ, but wants to experience it in the Cathedral setting as she thinks it will resonate here and fill the place with swelling sound.

We've still got plenty of time until our bus. What could be better than a stroll down to the marina and perhaps a beer or maybe two? But first, we must go and buy one of those heavy octagonal boxes, containing the Menorcan delicacy.

I might have known it. The signs were all there. Since we had seen them everywhere when we first arrived, at the Cathedral, we had seen not another sign of them, not a glimpse, nor another baker's shop either. The one we had seen before is closed. In fact, it looks as if it had been closed for years.

"Huh! I told you we should have got them when we saw them!" La-Belle-Dame-Sans-Merci is not amused.

Did she really say that? I can't remember. I thought it had been a mutual decision to leave them to later so she didn't have the nuisance of carrying them everywhere. Things had been going so well in this lovely place, but now, as usual, I have blown it again.

Emerging on the Plaça d'es Born again, we take the long way round, passing the palaces and the Teatre d'es Born, a late 19th century building and built to show those upstarts in Maó that anything they could build, the citizens of Ciutadella could build better – but when it came to actually experiencing the artistic fare this building was built to provide, the culture vultures of Ciutadella found it very unappetising indeed and the place fell into disrepair, though it has been restored now. If, like in Maó, it was operas which were staged, I don't blame them. In fact, I would say it marks them out as being more discerning than their rivals in Maó.

Next to the Ajuntament is the police station, which, to judge by the number of police cars and motorbikes parked outside, must be hosting a meeting of the entire police force of Menorca.

The road wends its way in a gentle curve and then turns back on itself along by the fish restaurants and the boats. To the left there is a paved area brimming over with restaurants through which we weave our way amongst the diners and then along a boardwalk which hugs the contours of the cliff which we take as far as it goes. It is certainly not boring but the path along by the restaurants, looking through the blur of masts to the other side, is much more appealing.

We must have walked for miles and I deserve a beer, in spite of my transgression with the octagonal boxes. And even Iona, who normally can't stand the stuff, except in the direst necessity, when they don't serve sparkling mineral water, decides to have one. Perhaps she's going to drown her sorrows. According to a pharmacist's sign I had seen, the temperature is 26 °. It doesn't seem that hot to me, as usually at that temperature, the sun drills a hole in my head and I have no such sensation today, but it's very pleasantly warm all the same and what a pleasant way to spend an October afternoon, with nothing more to do except watch the world go by: watch people stroll past; watch the little bubbles in my beer effervescing to join their fellows in the froth at the top; watch the sparrows hopping nearby in the hope of some crumbs, incredibly tame and clean; watch a dirty fly zoom in and drink from the ring of condensation which my glass has left on the table. I can actually see its tongue coming out and lapping up the liquid, and then it flies off, satisfied and refreshed. That Super-Tramp and poet, W.H. Davies would most certainly approve.

Refreshed ourselves, but still with plenty of time until our bus leaves at 3:30, we walk along the marina looking at the menus. Some of the restaurants have actually been carved out of the cliff face and look pretty exclusive but the good thing about Spain is that by law, the restaurants must offer a *menú del día,* so poor people like me can afford to go to the swankiest places, as long as you like the look of what's on the *menú del día* of course, which can often be not that exciting. The problem here, though, is going to be which one to choose.

The other side of the port has fewer eating places and is altogether much less classy than the other side, and yet, in my view, has the better view, for from here you can see the restaurants, which at night will be lit up, their lights reflected in the water, and if you raise your eyes you can see the city wall, the back of the Ajuntament and the Bastió de Sa Font, none of which would be visible from the other side. There is a restaurant here called *Es Moll* which I've noticed is mentioned in our guidebook with seats outside by the waterfront. It looks the perfect place to come when we get the car.

A cockerel crows triumphantly from somewhere near at hand. It's nearly three o'clock in the afternoon, for God's sake! Doesn't he know what time it is? Or maybe he's just made a conquest. Perhaps it's a sign. Perhaps La-Belle-Dame-Sans-Merci will not hold the incident of the pastries against me and Menorca may be consummated this very afternoon.

4. Facing the Music

The bus leaves the Plaça d'es Pins more or less on time and we are back in the apartment by four o' clock. Even if we were blind, we'd easily know that we were back: the nose is assaulted by the smell of cat pee and seems worse than ever and the dog that was whining yesterday sounds like *The Hound of the Baskervilles* now. It's coming from a villa just down to our right where the extended family is sitting at an extended table, having their Sunday lunch. It was underway when we left at noon and doesn't look as if it's about to stop either. It would be nice if they got the bloody dog to stop though. Why don't they throw it a bone or something? If they don't have one, they could give it the one I've got to pick with them.

When we come back from the pool two hours later, the gathering is beginning to break up and the dog has laryngitis, or at least has stopped barking. The couple from next door is sitting out the front. As I had surmised, they've got two little girls of school age and have been here a week already which means that they must have taken them out of school early. Still, they seem a nice enough family. I comment on the smell.

"Isn't it dreadful?" she says. "It's worse inside our apartment. I bought some disinfectant and lit scented candles and we can still smell it!"

Scented candles, eh? I like the sound of that, and adore the smell, being a bit of a candle fan. But I don't think I'd go to the trouble of disinfecting the place, not when it doesn't belong to me. Perhaps she is one of that peculiar breed of house-proud women. She also says that their bathroom floor is swimming, like ours. I tell her it's probably a design feature.

We sit out the front with the gin and T's. The family next door has gone out for something to eat. We'll be following them in a wee while but in the meantime, it is bliss to relax in the peace and quiet and catch as much of the setting sun as I can.

A car pulls up opposite and Jane, the rep, gets out. After she disappears from view, I hear her heels clip-clopping on the pavement and presently I hear snatches of her conversation. She appears to be talking to some people in an apartment three or four down to our left. Perhaps they are complaining about the smell.

"It's got faulty wiring in the bathroom, that's why I can't let you have it."

I can't make it out, but someone is making some lengthy response, then Jane's voice pipes up again. "Well, I'll let you see it, if you like..." She sounds slightly exasperated, like a mother giving in to a persistent child. Ghetto Blaster Woman wouldn't recognise that tone though. She just gives into them right away. Saves time I suppose.

Clip-clop. The heels don't sound too happy either, but brusque and business-like. She appears with a thick-set man wearing a red singlet with cut away shoulders, like the thin, hippy-looking man at the football yesterday was wearing, the type that Iona hates. Never mind the singlet, I don't like the look of *him*. His bullet head is shaved down to the wood, but he's got a moustache like a thick black leech clinging to his upper lip. He can't walk. He has to waddle, for if the circumference of his stomach is anything to go by, I imagine the thighs in his tracksuit bottoms are so thick he has to, to stop them rubbing together. I can see his biceps though - as thick as my thigh - and decorated with a tattoo of a dagger framed by a wreath. Some people have MOTHER

63

or RUBY or the name of someone dear to them, but he just has a dagger. I don't blame Jane for not arguing with him. He looks an ugly sort of customer and yet he has fathered at least one child, because a girl of about twelve is following in his wake.

Oh, my God! They're coming next door! Come to think of it, our neighbours on the right *have* been very quiet and we've never seen any sign of them. This explains it. The apartment is empty. Iona and I look at each other wordlessly, in dismay. She doesn't like the look of him either. There's a high wall between us, so we can only hear the sound of the door being opened, then we can't hear any more for a few moments, presumably they are inspecting the premises, then Jane's Liverpudlian vowels, definitely sounding exasperated now.

"Well, it's not safe, that's why we're not allowed to let it out. If you insist on taking it, you'll have to do so at your own risk and sign an indemnity form."

There is a pause. I'm not a religious person, but I pray to Someone very hard indeed. Surely no one in their right mind would take an apartment under such circumstances? If that bathroom is anything like ours and the one next door, swimming in water and with dodgy electrics, surely it wouldn't take much thinking about.

Right enough, it doesn't take him long.

"We'll take it." He sounds like a Geordie. A Geordie accent is my favourite of all the English accents and it is a matter of regret to me, that although my mother came from South Shields, she didn't sound like Jimmy Nail who played Oz in *Auf Wiedersehen, Pet.* But now, from him, from my new neighbour, the accent seems to lose its appeal.

In a few moments there is a procession past our door, father and daughter joined by a skinny little woman with ginger hair scraped back from her face into a pony tail, making her look severely old. They don't bother to pack suitcases, but carry their clothes, which seem to consist mainly of football tops, on hangers. They look like Manchester United's red, certainly not Newcastle's stripes, so maybe I've misplaced the accent, but I don't think so. Amongst his other faults, as I perceive them, he also appears to be a traitor.

It's dislike at first sight. His tattoos (I'm sure he must have more of them) and his appearance don't make him a bad person, but there's something belligerently arrogant about him which repels me. He looks the type, all brawn and no brain who bulldozes his way through life with absolutely no regard for other people, a bit like Ghetto Blaster Woman but in his case with the much more offensive weapon of his boorishness which he wields like a club. Naturally, one wants to get on with one's neighbours, but for what it's worth, I just can't see us exchanging words of wit and wisdom, becoming bosom buddies, discussing Wordsworth's *Lyrical Ballads* over a glass of chilled Chablis for instance.

He can hardly not see us, sitting just yards away, nor can we pretend not to notice what is going on, for that would be to instantly signal our ostracism of him. Apparent overtures of friendship must be made. I give him a nod of acknowledgement - it's the most I can muster and he nods back. A nodding acquaintance. I should think that's the most our relationship is likely to amount to.

On the second trip, what I feared most, happens. He is carrying a ghetto blaster. I'm not surprised. In fact, I expected no less. And what's worse, we're getting it right away. Within a moment, our peace, already destroyed, is shattered by a calamitous cacophony, the very same sort of insufferable din which Hélène was playing in the car, only in her case, dozens of decibels more quietly. This is obviously Music and Movement. It blares away to the empty apartment as they ferry what looks like a whole shop of clothes to and fro. It's no consolation to find my assessment of his character has been correct. Anyone who has not even moved in yet, but who can inflict this, not just on me, but the entire neighbourhood, is a boor of the first magnitude.

Right that does it! I can't stand it any more. I couldn't bear to even have eye contact with him again. I'm going to move round to the back. I'm pretty sure what the reaction would be if I asked him to turn it down, let alone off. Even if he didn't hit me, I know he wouldn't turn it down, and he would know it was bugging me so it would be tantamount to a declaration of hostilities. He might even turn it up. Better to pretend it isn't affecting me, then perhaps he won't deliberately keep playing it, for I have a feeling he didn't like the look of me either, and I can pretend that I am merely indifferent to him instead of hating his guts with a passion. Come back, Ghetto Blaster Woman, all is forgiven! If only you and your charms and your charming children were next door to us, we wouldn't have *him*!

I grab my gin and T and fume at our back door. There's actually more room round here and it's actually quite warm, although there's no sun. It's grim isn't it! All you have to do is just even think about how nice and peaceful it is and the gods read your mind: *So that's what you think, is it? Well, we'll see about that then, heh! heh! heh!* The merciful thing is that you can't hear the racket round here. Thank God we can do this. If we'd only had a balcony as is normally the case, there would have been no escape, like in Sorrento last year where I had been plagued by a trio of teenage girls and their ghetto blaster.

"What if they play the bloody thing all night and we can hear it through the walls?"

"They won't," says Iona. "They'll have to put it off to let the girl sleep."

But I'm not so sure. She's probably the type that ordinarily stays up half the night and even longer on holidays. I go inside again, to see if I can hear anything. Maybe now they've moved in, they no longer need the "music" to move to.

"It's all right in the bedroom, but you should hear the bloody din in the living room!"

"Well, we can't hear it here, so just forget about it."

I wish she were half as tolerant with me.

"Well, if we do hear it in the night, you can go and complain. It won't bother me," I lie. "I've got my own radio." It's not just cowardice. That type probably doesn't hit women. They don't mind head-butting a man, or kicking him where it really hurts, but their ethical code does not permit hitting women. I hope I've got that right - for Iona's sake.

Anyway, it's time for another gin and I need a large one this time and by the time it is finished and time to go for our meal, I am feeling a bit more mellow.

The din is still spewing from next door and they have their door open so everyone in the complex can hear it better. I steal a cautious glimpse in as we pass. There's no sign of them, but I can see the object of my misery on a table near the door. Typical! They're probably at Barry's Bar. I wish I had the courage to steal more than a just a glance at their apartment, but the bloody radio as well.

"Aren't you going to wear a jumper?" Iona asks.

"It's actually very mild."

"It may not be when we come back."

"It's OK. I'm hardy and you may kiss me." The gin must have been stronger than I thought. I would never normally make such a bad joke, not even in jest. I expect I'm just stressed. It doesn't even make sense, if you think about it.

The villas on the way to the Commercial Centre are lit up. Attractive enough by day, to my mind they look even more appealing by night. Which one would I buy if I won the lottery? What about this one here, for example? Set in garden of palm trees, it is L-shaped with a colonnaded terrace which follows the contours of the house with, on its longest side, where bougainvillea is being trained up the whitewashed walls, a long dark oak dining table with high-backed chairs, and on the short side, a cartwheel hanging on the wall with pot plants in a wooden stand beneath. I imagine the family dine out here all the time. Through the glass doors I can see a stone and brick fireplace. Even the dog kennel is splendid, a sort of mini villa complete with whitewashed walls and orange tiles on the roof.

But I think I prefer this one – a much grander affair with a much larger garden but not yet mature, with a curving convex terrace, ending in a two-storey cotton reel sort of tower. But as the road takes us further round the house, we are able to see that in fact, the tower only marks the beginning of a whole new wing which appears to have a flat roof with a balustrade and a chimney which serves a room below, unless it is some sort of fancy barbeque. It appears to be in utter darkness. Perhaps it is for sale, though there doesn't appear to be any advertising to that effect. Iona doesn't like it which is going to present her with a bit of a dilemma when I buy it when I win the lottery. I'm sure I'll find someone to live in it with me though, depending on how much money is left over after I buy the house.

Tonight *The Yangtse* has a handful of patrons I'm pleased to see, but we walk straight past it and all the other restaurants. We know which restaurant we are heading for – *Es Choix* which has a canvas screen with windows in it, so it's a bit like sitting in a tent and not quite alfresco, but is ambient enough, with pink tablecloths and wine glasses glistening in the candlelight. Unfortunately, however, there is a bit of noise pollution from the English bar across the street. The gods make sure you can't have everything, just to stop you feeling too happy, as I know only too well.

We order the fish and a white wine, Ca N'estruç, like last night also from Cataluña but this time 12% and which, I'm glad to see, is placed in an ice bucket by the side of the table and covered with a napkin. That's a good sign and doesn't always happen, like last night for example. The waiter is dressed in black trousers and a red shirt which clashes with violently with the tablecloths. As far as I can see, he seems to be the only one in charge and he has tables inside and outside to deal with, as well as a bar. Fortunately or unfortunately, he's not over-burdened with work. Across the street, the English bar is doing a roaring trade and, so I noticed, were the other English bars we passed.

He can afford to spend some time chatting with us, even if he can't afford much else unless business picks up. He asks us where we're from and when we tell him, he extols the virtues of Scotland, having spent a holiday there once. We tell him we've just arrived and haven't seen any of the island yet, but how wonderful Ciutadella is and having complimented each other's countries as much as we can, he goes off to place our order.

Outside, three boys of varying heights and therefore ages, presumably, attired in football tops, one unmistakably a Newcastle United supporter while the others in blue, could represent any number of clubs. The tallest, wearing a white baseball hat, is driving a baby buggy with panache, slaloming round the legs of prospective diners or perhaps just people out for a stroll, for the pedestrian precinct when we first came and which had been relatively quiet, is now well populated. Perhaps the parents have bribed the boys: *Here! Tak' this an' tak' yir brither oot furra walk* whilst they get down to the business of consummating Menorca and providing the brothers with yet another, in the fullness of time.

"Do you remember that family in Mallorca?" I ask Iona, pointing my wine glass vaguely in the direction of the boys with the baby buggy, and incidentally, if my geography is correct, also in the direction of the big-sister island.

Iona knows exactly to which family I am referring. Between the wine and the fish, we reminisce about the whole remarkable, not to say totally embarrassing incident, although we were only incidental witnesses, but in a privileged position, if that's the right word, to know this dysfunctional family better than most.

There we were, sitting outside (as usual) at a restaurant, built on a slope, where two boys aged about eleven and eight were having great fun letting the baby buggy roll down the hill with their two-year-old baby brother passenger aboard. One stood at the top and pushed it to send it on its way while the other caught it and then they changed places. It was good to see such brotherly co-operation and fair play. Perhaps, for all I knew, the little tot was having the time of his life, but the noise of the wheels rumbling over the flagstones was extremely irritating, not to mention their cries of triumph as they retrieved their brother intact and ran yelling up to the starting point again.

Iona and I were not the only ones who were concerned for the safety of the little one. Other diners were looking mildly alarmed but no one interfered. I was hesitant to do so myself, knowing all too well how some children do not take too kindly to guidance from their parents, let alone total strangers, and in any case, surely the mother must intervene soon? She couldn't be far away, could she? The child should already be tucked up in bed anyway. In fact, it was about time the eight year old was heading that way himself, holidays not withstanding.

The game was getting a bit boring - the baby didn't seem to be objecting to being used as a projectile weapon and the human cargo was safely gathered in each time. It needed a bit more excitement, something a bit more challenging. The solution was to take a running jump at it, to send the buggy down from the pre-arranged starting line at an ever-increasing rate of knots, to our and the other captive diners' ever-increasing alarm. But still we took no action and eventually the inevitable happened. The buggy toppled over long before the catcher could catch and skidded down the slope on its side, fortunately, not face down. The baby, if he had been sleeping, had an extremely rude awakening and if he had suffered any damage, it was certainly not to his lungs.

"Whit the fuck are ye daein' wi' that fuckin' wean? Get yir erses up here afore I leather the lot o' yis."

Like a *deus ex machina,* a voice resounded from the air somewhere above us. Although we could not see the speaker, the voice was as rough as a cheese grater, the sort of voice which could only be produced by years of dedication to the cancer stick. I bowed my head in shame for equably obviously the voice was unmistakably Scottish, certainly west coast, and if I had to be pressed for a precise location – Coatbridge - or perhaps, at a push, Airdrie, not more than half an hour's drive from where I live.

Our fellow diners looked up in consternation. Did they really hear what they had just heard? Perhaps they were amazed, wondering what foreign language was this – and yet, they must recognise the expletives, for even if they came from deepest, darkest Surbiton, if they had understood nothing else, they must, at the barest minimum, have recognised *those* words, the lingua franca of the curse world.

The next day, by sheer chance, we were able to put a face to the voice. It was the boys and the buggy I recognised coming towards us along the beach, the buggy as if propelled by steam power, for she whom I took to be the mother, was puffing out clouds of white smoke like a steam engine. She was accompanied by a younger woman who might have been her sister or just a friend, and a little girl who may have belonged to either, aged about ten.

As luck would have it, they decided to install themselves only yards from us and in front of us, which gave us the chance to observe them without appearing to stare. Oh, no! She's not going to is she? But she was and she did. Without wasting a moment, the mother proceeded to disrobe, liberating from a white *Bustenhalter* a pair of drooping bulbous dugs, scarcely any less white than that in which they were encased, swinging low to meet the rolls of fat at her stomach. She could easily have got a job in advertising as the Michelin man's wife. Her face also looked as hung-dog as her breasts; deeply etched with the vicissitudes of life so that although she looked about 55, I bet she was actually about 20 years younger. Even her hair looked tired of life and hung in long, lank strands. She was what we Scots call *hackit,* and the astonishing thing is that she got pregnant at all, never mind three times.

Her more comely companion, though she would not be winning any beauty contests either, spared us the spectacle of her topless torso, spread a towel and sat down beside her friend, facing the sea and the sun as they each lit up another fag. The boys and the girl were creating mayhem in the sea, splashing each other with gay abandon whilst the adults abandoned the toddler in favour of an earnest and serious conversation and had absolutely no idea that the toddler, naked apart from a disposable nappy, and although on unsteady legs, was nevertheless making steady progress further and further along the beach and out of all sight and sound. God knows where he was heading, least of all him.

At last he disappeared round a bend and was lost from view and as far as his mother was concerned, totally lost, for should she suddenly remember him now, she wouldn't have a clue in which direction to begin looking for him, though ironically, all the people in the immediate vicinity were obviously discussing the situation and having suspended their sunbathing or reading, not to mention their disbelief, as

Coleridge urged us to do when watching a drama, (only this was real life), were now sitting up following the youngster's progress and looking back at his mother, incredulous that all this time she had never spared him a moment's thought, nor apparently, had her friend. Like us, with each passing moment they were thinking: *Surely she must remember him now!*

But now, since he had disappeared from sight, Iona and I decided we could not let him get much further away - it was time to act. I'm not sure if I intended to speak to the fond parent or set off in pursuit of the youngster's gallant bid for freedom, but just as I was getting to my feet, I was beaten to it by a man who went over to speak to the mother. I couldn't hear too well what he was saying but he was pointing in the direction where the infant was last seen heading. She lumbered to her feet, said something inaudible as she followed the direction of the pointing finger and as she smiled in what I presumed was a gesture of gratitude, and not at what she imagined was the humour of the situation, I could see that there was a gap in her upper gums where two, if not three teeth should have been. Perhaps that's what she and her friend had been talking about – about who knocked her teeth out. Not a jealous husband, surely!

Just then, the boys ran up from the sea and after a vigorous towelling, were dispatched in pursuit of their human projectile of a brother and perhaps it was his use as this rather than concern for their sibling's safety or whereabouts, that lent wings to their heels as they scampered off in pursuit. It was astonishing at first, that the mother herself did not go in search of her son, but on reflection, by the time she had captured and confined her weapons of mass repulsion into the *Bustenhalter* again – for surely she would not have set off with those swinging about, not so much giving people an eyeful as more liable to hit them full in the eye – the child could be much further away. In any case, she hardly looked as if she could match the boys for speed.

No, what really *was* astonishing was that she did not stand and watch as the boys set off on their errand, but sat down again with her back to the proceedings and continued her absorbing conversation as if nothing had happened. Plainly we were not the only ones who could not believe this latest turn of events – all around us, people were looking at each other in horror and disbelief. But little did we suspect that we had not yet witnessed the climax of this scenario.

Never once did she turn round to see if the boys were coming back - and how many of them there were. Whatever their conversation was about, it scarcely seemed if it could be more important than the loss of the youngest of her brood. Indeed, we and the other spectators were keeping more of a lookout than she was.

Eventually, that which was lost, was now found - we could see them advancing across the sand; each brother had an arm and the little one's legs were more dragged than moving under their own locomotion. You see, Mother was right not to worry after all! Why didn't the biggest one pick him up and carry him, I wondered - for the little one was exercising his lungs in much the same manner as he did last night, but whether from this forced march or just anger at his recapture, it was impossible to say for certain.

Mother could scarcely fail to notice this and at last swivelled round to watch them approach but I imagined no one was surprised any more when she did not leap up to comfort him and calm him down, dry and wipe away his tears.

And, as they drew nearer, it became apparent that the infant's howling was only partly at least a result of his protest at his recapture, for there was a liquid brown stain overflowing the nappy and running down each leg. No wonder the boys didn't pick him up. I should think, if we really wanted to know where he'd been, we could follow the trail across the sand.

The mother at last was galvanised into action. Well, perhaps galvanised is hardly the *mot juste*. She seemed completely unflappable. Taking the child at arm's length, she handed him over to the young girl: *Here, Jessie, tak' the wean an' dook him in the watter.* Problem solved. Crisis? What crisis?

Not only did this incident confirm my opinion of the mother's lack of parenting skills, but it must also prove that, incredibly, the girl must be hers too. She had to be a close family member to be entrusted with, and to undertake such a task which she did without hesitation or protest, showing a maturity well beyond her tender years, not to say her mother.

Off she went, holding the child before her under his oxters, his legs wriggling like two recently excavated fat worms with pieces of earth still sticking to them, looking for all the world as if she had done this sort of thing before and often and no doubt she had. Meanwhile mother resumed her seat, watching operations from afar, as her daughter diddled her youngest in the water, nappy and all. But it wouldn't have surprised me if she was not even watching that at all, perhaps she was watching the swimmers, they themselves, blissfully unaware of the polluted waters in which they were happily splashing or perhaps she was just looking out at sea, like her thoughts, like her life.

I hadn't thought of that dysfunctional family until now when I saw those boys recklessly pushing their baby brother in his baby buggy. It's curious how such an incident can dredge up forgotten memories, possibly even ones so horrendous that they've been repressed.

Ah, here comes the fish at last. A good sign, as unlike last night, from the time it has taken, they must be cooking it from fresh - to order. The proof is in the eating and sure enough the fish is melt-in-the-mouth and has a delicious sauce, but there's no spoon and is far too good to waste, so however inefficient it may seem, I slurp it up with my fish knife, knowing that it would be crude and rude to pick up the plate and just drink that nectar right off after last night's reprimand in *The Yangtse*. At this rate, I'm never going to get all this sauce up and if there's one thing I like, apart from value for money, it's this sauce. But I just can't win.

"For God's sake, have you absolutely no manners? People are looking!"

What people? The place is practically empty and I doubt if the few that are here have any interest in looking at me, seemingly engaged in their own conversations. I, however, can see across to the bar opposite where a big screen is showing a football match of some significance – but only to the Spanish or the fanatical. I can't see it properly as there's a head directly in front of the screen sporting a baseball hat, fashionably worn back to front, with an earring, like gypsy Rose Lee, dangling from the left ear. I am not too sure of the symbolism, but I gather that the siting of the earring is crucial to advertising one's sexual orientation. My problem is that I don't remember which ear means what. Presumably if you have one in each ear as I have occasionally seen, it means you are ambidextrous. Anyway, he can't see me, so he doesn't care if I drink the sauce off my knife.

To my left there is a woman with "gold" hair who hasn't noticed me either as she is writing a postcard, laboriously, between courses. You can practically see her licking the pencil. Then I hear her say to her companion, so ingenuously that she doesn't even have the sense to lower her voice: *How do you spell soon – s-u-n or s-o-n?* Poor spelling, it seems, is not confined to the menu we'd seen yesterday advertising the unbelievably cheap meal, but that was someone writing in a foreign language. This is a native of Yorkshire unless I'm much mistaken.

After that, I am spellbound and can't say anything else in case I miss hearing her ask for another spelling, indeed to find out if her partner can do it - and neither can Iona. She has literally cast a spell upon us you could say, and I would have said to Iona, had I not been banned from punishing her with puns.

Unlike in Skye, where we had a sorbet thrown in as a palate freshener, between courses, here you can have it as a sweet. Iona chooses lemon flavour, as I knew she would. I have mango. It comes in martini glasses, very quickly, which is good news as it may sweeten her up and not all may yet be lost regarding the consummation of Menorca after my recent solecism and the mistake I made earlier in the day. Only two today. I'm improving.

The bill is so long in coming, I wonder if the *patron-*cum-waiter and perhaps even the chef, has forgotten about us, or is he just too busy working inside? What's to prevent us from doing a runner?

"Put on your running shoes, let's go!"

It's meant to be a joke - as if I would have any serious intent of slipping out of this tent without paying!

She doesn't think that's very funny. Better if I shut up and stop while I'm ahead – if I am ahead.

It's no good. We could sit here till doomsday, waiting for the bill. Who's meant to be doing the waiting here, us or him? We go inside. There's no one else there and we immediately spot the red shirt behind the bar. He appears to be doing some sums.

I hand him my Visa card, but for some reason, his machine seems reluctant to accept it. While we wait, I notice the range of Glenmorangies on the shelf behind him. He doesn't have any other malts, as far as I can see.

"That's a very impressive range of Glenmorangies you've got there," I tell him, making polite conversation whilst we wait for the reluctant machine to burst into life.

"I compliment you on your choice. It's a very good brand
– one of my favourites, in fact. As a matter of fact, there's
some there I've never tried and I'm from Scotland. Ha! Ha!"
Even to me my laughter sounds hollow and forced.

In Spain on earlier occasions, I have sometimes been
presented with a glass of Spanish brandy at the end of the
meal and in Portugal, a glass of port, and in Greece, a Metaxa
if you're really really lucky, but more often a *raki* which is
so vile, they can only give it away, but alas on this occasion,
I'm not going to try a malt whisky, not unless I buy it myself,
that is. The card machine suddenly whirrs into life. I leave a
bigger than normal tip because he has been so pleasant, even
if he hasn't given me a free whisky, and because I haven't
any change anyway.

"Really, you're so obvious," says La-Belle-Dame-Sans-
Merci when we get outside.

"What?"

"Trying to wangle a free whisky out of that poor man."

"What, me?"

"Yes, you! Can't you see, he's not doing very well?
Don't you want him to succeed in his business?"

The words are familiar. I remember her saying the
same thing to me not so long ago, in that restaurant in Skye
where we had the sorbets between courses, and recently
under new ownership, when I helped myself to a handful of
Pandrops as I was, just like here, waiting for my Visa card
to be processed. The intention had been, after this romantic
(and costly) meal to sweeten up my breath, get rid of any
lingering fishy taste (for as usual we had fish) just in case
she had had any intentions of consummating Skye. It seems
I dropped myself right in it when I took those Pandrops,
because, dear reader, she didn't.

Now, though the atmosphere may have chilled between
us slightly, it's still a very mild evening and I don't feel the
need for a jumper, though Iona is glad of hers and even

shivers slightly. I may be hardy, but I have a feeling she's not going to kiss me, let alone grab me in a half-nelson in a fit of unbridled passion when we get back. I should never have tried to wangle a free whisky.

No, it's much more likely we'll be going back to face the music and one thing's for sure, if we do, I'll be making a big song about it and the only dancing I'll be doing will be in rage.

5. Making for Mao

I'm standing outside reception looking up and down the road, waiting for the car, wondering if it will come or not, wondering what I'll do if it doesn't show up. It's already five minutes past the time it was due. I'm not feeling very good and I could do without this anxiety.

It was a two-and-a-half-play night which means that I listened to three and a half hours of plays on my Walkman before I got to sleep. The bad night was nothing to do with the new neighbours next door. It was a warm night and we had the window open, but only the sound of the "nightingales" penetrated the darkness of our room. Not that they kept me awake either, I was just being a worse insomniac than usual.

When at last, I did get off to sleep, I had some bad dreams which is unusual for me. I usually don't have any dreams at all, although they say that everybody dreams. I tell Iona I don't sleep long enough to have a dream.

It started off with my friend Pete. He had green hair and a skirt. He wasn't doing anything, he was just there, and it was not a pretty sight. He's built like a Suomo wrestler, an anorexic Suomo wrestler perhaps, but he's still an impressive sight. He wanted to know what I thought of his outfit. How could I tell him that that skirt just didn't suit him for Pete's sake!

Then the scene shifted. I was back in the classroom, a sure sign that I was having a nightmare. There were no boys, only the fifth and sixth year girls and they were deliberately teasing me, some with the top buttons of their blouses unbuttoned, others using their desks as a sort of super support bra, resting their breasts on the lids and looking at me provocatively. Some people would say that wasn't a nightmare, but it was because I knew I was a teacher and I musn't touch, but it was pretty nearly touch and go until the scene shifted again.

This time I was in my colleague, Susan's, new house. She was having a housewarming party and I had to make a speech. Some people think that speaking in public is a terrifying experience. That didn't bother me, but it still became a nightmare because no one was listening, just talking in groups, sipping their drinks, not even looking at me. I think I must be worrying that people are ignoring me. And to cap it all, I was desperate to go to the loo but I knew that there were pupils in there smoking and I couldn't go.

That's all I can remember. Probably I woke up then. That's the best thing to do in dreams when you're in a tight situation but here I am waiting for a car which may or may not show up and that could just be the start of my problems as I still have to sort out what happened to my original booking. This could be the real nightmare and I can't just waken up and walk away from it.

Ah, this could be it! Oh, no! If this is it, they've given me a much bigger car than I wanted. This is going to cost me a fortune. It is the rental company right enough and the driver wants to know if I am Mr Allison. Good grief! This does not bode well, but it transpires this is not my car either; the driver wants me to accompany him to the office in it. It sounds a bit ominous, like a policeman asking you to accompany him to the station. I tell him I am just going to tell my wife where I'm going and like Titus Oates, I may be some time, and we're off.

We go along streets and roads which I've never seen before. I hope to God I'll find my way back without Iona the

Navigator who usually tells me where to go and not always politely either.

"It's a one way system," says the driver, as we drive down a smart street lined with posh villas with swimming pools. He brakes suddenly and swerves to avoid a dog which had stepped off the pavement without so much as a thought about the highway code. He tells me that he killed one once before. It went right over the top of the car.

That's nothing. I tell him how on one black, wet, winter night, I killed a black bullock which had escaped from its field. I bemoan how I was found to be at fault according to the insurance company as under Scottish law apparently, cattle being before cars, chronologically speaking, they have the right of way. But what if the bullock is drunk? Who's to blame then? I didn't even get the steaks. There's just no justice.

With this cheery conversation, we duly arrive at the office in what otherwise might have been an uncomfortable silence had it not been for the almost sacrificial dog. I am pleased to see that I recognise where I am, that the Commercial Centre is further down the street and that the office is near another Chinese restaurant festooned with bright red Chinese lanterns hanging like harvest moons over the frontage.

There's just the two of them in the office, my driver and a girl, probably the one I was talking to earlier. She's talking to a customer – a prospective customer actually because he has forgotten his driving licence and he's trying to persuade them to let him have a car. This happened to me once in Cyprus but they accepted my passport, though what that has to do with driving I don't know, apart from providing evidence of who I am in case I absconded with it, I suppose.

But they're having none of it here. My driver is the boss, so he has to get involved, leaving me to sit there pretending

I can't hear anything. The client wants to phone his son, so his son can read the number of his licence over the phone, though you can actually work it out as it's just your name and date of birth jumbled up, if you have a model to work from, like mine, but I'm saying nothing. In any case, that won't do either.

The client tries a different tack - he wants to know what if his son faxed it? No deal. What if they phoned DVLC in Swansea (as if they would)? No way, José! He's just not getting the message is he? He's not getting a car. Only the original licence will do. Poor bugger, that's probably his whole holiday ruined. He goes away dejectedly. He's probably terrified of what his wife is going to say when he comes back without a car: *I told you to check you had your licence didn't I? And did you?* He's really in for it now. Imagine being stuck in your resort with a wife who's not speaking to you except to tell you what a bloody fool you are. They'll just have to resort to going on the expensive excursions or stick it out and get a divorce when they get back.

Clever me has my driving licence. I've even thought to bring it with me, here, to the office. They must have found my paperwork after all or else it has just been faxed to them, so it's all sorted apart from the additional insurance which means that if I did have an accident, I could walk away from it without paying any excess. What's the excess? €600!!! What's the premium? €22. I could buy quite a lot of wine for that at Spanish prices. It's also two thirds of what we have typically been paying for a meal, so if I don't take the insurance, it amounts to almost one night's free tea.

What should I do? Dilemmas, I hate them and Iona's not here to ask her advice. She'd just leave it up to me anyway. The driving is what I do on holiday. It's my use. It isn't thinking of *her*, I repeat, not an association of ideas, which makes me think of the dog, but I do remember it and I think

€7 a day is probably worth it for the peace of mind. If there are mad dogs in Menorca who don't know their highway code, there will certainly be some Englishmen. But then I think about the almost free meal or the bottles of gin I could buy for that and then I think what a brilliant driver I am, (not nearly as good as my son George, who is the nonpareil) three times across the American continent coast to coast and all over Europe in God knows how many countries, even in Italy, and never an incident, in thousands of miles. And I think this is just a little totty wee island and it's very unlikely I'd be involved in an accident.

"Nah! I'll not bother!" I say it as if I were sure I meant it. I just hope it's the right decision. I don't know how much €600 is in real money, but it sounds like a lot more gin than even I could carry home.

I get the keys to a Hyundai Atos Prima GLS. I'm told it's an upgrade, but I'm often told that, more times than I have a right to expect to be lucky and more times than coincidence would suggest, but it is a GLS so perhaps it's true. I'm also given a map which has some phone numbers on it in case of emergencies and that's it - I'm off in my car from Carefree Car Rentals.

But where are *we* off to? Iona suggests we go to Maó or Mahón, which lies right at the other side of the island. The family from hell, which had been dormant when I left has now resurrected itself, at least the parents have, but there is no sign of the girl and no sound of the radio as yet, so presumably they are letting her sleep on. I don't mind where I go, just as long as I get away from here before they put on her "music" to get up to.

"That's a capital idea!" I reply. Iona does have all the best ideas, but she looks at me sharply as if she suspects me of taking the Michael. But why *not* go there? It's only 45 kilometres from coast to coast, from the second biggest town of Ciutadella to Maó, the first and capital city, across this kidney bean shape of an island. That's not even 30 miles, one of the metric conversions which, amazingly, I *can* do.

Just out of Ciutadella, we pass one of Menorca's foremost prehistoric burial sites, the Naveta d'es Tudons. We can see it quite easily from the road, a honey-coloured stone building which looks like an upturned bread tin. There's also a bus in the car park and a trail of tourists strung out across the fields, making their way to have a closer look at it, which dispels any slight intention or temptation we may have had to visit it ourselves. The idea is to get to Maó, like the panel game on Radio 4, without any hesitation or deviation and hopefully without repetition, and, as long as we don't get lost, we should be there in a matter of minutes. We can stop at places on the way back and hopefully we can time our visit to the Naveta when there's not a bus. It's got one small entrance, like a hive, and you can imagine how long it would take to get a bus load in and out of there.

So we pass through Ferreries, Menorca's highest town apparently, although its elevation is only 150 meters, with a couple of massive leather and shoe factories on its outskirts. I'm glad we're not stopping, but I suppose it's really just a stay of execution.

Similarly, we bypass Es Mercadal with its ancient, attractive windmill a prominent landmark. It's an ancient market town, as its name suggests, and lies at the midway point between Maó and Ciutadella. Where Ferreries has its posh, designer shoes, Es Mercadal specialises in *abarca,* shoes whose soles are made from car tyres. I imagine you go into one of these shops and examine the treads: *These look as if they've done 20,000 kilometres. I was looking for some that have only done about 5 or 8k.*

I'm not sure if there's rivalry between these two towns or not, but if Es Mercadal lost out to Ferreries in the shoe department, it rose to greater heights as far as mountains are concerned, for whilst Ferreries nestles at the foot of

Menorca's second highest mountain, S'Enclusa, Es Mercadal lies at the bottom of the highest, Monte Toro. Having said that, it's only 358 meters but Menorca is so small you're meant to be able to see all round the island from there. This information is courtesy of Iona who is reading the guidebook as we drive through.

"Sounds like a load of bull, if you ask me."

"Well no one is and if you can't do better than that, just shut up. I told you yesterday."

Yes, she certainly did that all right.

We're looking for a road after Es Mercadal which will take us off the busy main C 721. It's not really a deviation, because we're looking for the Cami d'en Kane. The Cami d'en Kane is the original road which ran like a spine across the island and which the modern C721 largely follows. It gets its name from Sir Richard Kane, the First citizen of Menorca in the early 18th century. He was the Lieutenant-Governor and although he may have been Kane by name, he turned out to be a very able governor, as I would have liked to have pointed out to Iona.

His first act was to build this trans-island highway. That sounds a good enough idea on the face of it, but I imagine he raised a few hackles because he funded it by slapping a tax on alcohol. What *is* certain is that he annoyed the inhabitants of Ciutadella by transferring the capital from there to Maó in 1722 because of its vastly superior natural deep-water harbour, reputedly the second largest natural harbour in the world after Pearl Harbour. And, amongst other innovations, he introduced Friesian cows which even today, form the basis of the Menorcan cheese industry. So it's all thanks to Kane that that's how Maó's the capital now and the fields are dotted with Friesian cattle, which unfortunately, are black and white so if you were to meet one on the road coming back from Maó, you couldn't greet it with: *How's Maó, now, brown cow?* Which is a pity as it would have been good for your elocution.

Although we are keeping a close lookout for it, nevertheless we go shooting past the Cami d'en Kane. To do a three point turn here to return to the Cami would be more like kamikaze, so I have to go on for a mile or two until I can find a place to turn. So much for no repetition.

It's a pleasant, quiet country road this through rolling countryside and pine trees. The curious thing is that there are black and white striped plastic bags hanging from the branches of a good number of trees. What can it mean? Surely not that Dunfermline Athletic have won a magnificent victory here and their supporters have hung out the bunting in celebration? I stop the car and try to see what it could be, but the problem is that the bags are out of reach. Through the zoom lens of the camera I can get a closer look, but it's still unsatisfactory. I can see a crest of some sort, possibly the logo of some university. Perhaps they are collecting bugs or something, but who can tell? Maybe they are just doing it to litter up the countryside or make us wonder what the bags are for, to bug us.

We bypass Alaior, Menorca's third largest town, and guess what they make there? That's right, more bloody shoes! But its main industry is cheese-making which, no doubt, they got into after they found out that Ferreries and Es Mercadal had got not just a toehold in the market, but both feet, one catering for the poor souls of Menorca and the other, the rich, and it takes no great feat of the intellect to realise that there is no room for a middle man unless he is Jake the Peg.

It may be a secondary road but it's first class as far as I am concerned and as straight as a die and we're extremely unlikely to do that, let alone have a minor bump as there is so little traffic. Good decision not to pay for the excess waiver. I was right not to waiver, but make a firm decision without hardly any hesitation. Presumably all the traffic is on the "good" road, so we cover the last 12 km to Maó in no time.

So where do we park? There's a sign to a multi-story car park, but we see it too late and miss it. Fortunately, it seems to be the main square and we can go round again if I can get in the right lane. The problem is there are road works and every car in Menorca seems to have chosen this precise moment to converge at this spot.

What's this? Bloody hell! The car in front is reversing straight at me! I lean on my horn. He's got no idea I'm there, reversing into a space at the side of the road that I hadn't even noticed. That's all I need, just one idiot to reverse into me and even although it's not my fault, it could be hell to prove it, perhaps not at all, given the language barrier, or even without it. If a car is bumped in the behind it's always the driver who is following who's deemed to be at fault, even if the driver in front stops suddenly, for no apparent reason. You're always meant to be able to stop in time and maybe that includes the car in front hurtling back towards you. You should always be prepared for that, naturally.

I've just been here a couple of minutes and almost been in an accident already. If I'd paid the extra insurance, I could just have let the insurance companies argue it out, instead of paying God knows what, perhaps the whole excess, because it doesn't take too much of a bump to run a bill of excessive proportions given the price those latter-day highway robbers, the garages, charge per hour. I knew I was no good at making the right decisions.

We get into the multi-storey at the second attempt. €1.66 for an hour. How the hell did they arrive at a price like that? Probably something to do with rounding it up from what it was in pesetas, an added bonus, a hidden extra of the common currency, just like decimalisation, a good way to bury a price hike by confusing the innumerate like me, or the aged, who can't get used to the new coinage. I wholeheartedly agree with the confused and frustrated old lady whose letter I read in the paper at the time of decimalisation, who pleaded with the voice of reason, for compassion for the elderly: *If you must introduce decimalisation, why don't you wait until all the old people are dead?* That's right. That would be the best time for us to join the euro, when people like me have gone to heaven. Fortunately, for the Europhiles, that may, unfortunately, may not be before too long. I may be innumerate, but I don't need all of the fingers on one hand to count the number of years I've got left before, if genetics count for anything, I reach my father's death age of 59.

The car park is in the Plaça de S'Esplanada, the main square of the city and laid out by the British. Apart from its size, there is nothing special about it, a far cry from the Plaça d'es Born, apart from a goodly number of trees, some of which are already donning their autumnal foliage. Nothing to detain us here, so we head for the exit and take the Carer Ses Moreres which will take us to the port, ultimately.

It's a busy street, hoaching with voluble pedestrians. My ears and eyes, like cicadas to me and nightingales to Keats, are *deceiving elves*, telling me that I am back in Britain, possibly in an elegant street somewhere in London, such is the British influence in architectural style. And yet, not quite, for the uniformity so beloved of the British, creating row upon row, street upon street, until they create whole estates of identical houses, whole towns of them even, is dispensed with here and has been adapted to the local style. For example, here the façade of the building opposite has been painted deep red and the windows with their green shutters, picked out in white with a wrought iron balcony beneath them. Next to that is a much plainer edifice with white mortar round the stonework, retaining its British conservatism, while next to that, a plain white façade is relieved by the addition of green shutters, but especially by

89

a *boinder* looking more like an elaborately boxed in balcony than a bow window.

Boinders seem to be Maó's speciality in fact, much more elaborate than any we saw in Ciutadella. This one for example, in brown and white, is so big that it takes up half the façade and the panes have delicate frosted engravings on them, such as you might expect to see on an expensive glass vase or on one of those oil lamps they used to have in the olden days. Behind the frosted glass, I can see a fan fluttering as a faceless woman tries to keep cool as she, unseen, sees the activity in the street below. Perhaps, like the Lady of Shallot, she has been sitting there for an age, safe as long as she does not look at the scene directly but through the patterned glass, and as long as some handsome knight does not stroll by, or other eligible knights such as Sir Cliff Richard.

There's a good chance if he should come, he could be Scottish if the abundance of Scottish accents is anything to go by and yet - perhaps not. There seems little likelihood of one my compatriots tempting the lady to look through the clear glass to get a better view. She can have her choice: bandy legs, bald heads, beer bellies, ginger hair and tattoos. It could be a Scottish scene on an exceptionally warm day and the cream of Scottish manhood has stripped down to show off its talents to best advantage, a chance it rarely gets to do at home.

Unsurprisingly, the mysterious woman with the fan is impervious to these charms. The fan flutters with rhythmic regularity, but not the heart with sudden irregularity at such sights – she is no fan of theirs evidently and probably because she does not expect the unexpected, hasn't noticed me. I'd better move off sharply, in case she does. But just a minute, perhaps she's a really rich widow, looking for a companion and might make me an offer, so I linger about a bit, pretending to adjust my socks in my sandals. Only joking! Of course I don't have any socks on! As if I would dare - as if La-Belle-Dame-Sans-Merci would let me out looking a sight like that.

There's a pair of the female of the Scottish species in front of me now, jabbering away, shopping bags weighed down with red, freckled arms. If they are not Glaswegians, then their accents pronounce them unmistakably from the west of the country. Yes, it's easy to suspend disbelief and imagine oneself in Sauchiehall Street on a sale day, though we are in fact facing the house of Dr Orfila (1787 –1853), the father of modern toxicology. His head is seen in profile on a circular plaque on the wall and there is a bronze bust on the street outside which now bears his name, though in actual fact, according to our map, we are still on the Carrer Ses Moreres, which turns into the Carrer Hannover as it crosses the Carrer de sa Bastió or, if you prefer, you can call it the Costa de sa Plaça, because apparently, that is Hannover's more Spanish name. If only naming a street were as straight forward as it is straight.

A street by any other name, call it what you will, it could, *boinders* excepted, be a Georgian street in London. And here's a window, a *boinder* all right, at the corner of the street - the mother of all *boinders,* bending in a graceful sweep along the façade and continued round the corner with graceful feminine curves, far too sexy for an English street, yet this overall English impression is further enhanced by accents which betray the speakers as coming from south of the border. And if my ears alone did not provide sufficient evidence for this deduction, then my eyes surely would, for England football shirts abound everywhere, not to mention people who don't require this kind of advertising to look unmistakably English.

So it would appear that this place has not just been invaded by the Scots, but the English too - the British are back all right - with a vengeance. And, according to our guidebook, whilst British tourists make up only 11% of Mallorca's visitors, they form an astonishing 60% of Menorca's. You can't always believe what you believe in guidebooks, as I have found out, but I can believe this all right.

We have arrived at the Plaça Real, an unremarkable square, despite its grand name and take the Carrer S' Arravaleta, itself an unremarkable street of shops, to the Plaça Carme, dominated by the Església del Carme, a forbidding Carmelite church dating from 1750. Up to our left, we can see The Església de Santa Maria, another formidable construction, founded by Alphonso III in 1287 to commemorate his defeat of the Moors and the re-conquest of the island, though the building we see now dates from much later, in the days when churches looked more like fortresses than places of worship.

Indeed, The Església del Carme looks as if it *has* been in the wars. Its towering façade is pockmarked with holes and a pair of marble columns which once stood at either side of the main door, look as if they have been sawn down to stumps like the teeth of a hippopotamus. It looks as if it may, at one time, have supported a portico which may have given the church, once, a more prepossessing appearance. I may not be a fan of the over-blown elaboration which I had been accustomed to on my Italian Journey last year, but this is just not plain, but plain crumbling to bits.

There are some people sitting on the steps but the big green doors at the top are shut. Rats! If it looks better in the inside, which I doubt, we will not be able to find out, and frankly, I can do without finding out. It does, however, boast some cloisters and if there's any part of a church I *do* like, it's the cloisters, even if they are without the church and all churches in my Protestant religion, or at least in the faith I was brought up in, *are* without them, which I think is a mistake and a pity.

To the left, in a lighter-coloured stone, is an extension which does not marry well with the church, more than a little due to the way it projects beyond the façade of the church and emphasises the fact that it is a recent extension. Above the open door is a curious round porthole and further up, just beneath the overhanging ridge of the roof, three tiny windows. To the right of the door, in big black letters is written MERCAT. The market evidently and also the cloisters, the latest rôle in a list of previous uses as a prison, law school and just plain, ordinary school.

It comes as no surprise to find that these cloisters are a disappointment – everything in Maó so far has been, apart from the *boinders*. Inside, the market is drab and crowded with none of the colour or the variety or the bustle of human activity that you think of when you imagine a continental market, and passing to the outside, it's horrifying to see what they've done to the cloisters.

We find ourselves in a large open area, with on the left, an enormous stage on which a diminutive figure wearing a coolie hat, no doubt to convey an air of verisimilitude, is demonstrating t'ai chi to an audience of what seems to be mostly senior citizens, who are emulating his arcane movements as if they had been caught on slow motion camera. But perhaps, for them, they *are* moving in real time, just as fast as they possibly can.

If that was a bit of a shock, it is even more shocking to see what they have done to the cloisters at the other side. Here we can see a row of prefabricated shops, all shut, with glass doors and frontages painted in dull battleship grey, plonked right in front of the arches so all you can see of them are the tops which have been filled in, God forbid, with glass or Perspex. And, as a sort of supreme insult, tacked onto the last shop, they have dumped the public toilets in the same grey, a featureless blank wall, apart from the little sign with the universal figures of a man and a woman and the letters WC to announce its function.

Functional is certainly the name for it, for a thing of beauty it is not, nor is this row of shops, nor the cloisters – or what you can see of them. These may never have been the best cloisters in the world to start with, but now, after what the burghers of Maó have done to them, they could certainly be contenders, and most likely, winners, of the worst cloisters in the world competition. Certainly, in all my travels, this is without doubt, the worst cloisters I have ever seen in my life.

Emerging disappointed, but not deterred from further exploration of Maó, we turn our back on the Església del Carme, literally and metaphorically, and head downhill towards the Església de Santa Maria which, sitting on the top of the next rise, dominates the landscape. It's a pleasantly warm-coloured building with a not displeasing campanile rising above the red tiles with a row of round windows like portholes peeping shyly over, at last, a huddle of more traditional-looking white houses, the first we have seen since we came to Maó and which look as if they may have gathered together in the shadow of the huge church for protection, a last stand against the all-pervasive encroachment of English architecture.

The portholes make it not unlike a huge ship, but even it, with its cliff-like walls, is dwarfed by the real thing. We come upon it unexpectedly, heading down the hill towards Santa Maria. There is a gap between the houses, a passageway and, at the end of it, the most incredible sight – a startlingly white wall pierced with serried rows of oblong black rectangles – the windows of a cruise liner which seems to block off the passageway. It looks as if it could go on and on and up and up for ever, almost, if we went to the balustrades at the end of the passage, we could reach out and touch it.

In fact it is far below us, in the harbour, naturally, and its huge size is emphasised by the way it towers over the buildings at the quayside, as if one port of call had included Lilliput. No wonder there are so many Brits about. This ship, this floating hotel, this moving wall of windows on the world, must contain thousands of passengers and they have all disembarked and invaded in just the hour or so it takes to disgorge a whole ship of passengers only a short walk uphill to the city centre. That's the curse of cruises that they don't tell you about – you are all deposited in the same place at the same time and some of these liners contain more passengers than some towns I have been in. Like this one evidently.

And if it's not within walking distance, even if you are not a geriatric, fleets of buses will disgorge you at your location. Want to climb the Leaning Tower of Pisa? Forget it! Wherever you go, you'll never see the place but in the company of hundreds of people. And it was just our luck to choose this day the ship's in town, though I wouldn't mind betting that probably every day is cruise ship day in Maó. I wonder when departure time is? It will probably be hours from now before we get Maó to ourselves. Good for the shop-keepers, but not good for me. It's not that I'm against people; I really love them, the female of the species especially (if only they would let me) - it's just I prefer to have a little bit of space to look at things.

From our vantage point, high above the harbour, we can see a road winding down between groves of palm and citrus trees to the harbour-side where white houses stretch along the waterfront. This looks a bit more like it – this must be where the real Maó is. This is where we should head for, never mind Santa Maria, even if it does have a famous organ built in 1809 by that well-known Swiss, Johann Kyburz, who was a bit of an expert when it came to making organs apparently. It was imported from Barcelona by the British during the Napoleonic wars. No, I'll give the Swiss a miss.

Besides, I have done my homework and I know that at the bottom of this long and winding road, somewhere off to the left, is where the famous Xoriguer gin distillery is to be found.

We pass the fish market, recommended by our guidebook as a sight worth seeing. Presumably it means actually going there at the crack of dawn, when the catch has just been landed. It's 11:47 now and the big iron gates which have the legend *Mercado de Pescados* picked out in white above them are firmly closed and possibly have been for hours. Not another disappointment. Dead fish on the slab, the sight and smell of them, have never been high on my list of attractions, and even less Iona's, for whom the underwater world is worse than anything Hieronymus Bosch imagined in his worst nightmares.

As a boy I used to keep the best on my plate till last, got rid of the nasty vegetables first. Our guidebook suggests we can continue the city tour from here as an alternative before going down to the port, so at the top of the Costa de Ses Voltes, we ignore the temptation and the steps which would have taken us down to, seemingly, the best that Maó has to offer, and instead continue through the Plaça d'Espanya which the Plaça del Carme seems to have become, without any obvious division or break, or for any good reason either, just as the Carrer de Ses Moreres re-invented itself. And like all the other squares in this town, this does not impress me at all.

The Plaça Conquesta, however, where we now find ourselves, is by far the best square we have come to in this city. It even looks as if it may actually be square, the rigidity of the form less conducive perhaps to aesthetic appreciation, yet it is by far the most pleasant place we have found in this city up till now. It might be due to the huge circular terracotta pots filled with colourful flowers or the warm, honey-coloured stone of the Santa Maria or a combination of them both, but not the architecture itself, which, although plain, is pleasing enough, but not exciting enough to inspire admiration.

No, what I like about this place, or Plaça, is that it is practically deserted apart from a few people taking lunch. Isn't that a remarkable thing! In this city of 25,000 inhabitants, almost half the entire island, not to mention the hordes of invading Brits, we have got this place practically to ourselves! In fact, since our arrival, whether it is merely coincidence or as a result of our appearance, or, more probably, just mine – many of the few are packing up and heading back to work, presumably. About time too! There's nothing like the sight of people heading off back to work more calculated to lift your spirits and make you really feel on holiday than that. Come on! Come on! Get a bloody move on! You're going to be late!

The first rule of successful city exploring is – if you find an empty bench, sit on it and let the feet recover. Although it is perhaps just a little bit early for us to take lunch, our breakfast I imagine having been quite a few hours later than the office workers who have just consumed their lunch and left, we may as well kill two birds with one stone, and take advantage of the vacant range and choice of seats, and have our lunch now too.

And talking of killing birds, there's a statue here of an old bird who must have killed a few in his time, or if he did not do so personally, at least was responsible, not for a few, but for the deaths of a great many. For it is a statue donated by Franco, of all people, of the 18 year-old king Alphonso III, looking extremely youthful, with long flowing locks, leaning on a sword almost as big as himself, who drove the Moors out of Menorca in what was called The Reconquista, in 1287. He may have had a poofy name and a hairstyle to match, but that doesn't mean to say he was a push-over, even although his nickname was The Liberal since he bent over backwards to satisfy as many of his followers' requests as he could, donating land especially to the Franciscans and to the St Clares, which is curious as I thought they were meant to be devoted to poverty, so they were no doubt relieved when Alfonso's successor, Jaume II who thought he was far too liberal, took the lands off them again. Phew! Alfonso nearly landed them in it there, I would have said to Iona, if I had been allowed.

Jaume II was Alphonso's uncle, and quite different from his nephew, and in my view, in spite of the aforementioned taking the lands back from the Church, more deserving of the nickname Liberal than his brother. He started the building of churches and monasteries. He founded Alaior and Es Mercadal to stimulate trade and he also patronised the arts, most notably in his patronage of the Mallorcan Franciscan friar and poet, Ramón Llull. (I've never read any of his poems, but he must have been an 'ell of a poet if his surname is anything to go by).

No, the soubriquet Liberal for Alphonso disguised a much harder man. He was actually ex-communicated by the pope (for a short time) for his atrocities in the conquest of Mallorca two years earlier and, dear reader, we are in 13th century Spain, for God's sake, not exactly noted for its benevolent treatment of prisoners, so what went on in his name, one shudders to imagine. But two years later, you can get an idea of how much he'd mellowed. His final solution as what to do with those Moors who could not afford to pay a ransom or who were too weak or too young to work as slaves, was to take them out to sea and drown them. You may call me cynical if you wish, but I think I am beginning to form a suspicion of an idea why he left all those lands to those religious orders. Could it possibly be an insurance policy for his immortal soul - a sort of get out of hell card for his soul for former atrocities committed. In which case Jaume really dropped him in it, didn't he!

And maybe he had a premonition, for Alphonso died in 1291, aged only 25. Live hard, live fast, die young could have been his motto, could have been his epitaph, for it took only two weeks to subdue the Moors and there were Moors no more, or at least a lot less, like the tombstone of Lester Moore in Tomb City, Arizona which reads:

> *Here lies Lester Moore*
> *No less no more*
> *No Lester Moore.*

Amazingly, I'm not the fount of all knowledge about Alphonso. I have merely been reading and paraphrasing the guidebook whilst Iona has been extricating our delicious repast from her rucksack which she had prepared earlier and which she has been lugging about, not that it's a heavy lunch, for neither of us like a big meal in the middle of the day.

I read on, telling her that the statue is described as crude, but I don't think it is crude at all, and neither does Iona. In fact, the only thing in this square that could be described as crude, (apart from me) are our sandwiches. For they are what the French call *crudités*: cold meat, lettuce and tomato in a baguette. Crude by name and crude by nature for they have not survived the journey well, though of course as Iona slaps the filling back on the bottom layer and presses the top firmly back on, I would never be so crude or so stupid as to say so.

There is an arched passage at the bottom of the square, a narrow exit between two sides of the Plaça which reminds me of the Corridoio Vasariano in Florence and through which I can see a tantalising glimpse of blue. I bet there's a really good panoramic view of the harbour from there. Iona has finished her lunch and moved off to explore. Ever since I plonked my bum on the sunny side of the seat, whilst Iona sat on the shady side, I have been eyeing that intriguing passageway and longing to walk down it, but first I have a closer look at the young Alphonso. Is it crude? No, it certainly isn't. Can't think why the writer of the guide thought so. I've seen some crude things in my life, and this isn't one of them.

Actually, I'm just wasting time, savouring the scene I expect to see at the far end of that passage, enjoying the anticipation, prolonging the moment before that passage gives up its secrets. Meanwhile, Iona, my very own Belle Dame Sans Merci, like Keats's knight in the poem of that name, is palely loitering and beckoning on me to get a move on, so, like a good husband - didn't I promise to obey - I obediently turn my back on Alphonso and trot off to join her.

Of course, it's a bit of a disappointment as all things I look forward to generally turn out to be. It's impossible to look across to the other side of the harbour because of that bloody big liner and there is another drawn up behind it, though it looks more like a toy boat in comparison. Looking up to the right though, we can see the Església del Carme perched on its bastion like an eagle's eyrie and far below us, beyond the dovetailed red roofs of the houses, there is the gable end of a white building on which the Xoriguer gin logo is displayed. Don't worry Xoriguer, we're coming and we'll find you, but first we're going to finish our exploration of the city while we're up here.

So it's back through the passage, through the square with its cobbled surface marked out in squares like a giant chessboard and taking the Carrer Alphonso III, we arrive shortly at the Plaça de la Constitució and the administrative centre of Maó, the Ajuntament, or Town Hall.

It's an imposing edifice with wrought iron grilles on the lower part of the windows and balconies and with the Spanish flag fluttering above the entrance. Round the side, as we approach it, is a clock with big Roman numerals, the kind you used to see, if I am not mistaken, in railway stations when I was a boy. It was a personal gift by Sir Richard Kane who, presumably, thought it was about time he did something else for the Menorcans apart from building roads and introducing cattle and other capital ideas like making Maó the first city.

They're roughly the same distance apart, Glasgow and Edinburgh and Maó and Ciutadella and I can just imagine the furore there would be if anybody tried shifting the capital of Scotland from Edinburgh to Glasgow. The guidebook doesn't say if the good citizens of Ciutadella raised Cain or not, but there were letters of complaint to London and the Government had to issue an open letter entitled *A Vindication of Colonel Kane*, like Tammy Wynette, standing by their man.

Anyway, this was where he stayed when he was governor, but the building we see now dates from seventy years after his death. It's not a patch on Ciutadella's Ajuntament, but nothing we have seen yet in this place is, even the harbour, from what we have seen of it. Just because it's bigger, doesn't mean to say it is better, a maxim which applies to many other things in life, not just harbours. But perhaps it is another thing we should thank Colonel Kane for, for if he had not moved the capital here, I bet that Ciutadella would have lost a lot of its charm.

With our back to the Ajuntament, the toffee-coloured Església de Santa Maria is just a stone's throw away on our left but we leave it alone. It's so big, you can hardly miss it, even if like Iona, you can't throw stones for toffee. Since we have no intention of going in, it doesn't seem to be worth going any nearer to take a closer look since what we can see from here doesn't look that inspiring, apart from its colossal size.

So, we continue on our way. The Carrer de Sant Roc seems to be the Carrer Alphonso's alter ego, for that is what it is called now though it has not deviated from it by so much as a millimetre. It's a narrow street which looks intriguing, not for itself, but at the end there is all that remains of the city walls and the Portal de Sant Roc, built to repel that notorious pirate, Barbarossa.

But we're not going there just yet. We are seduced by The Carrer Isabel II which, we are told, has some very fine Georgian mansions, not to mention the Gobierno Militar or Military Governor's Residence and barracks. But we've just been looking at his residence, haven't we? What did he want with two residences? That's a bit greedy surely, but if you're the governor, I suppose you can have anything you want – unless the guidebook is wrong of course, because it says that this was where he stayed when he came from Ciutadella and that he moved in here when Maó became the capital and that he extended it. Perhaps he used the other place whilst the builders were in.

Anyway, we are not there yet as a little alley leads us down to a *mirador* where we will try again to have a bird's eye view of the harbour. This time we are more successful, being nearer to the harbour mouth (though it is still a considerable distance away) with the liner now a good bit further upstream so instead of looking at it sternly for blocking our view, we are now looking at it in the stern. Now we can see just how wide the harbour is - and how long. And, as I suspected, it is just too big to be beautiful – it has none of the charm of Ciutadella's harbour, though it is not without its own interest.

We are standing right at the edge of a cliff. It's a sheer drop over the crude concrete barrier they have built here. We can look down to the backs of the white houses below with their miniscule and claustrophobic gardens and if we look up, we can see the backs of the Georgian houses on the Carrer Isabel, much plainer than the façades but with *boinders* facing out to sea, though of course the houses could be seen by absolutely every ship or small boat which came to Maó. You would have thought that they would have presented their best face to the sea to impress the visitors whose first sight of Mao must have been these houses as they sailed into the harbour. There must have been millions of them over the centuries; there are hundreds of them here now.

A flotilla of small craft is lining the quay on this side. By the looks of it, every family in Maó must have a boat and, to paraphrase Henry Ford, you can have any colour you like as long as it's white, for there is a thin line of white sails and boats hugging the quay, as far as the eye can see in both directions, and from our elevated position, looking like waves breaking on the shore.

Only the waves are not breaking, but seem suspended in time, as if we are looking at a still-life scene. There are hundreds of ships and the harbour, though vast, could hardly be described as an ocean but there is no motion at all amongst the little craft, bound, like the two liners, to the water's edge - yet for all that, Coleridge's *painted ship upon a painted ocean* comes to mind. An oil tanker lies idle in mid stream, whilst some strange vessel, like some sort of hybrid between a trawler and a midget submarine and painted a vivid red, coquettishly provides a splash of colour. But that's the only splash it makes as it too lies harboured between the two liners. Only a bright yellow launch, now suddenly appearing from behind the Brobdingnagian liner, and scudding out to sea over the motionless blue of the water, incredibly, provides any movement or any sign of human activity at all out of those hundreds and hundreds of boats. Where could all the people be, the owners of all these boats? I think I know. Working to pay for them; weekend sailors, perhaps – weakened bank balances, certainly.

The other side of that great gash in the land known as the harbour is quite flat, which, considering the precipitous cliffs on this side, where I am now standing, is quite astonishing but, unsurprisingly, that is where the industrial shipping is located, where they have the docks, and tanker terminals, never the prettiest of sights, and up to the right is the Illa Pinto, an artificial island created by the British, though our guide does not say why - unless it was to hold prisoners or keep fever victims in quarantine.

Closer now, down to the left, is the Destilerias Xoriguer. I can see the name painted on the gable end of the building, echoing the colours of the mystery vessel and the launch. If I could launch myself from here, I could be there in a minute but we're not going directly there. It wasn't intended to be the last stop on our visit, but now it looks as if it will be. With a bit of luck, it could turn out to be the best and from what we have seen so far of Maó, there's every chance it will be. So hang on, Xoriguer, however you pronounce your name, X marks the spot, we know where you are and we're coming, so whatever you do, don't close until I have sampled your produce.

Back on the Carrer Isabel, there are indeed some splendid *boinders* and, gleaming white, as though made out of icing, is the Gobierno Militar. I think it's safe to say this is the most impressive building we have yet come across in Maó. It's a U-shaped affair built round a courtyard in which a number of cars conspire to detract from the effect of the cloister-like appearance by blocking our view. If it's not bloody boats, it's bloody cars.

On the left hand side, jutting out onto the street, there is an ornate *boinder* and the courtyard is fenced off from the street with iron railings and between two slim pillars, a pair of wrought iron gates which are open. I can't get rid of the cars, but I can step through the gates and get a better view of the best building in Maó without it being cut into strips by the railings. That's better. Now I have an uninterrupted view of the two identical wings, mirror images of each other, each with two tiers of arched windows, looking across the courtyard at each other, every window blank with closed green shutters.

At the far end, the two wings are joined by a linking block in the same style, only the arched windows appear to be broader though still shuttered and there is a coat of arms in the centre of some Dutch-style frilly ornamentation. Over the centre of the west wing, the Spanish flag is standing stiffly at the top of its pole, though down here I had not noticed any breeze. I also hadn't noticed till now that the Xoriguer colours are the same as the Spanish flag. Probably not a coincidence. I wonder if gin is the national drink of Spain? It wouldn't surprise me it were. I certainly have plenty of it when I am over here anyway. I am also wondering why every single shutter in this place is closed. It must be as dark as Hades in there and almost a criminal act to shut out the sunlight like that. I'm glad I'm not a Menorcan taxpayer footing the electricity bill for this place anyway.

I am musing on this, standing with my back to the building as Iona, across the street, is preparing to take a photograph of Maó's most photogenic, or one of them at least. But something is wrong – she is lowering the camera and shouting my name.

"What? What's the problem, Houston?" I call back. Perhaps my Panama is not at a rakish enough angle and she can see too much of my face.

Before she has time to answer, a voice behind me commands: "No photography allowed. No photographs. Not allowed in here."

I turn round to see that the voice belongs to a big burly policeman advancing towards me, his moon of a face a yard behind his paunch. I can see from his approach that he means business and that he clearly thinks that I have no business here. Having sorted out David Bailey over there, it's now my turn.

"Not allowed in here."

There was a time, a long time ago, when I would have turned and fled, but age has made me bold. I stand my ground.

"Eh? Not allowed? Where does it say that?" Just to make sure, and since I am already certain there are none – they would surely have been prominently displayed on the pillars or the railings - I make a great pantomime of looking around for a camera with a dirty great red line through it or a silhouette of a man with a camera similarly being struck through or crossed out.

There's no answer to that – at least not in words. The unsmiling policeman is a man of few words or English ones at least, and perhaps he doesn't know what I'm saying, but anyway, he's not prepared to argue the toss. In the battle of the bellies I am a non-starter and he's pushing his paunch at me. Before push comes to shove and paunch comes to punch, I'll leave but not before I have one parting shot.

"Why? Why am I not allowed here? Why no photography?"

"Military."

"Military?"

"Yes, military."

Ah, right that explains it. Those cars which look like dozens of others, must be tanks of some sort. And behind those windows in the house with the green shutters, they must be devising some sort of fiendish military strategy and that's why the shutters are always closed, even the ones on the upper storeys in case someone like me with a zoom lens on his camera and with the ability to penetrate closed shutters, takes a photograph of the documents marked **Most Secret**. Perhaps it's a plan on how to deal with the British problem – what's to be done about this latest invasion, all those beer bellies, tattoos, shaved heads, body piercings, red arms and freckles which are making the streets of Maó look a scary place to be. Then, if they sort that little problem out, they might turn their attention to the men.

We turn right up the street, admiring the occasional *boinder,* heading for another interesting-looking building at the top of the street. The street is narrow and we can't see all of the façade yet, but it can see us. One Cyclops eye is watching us as we approach, then, as we come nearer, another bigger one, higher up, pops into view. In this way, the Església de St Francesc gradually reveals all of its façade, until, as we emerge from the Carrer Isabel, we can see that there is another window to match the one on the left and an impressively deep Romanesque doorway. I think it is mainly due to that doorway which makes the church look incredibly old and tired, though it might be the juxtaposition of its red sandstone construction with its much paler cloisters which now houses the Museu de Menorca.

It may look old and tired, but for my money, it is the best looking church in Maó and since I don't need any of it to enter and the door is invitingly open, we decide to pop in and have a peep. After all, it had been peeping on us, so it only seems right to respond in kind.

It's dark in here, but it has more to do with the lack of lighting than the décor of the place which is actually quite light – the red sandstone, actually quite pink in here, with white walled chapels and not too much clutter, is actually a lot better than I had expected and a lot better than many Catholic churches I have seen. Where it goes wrong is the altar, which seems to cast a shadow of gloom over the whole place with its heavy gilt panels and paintings so dark it's impossible to make out what they represent.

But there's a real find, a complete contrast, a complete surprise to find such a light and airy chapel in a place like this. We are in the Chapel of the Immaculate Conception and there is something instantly numinous about it which takes the breath away, makes Iona and me talk in hushed whispers. Octagonal in shape, light floods in from an oculus, bathing the place in light. The walls are white and barley-sugared pillars, in the lighter coloured stone of the cloisters and intricately carved in a vine design, twist up to support balustraded balconies. Above the pillars, on the wall, there is another foliage design, a bunch of flowers, possibly roses, wilting in their vases. The wilting shape, I concede, is more pleasing in plaster than a fully alive spray and like Keats's lover endlessly pursuing the object of his desire round the *Grecian Urn* without ever having his wicked way with her, these flowers will wilt no more and never die. And above these immortal plants there is a flowery frieze running round the oculus, like the border we have on the wallpaper in our bedroom at home. If it all sounds a bit too flowery, it might be if the flowers were real or God forbid, on wallpaper, but here in the plaster, it not only looks acceptable but to my mind, very good.

This style is called churrigueresque after its inventor, José Churriguera. You may call me an art ignoramus if you like and you'd be right, but I've never heard of it before, and as far as I can remember, never have seen it before, and I am an instant convert. There are brightly polished wooden benches all around the octagon and some real potted plants, or rather foliage, either by intent or design, drooping their leaves in empathy with their plaster cousins. I wouldn't mind coming here every week as long as I could have this place all to myself, like now, to spend in contemplation. Yes, I have a new hero. The architect was Francesc Herrara. Hurrah for you Francesc! I see you nearly had a woman's name, maybe it's due to that, your feminine side coming out, that makes this place so great. They can keep their Military Palace. This is by far the best that Maó has had to offer, perhaps the best that Menorca has to offer – and to think that I nearly missed it and it was little more than a whim which brought us in here!

Only yards away from the church, is another of these occasional *miradors*, and we can't resist another glimpse of the port. From our heady height, we look down on the scene, much as before but by now there's a little more activity. White wakes furrow the field of blue water far below as powerboats nose out to sea. It looks as if siesta time is over, but not for the massed ranks of sailing boats still moored along the waterfront.

Before we go down there, we have one final thing to see on our city tour – the Portal de Sant Roc. An appropriate name for the last remaining city gates from the medieval period, for, as solid as a rock, two great square towers soar above us, connected by an arch. The arch has a great slit where the portcullis must have been. The gates have been standing there since 1359 and look impregnable, yet the poor inhabitants of Maó were not protected from the Ottoman admiral Khair ed-Din whom the world knows better as Barbarossa or Redbeard who, in 1535 sacked Maó and killed or enslaved more than half the population. No doubt the red beard is a reference to the depth in which he was immersed in blood for gingers are not exactly thick on the ground in Turkey I would have said. Unfortunately, as we saw on the monument in Ciutadella, he was a sort of advance party, for the Turks came back twenty years later and did the same there, evening things up in the inter-city rivalry stakes as far as massacres were concerned.

At the bottom of the Costa de Ses Voltes, we pass speedily through the market lying in ambush and look up at where we have been, at the backs of the Georgian mansions on the Carrer Isabel. This, like Naples, is how one should approach Maó for the first time - from the seaward side. Not that it's a thing of beauty exactly, more a striking sight. Like a secondary cliff, stacked on top of the natural limestone, the houses shamble together, a higgledy-piggledy collection of white; not one house the same, not in height nor in width nor in style, but clamjamfried together in a ragged ribbon running the length of the cliff until the mass of the Eslégsia de St Francesc suddenly brings them up short.

We walk along the car parking for the ferry, empty of cars. Apparently no ferry is due which is good as it allows us a better view of the cliff and the houses, with the palm trees which parallel the road as perspective. It also gets us away from the annoying buzz of the traffic, and besides, it lets me walk in the sun.

Journey's end at last – the gin distillery – a white, two-storeyed house with *Gin Xoriguer* in red letters prominently displayed on a board on the roof and another over the door which also has a green awning. There's no mistaking we are in the right place but it looks nothing like the Scottish equivalent of a distillery. In fact, it is nothing more than a glorified shop, though there are copper stills behind a glass window. Still by name and still by nature. If there's any distilling going on there, it's the equivalent of watching paint dry. We're plainly not going to get a tour or an explanation of the process. Why don't they just call it the Xoriguer Gin Shop – because that's just what it is.

It could be called Aladdin's cave though. It looks like a cave, a long room with a vaulted ceiling and shelves of bottles standing sentry all around the room, but in the middle of the room – barrels and barrels, upended to form tables, and on the barrels, bottles and bottles of gin and on a table beside the barrels, a tray of shot glasses, like giants' thimbles, bottoms up, giving the thumbs up to free samples. It's as if I have landed on the other side of the rainbow. I had no idea there were so many different types of gin – and so many different colours! It's like looking through a prism at the range of gins on display and all ready for the sampling. But where do I begin?

I pick up a glass, then, although it is clear glass, a dark green bottle. Iona picks up a glass and looks at me darkly.

"Remember you're driving," she says.

Don't I know it! All this free booze – for there seems to be no limit to the amount one can sample. There is a person at the till by the door, but no one, as in other distilleries I have visited, who pours the sample for you upon which you feel obliged to comment, yet not too favourably so you don't have to spend the best part of half a hundred pounds buying it and who then tells you, after your second sample, that the next one is your last. It looks as if you could sample as many as you want here, and if you find one you really, really like, you could take a bottleful of giant thimbles home inside you. You might even be persuaded to buy a bottle.

But it's no good. I have La-Belle-Dame-Sans-Merci with me, as officious a policeman as the one at the Gobierno Militar. Worse even – I have to live with her. I shall have to be selective, but how shall I choose out of all these bottles? And how many will I be allowed before I'm told: *The next is your last.*

Well, I'll stick with this one anyway – it's such an attractive colour and for someone who's a bit green about flavoured gins, green seems as good a place as any to start. If it tastes as good as it looks, it should be delicious. Crème de menthe gin. I might have guessed. Maybe I should let Iona try it first.

"Do you want to try this first?" I ask her, showing her the bottle.

She hesitates, but not for long. Like me, she is seduced by the colour. She smells, she sips, her lips twitch like a rabbit's, she sips some more and hands the glass over for me to try.

"Well, what do you think of it?" I ask before I taste it myself.

"Not much."

But then she's not really an aficionado of things alcoholic. I think it's quite pleasant, if you like that sort of thing. It might have been a better idea to have that one last and to have breathed peppermint over any policeman if I were unlucky enough to be stopped.

She's found a crème de cacao for herself. She's a coffeeholic so that should suit her - and it does. Her other passion is for lemons and in a flash it comes to me, that the answer is a lemon. Give the gin police a lemon. It's bound to sweeten her up.

"There's bound to be a lemon flavoured one about here somewhere, there's bound to be."

She sees the wisdom of my words and goes off to search. Right, now that she's occupied, what shall I have first? If she likes lemons, I like oranges, more precisely tangerines, and there's one here, a beautiful tangerine colour – and it *is* as good as it looks.

What! She's back already!

"Did you find it?"

"Yes."

"And what did you think of it?"

"OK."

Oh well, not much chance of that sweetening her up then. Back to plan B obviously.

Well, if I am to be restricted, and I am, I may as well go for the unusual. Our guidebook has some recommendations. There's *calent*, for example. I know I'm not going to like it before I even taste it, even before I smell it. I don't even like the colour – a dirty shade of brown, not a nice beery brown, more an upset tummy sort of brown. Apart from the gin base, it is made from aniseed and cinnamon and saffron. You could have fooled me. It's only the aniseed I can taste and it's the aniseed I don't like. Ah, well! Down the hatch! Aaargh! Horrible! Something to take the taste away – quick!

It's a case out of out of the frying pan into the fire. The next on the list is *palo* – a licquorice-tasting liqueur made from carob seeds. Oh my God! Yes, I think that's even worse.

"One more only," says the drinks police.

"Thank God for that!" I say wholeheartedly.

There's only one left on my list anyway – *hierbas*. At least it is a pretty lime-green colour. It's made of daisies, well camomile actually. Well, it has to be better than the others, and it is, even although it is sickly sweet - but it does take the taste away.

We're not going to buy any of those, that's for sure. No we'll stick to the straight gin. As well as the conventional bottles, they sell it in the attractive imitation earthenware flasks called *canecas* with a little lug on the shoulder. I can just see British sailors crooking their forefinger in and presumably, by the use of this handy stabilising device, just glugging the stuff straight back. And that's another thing that the British did for the Menorcans – they introduced gin to the island in the late 18th century. I should imagine that was one thing which did go down well with the natives even if they weren't too fussy about the roads and the cows and the cheese and the capital being moved.

Yes, this would make a pretty good souvenir. Apart from the flask-like shape of the bottles, the label is very attractive with an old-fashioned windmill in full sail against an azure sky. The problem is they are quite heavy and possibly rather fragile, when you remember how our bags will be at the mercy of beefy baggage handlers. As I already said, what we normally do to counteract this difficulty and also to keep within our baggage weight allowance, is to transfer our alcohol from the glass bottles into plastic bottles which once held fizzy drinks. Strong, light and baggage-handler-proof.

What are we to do? We, well I suppose I mean me really, would really like to take one of these *canecas* home. Apart from wanting one for myself, it would make a good present for Hélène, whose e-mail moniker, for some reason, leads me to suspect she is partial to the odd glass of gin: *ginsuperstar.* Then Iona has an idea.

"Why don't you get two of the little flasks and a glass bottle? Then you can put the glass bottle into a plastic bottle and use it to top up the flasks."

Brilliant! Why didn't I think of that? The small, 50 cl *canecas* don't weigh that much really. She just got one thing wrong – each baby *caneca* needs a big, parent bottle to accompany it on that flight home, surely. Have I got the bottle to buy another litre bottle? I have - when her back is turned.

By the time she reaches me at the till, it is too late – the plastic is already having its numbers read, being digested by the machine whose whirring, churning sounds are nothing but so reminiscent of gastric juices getting to work on the latest offering as they reduce my bank balance.

"What's that?" says La-Belle-Dame-Sans-Merci looking disapprovingly at the extra litre glass bottle, but holding back from creating a scene in front of the cashier.

I could have attempted levity such as: *I think it's called a clone* but there is something about her expression which tells me it would be best to leave the clone idea alone.

"I think they are called *canecas,* dear," I say, instead, ingenuously.

She flounces out of the shop. Too late, I know I've made a mistake. I should not have patronised her by calling her *dear.* It's one thing to make an idiotic remark, but a totally different thing to address her with terms of endearment. I never do that and will no doubt pay for it dearly. I'll have to face the music sooner or later. I think I'd rather face the "music" back at the apartment. No not really.

She's waiting for me outside - my Chinese wife, Scow Ling. Of my two other wives, Frau Ning and La-Belle-Dame-Sans-Merci, she's the one I'm most scared of.

"There was absolutely no need for that. You don't need all that gin. You've got a full bottle, practically, at the apartment. Not to mention we are swimming in it at home."

I agree. That's my fault. I was wrong there. I should have made sure that we had drunk more of it before we came here. But the problem is I only drink gin in the summer and only on warm sunny days at that, so stocks have been building up. In spite of that, I do need more actually, but I'm not a complete idiot, this is not the time to point out that I don't intend to drink it all at once, especially not tonight, (when she may have *had* consummation plans) or give her a lecture in economics, on how, by buying at source, I've saved more money than I can calculate (though it would not have to be much before I ran out of fingers); or to pose the question on how can I be expected to run an import business of the best gin in Europe (and one of the cheapest) if I'm not allowed to import any? I say nothing – the safest way to express myself at the moment. Instead I put on my hangdog expression.

"And if you think that I'm carrying any of that, then you've got another think coming!"

Having won the argument, but not completely mollified, she and I turn our backs on the so-called distillery but not on each other, and as we walk side by side by side, we must look like any other happily married couple. Little do they know that one of us has to bear the burden of a tiresome husband while the other has merely tired arms being burdened down with gin – if that's the correct word for something you really don't mind carrying. We have an appointment with a parking meter, and without any hesitation or deviation, we must go directly there and if we do so, we should arrive in time and avoid a fine, which is fine with me as there is nothing left in Maó that I desperately want to see anyhow.

115

True to her word, although she has the knapsack on her back, La-Belle-Dame-Sans-Merci absolutely refuses to carry any of my purchases, even when she sees me puffing up the Costa de Ses Voltes (it was all right coming down, unladen; it's something else carrying two heavy bags up, even if they are balanced) - not to mention the long trek back the way we had come, which hadn't seemed that far then.

By my watch, we've used our parking time up to the limit, actually beyond, depending on whether you're looking at his or her watch. We have a matching pair, as we complement each other so well. It's not like me to be ahead of the time, but even by hers, we don't have much time on our hands. In fact, it could all boil down to how rigorous and efficient the car park attendants are here.

In any case, we can't afford to stop and rest, let the bags rest for a moment on the pavement, let my arms spring back to their sockets. No, I must huff and puff and even when I've had enough, I must conjure up some more energy and huff and puff some more. The gin may have been cheap but I am paying the price now and I hope La-Belle-Dame-Sans-Merci is satisfied. I can't say for sure, but her back still looks cross to me. If I'm the cross she has to bear, why doesn't she give me a piggy back, I'd like to know? But she is steaming ahead to defer any parking fines, hopefully, by saying I'm just coming. To heaven, I should think before the car, by the thumping of my heart.

By the time we eventually return to the Plaça de S'Esplanada, my shoulders are breaking. I feel as if my knuckles have been scraping the ground and anyone watching might have mistaken me for an anthropoid recently liberated from the zoo with a peculiar sense of dress, for I am sporting my normal holiday ensemble of swimming trunks and Panama hat. Anyway, that'll teach me not to try and make a monkey out of my trouble and strife.

Long before we reach the car, I notice with relief there is not a piece of paper tucked beneath the windscreen wipers. With even greater relief, I lay down my burden and as I do so I reflect, as the pain gradually leaves my lungs and shoulders and my breathing returns to normal, that it wasn't so much a case of being a bottle too far for La-Belle-Dame-Sans-Merci but too far for me with two.

6. The Deserted Villages

It's one thing going into a city, it's another thing finding one's way out again, especially when that place is a small place and there are no signs to it, as far as we can see. We're looking for the road to Sant Lluís, heading for the coast and the Talayotic site of Trepucó.

These Talayotic sites are a bit of a Menorcan speciality, although they do exist in Mallorca. The Talayotic period dates from c1400 BC – c800 BC. The word derives from the Arabic *atalaya* meaning watchtower and several of these conical towers, or their remains, are scattered throughout the island. But there is one thing which Menorca has uniquely - *taulas,* (the Catalan word for tables, though you can see that they got it from the Latin *tabula*) - great T shaped structures, with a grove in the flat stone at the top to keep it firmly embedded on the upright.

They are a bit of a mystery, these *talayots*. Although they are called watchtowers, it seems unlikely that this was their function since few are situated near the coast from whence invaders would come and, intriguingly, there is no internal staircase.

Similarly, no one knows what the function of the *taula* was. It seems likely that it had some sort of religious significance. They are found in a circular, rectangular, or horseshoe enclosure, bounded by a low wall, while the remains of dwellings have been found outside this perimeter wall. There is only ever one *taula,* though there may be more than one *talayot,* (why would you need more than one watchtower?) so it seems certain that they were the central, focal point of the settlement. One theory is that they were a stylised representation of a bull, bull-worship being not uncommon in Mediterranean societies, most notably of course, by the Minoans. This theory was given further credence by the unearthing of a bronze bull at the Talayotic site of Torralba d'en Salord, near Alaior, together with fire pits containing charred bones and amphorae which suggest that some sort of ritual or sacrifice took place there.

"Do you know the way to Sant Lluís?"

I have a song for every occasion and this is the time for this one, but not to voice it aloud. It's a rhetorical question. Plainly Iona the Navigator does not know the answer as we emerge from one more identically anonymous industrial zone and come to yet another roundabout, with yet again no sign of a sign to Sant Lluís and she's becoming increasingly frustrated and irritated. Clearly, we have taken a wrong turning somewhere and we're off the beaten track, exploring parts of Menorca which other tourists normally do not see. That's the good thing about being an independent traveller, you see things and go places that the tour operators don't bother with: *Over to your left you can see another factory and coming up on your right, an exceptionally ugly electricity sub-station.* Fascinating! All we can do is keep on going, trust to instinct and our general sense of direction and hope we eventually come across a sign.

And at last we do and like buses which all appear together, we also see the sign to Trepucó off to the left – but first we have to cross the road. Traffic is thundering past in an apparently unending stream, trucks shaking the car with the displaced air as they hurtle past. I don't like this one little bit: *We've gotta get out of this place or it's the last thing we'll ever do.* Another song for another occasion but I'm feeling far too nervous to sing it now. It would just come out as a croak. In fact, nervous or not, it would still sound like that. I must have missed the day musical skills were being handed out.

The road is straight and at last, I think I can see a gap coming. It's not the sort of gap that I would normally consider a gap, but we've been here far too long already. It would only take a blow-out or a moment's inattention from the driver of one of these juggernauts and we'd be mincemeat. I grip the wheel tighter, check I'm in first gear, handbrake off, keep the engine on high revs, and as the oncoming truck shudders past, spin the wheel sharply to the left and engage the clutch. God help us if the engine stalls now. But it doesn't and we're safely across and heading for the ancient site.

"Bloody hell! What are you trying to do – get us killed?"

"Well, did you want to sit there till kingdom come?"

"We just about bloody well did!" Iona has just relaxed her grip on the sides of her seat and is staring straight ahead as if expecting to see the pearly gates on the horizon and can't believe they are nowhere to be seen. Her face is red, not chalk white, which means she's more furious with me than terrified but I have chalked up one more crime and all in the space of less than half an hour. Not bad going, even for me.

"Look, just let me do the driving, OK and you do the navigating." I'm a bit rattled myself, truth to tell. It was a closer encounter with I don't know how many tons of metal relentlessly hurtling towards us than even I had realised or would care to admit, but I hope my allusion to the navigating will remind her she is not quite perfect herself.

The truth is she's too timid a driver and we *would* still have been sitting there for God knows how long, in imminent danger of being mowed down. That's why we stick to what we each do best. I do all the driving on the continent while she, as an ex-geography teacher, likes looking at maps anyway and, generally speaking, she *is* a better navigator than me, our recent detour not withstanding.

When we get to Trepucó, I am pleased to see there are no cars in the car park. That's the other good thing about driving yourself around, apart from the excitement of the driving experience itself, because if you're lucky, you might well end up at a site and have the place to yourself, like we have now, whereas, by definition, if you go on a bus tour, you are bound to arrive with a whole lot of other people, like those we had seen visiting the Naveta d'es Tudons this morning.

A path, bordered by two dykes, leads to the *talayot* at the end. This is one of the circular, conical ones, tapering inwards, though I estimate all that remains is the lower third, which meant it must have been some height as I reckon it's about thirty feet high as it stands now. A notice nearby states categorically that *talayots* were defence towers and that the living area was near the top. I expect they flew up as, true enough, just as the guidebook said, there are no stairs. Right enough, they would be in a hurry if they were being attacked and you wouldn't want stairs which the attackers could climb up and get you, would you?

There were four on this site, though only this and a smaller one remain today. Watchtower or defence tower? You pays your money and you takes your choice. Or rather you don't, for another good thing about this place is it's not only people-free, but free in my favourite sense of the word too. I don't see why they couldn't have been both watchtower and defence tower though. Some people think they may have been guard-houses or meeting places or tombs or farmhouses or storehouses or dwelling houses. Or maybe they haven't got a clue. Actually that's part of the appeal of them to me.

There's another notice board which tells us about the *taula*. It had a religious significance. Well, the guidebook and notice agree on that then. It also says that some people think that it was the central column of what was a roofed structure. Well that sounds a bit boring. I think I'll go for the religious thing. Perhaps it was a sacrificial altar. That's a bit more interesting. Pity about the victims though.

This is the tallest *taula* in Menorca, which makes it the largest *taula* in the world and here we are, the only two people in the world at it. Isn't that a remarkable thing? Then again, possibly not. I'd never heard of these things before I came here. There are only three Great Pyramids of Giza and one leaning tower of Pisa and you can never ever be alone with them, even if you stood there for as long as these stones have been standing – about 3,000 years. And when you think about it, these walls have been standing a lot longer than the city walls of Maó which have been reduced to fragments long ago, whilst here, these walls, without the benefit of cement and mortar, are still here. And that *really* is an amazing thing, especially when you bear in mind that the French were here, that this was their headquarters in 1782 when Britain was at war with the Spanish and the French (as usual) but this time taking them on together. Expecting an attack, although he had vastly superior forces, the French commander, the Duc de Crillon, built star-shaped defences which we are meant to be able to see, but which I can't make out, possibly because it looks like a pile of rubble. I wonder now, where on earth could the French possibly have got the stones from?

Incidentally, against overwhelming odds, the British were forced to hole up in Fort Sant Felip, at the mouth of the harbour, on this, the southern side of the bay. They never came near this place, never mind attack it, and in the end were starved out and finally were unceremoniously booted out of Menorca. One up for the French.

Maó may be heavily influenced by the British, but Sant Lluís is French (I would never have guessed from the name) and that's where we are headed next. We're not heading there especially; it just happens to be en route as they say in France, for the coast, but it does have a windmill, quite famous in these parts apparently, the Molí de Dalt, like the one on the label of the Xoriguer gin bottle and I want to stop off on the way and see it. I am a bit of an old windmill fan.

Sant Lluís was built by the Duc de Richelieu in 1756 (not the one in *The Three Musketeers* – he died in 1642), when, on another occasion, we allowed the French to throw us out of Menorca, the first time, actually, and named after Louis IX who died on crusade in 1270, and, having been responsible for bashing a goodly number of infidels over the head, became a saint.

What's of interest here is that the British lost Menorca due to the incompetency of Admiral Byng who was sent out to relieve the British force, but after a skirmish with a French squadron, turned tail and ran, leaving the British no option but to surrender. For his pains, Admiral Byng was shot as an example to the others, or as Voltaire famously put it: *Pour encourager les autres.*

You can't miss the windmill – it's just about the first thing that you see as you come into Sant Lluís but there's nowhere to stop, not a single parking place. There's no alternative but to head on down the narrow street, getting further and further away from the windmill, and even if there were a place, I'd have to stop and reverse in and hold up the traffic whilst I manoeuvred. With that queue of traffic impatiently piling up, it would be enough to make me misjudge it and then I'd get even more flustered and in the end give up anyway with Spanish curses ringing in my ears.

At least this gives us a chance to see the town, and it's enough to know it's not worth getting out to explore any further. I take a left at the square and turn back on a parallel street. No parking here either. Ah, there's the windmill again, but still no place to park. But wait a minute, we have come to a little square and there's suddenly lots of parking. How can that be? I pull in.

"You can't park here," says Iona in panic. "This is a taxi rank!"

Right enough, so it is. TAXI is written on the road, plainly, for all to see.

"Well, where else? Besides, there's plenty of room for the taxis."

That's what I say, but actually I'm not too happy about it myself. The last thing I want is a fine – I'd not be able to get over it for days - but I do want to have a closer look at the windmill and take a photo of it. I suppose it's the Don Quixote in me. I decide I'm going to risk it and reach in the back for the camera, but Iona shows no sign of following suit.

"What's the matter? Are you not coming?"

"It's not worth it. You can see it all from here anyway," she adds pointedly as if she sees little point in getting any closer to it. Evidently she thinks I'm more like Sancho Panza's ass than the Don himself.

I'm glad about that, I mean that she's staying in the car. She may not be able to move it but perhaps she could persuade the traffic cop not to give us a ticket or pacify an irate taxi driver or perhaps we could even make some money by taking someone somewhere.

"Right. I won't be long," and I hustle up the side of the square to the top of the street where the giant waits, ready to do battle.

It is cylindrical, blindingly white, with a broad light-blue stripe at the bottom and at the top, a poky hat divided into white and light-blue segments. There are no sails, but the frames for them, looking delicate, a lattice work of rectangular holes, (more holes than substance it seems) are there, immense, the one at the top at least as high again as the windmill itself and all joined at their extremities to form a hexagon, reminding me of a spider's web. The whole thing seems to grow out of a white square building at the base, but to investigate properly, I'd have to cross the road and walk round the block. Should I? Probably this is as good a view of the windmill as I'll get anyway. But after all the bother of trying to find a parking place, it would be a pity to waste it. Why not – if I'm very quick.

Just as I make the decision, there is a toot of a car horn. I turn round, and to my horror, I see a police car pulled up behind my car and Iona waving frantically from behind the windscreen. Oh, no! Bloody hell! It was a very nice windmill, but not worth getting a fine for. Trust this to happen. I'll never hear the end of this from La-Belle-Dame-Sans-Merci. If I get back really quickly, maybe the cop will let me off and save himself some paperwork.

I gallop towards the car, already planning what I'll say: *A taxi rank! Really! I never noticed! Well, well, would you believe it! We don't have them like that in England (no point in disgracing your country). Well, thanks for pointing that out to me, officer. I'll certainly know where not to park in future. I was just taking a look at your lovely windmill there. I wasn't gone long, but I just couldn't resist taking a photo of it. It's the best I have ever seen. And your village is lovely too.* Actually, perhaps not the last bit – he'd think I was winding him up, when in fact, what I'm trying to do, like the windmill, is take the wind out of his sails, and he'd forget about the fine.

I'm sweating when I get back to the car, but I think it is more to do with fear than effort. I decide I'll keep my eyes down, not look at the police car at all, act normally, pretend it's not there. I open the back door, sling the camera on the back seat and fall into the driver's seat.

"I told you not to park here!"

"I know, I know!" I say irritably, switching on and looking in the rear mirror, but I can't see anything happening. Why didn't I listen to her? If I get out of here fast, the cop may not have time to get out of the car before I'm gone. I put on my indicator and begin to move out. Still no sign of any activity from behind. The coast is clear, at least as far as pulling out onto the road is concerned, but twenty yards away, at the top of the street is a Give Way sign and I have to stop. Well, this is the moment of truth. Either he'll follow me, or he'll let me go.

"Oh, no! He's following me," I announce to Iona. There's a hard lump in my throat. My palms are sweaty.

She sighs heavily. "Well, it's your own fault. I told you not to park there – all for the sake of a bloody windmill!"

I'll never hear the end of this, and it'll be bad enough having to pay the fine. I'll balance it up and punish myself by not importing any more cheap Spanish booze. That scarcely makes me feel any better. Just as well I have got what I did get from the distillery. I'm glad for all the pain of the shoulder blades now. I wish I'd made it worse.

The cop car is behind me now. Please, please, let there be a break in the traffic soon, before he can get out and speak to me. What if he'd been signing me to wait from the car, but I hadn't seen him? Now I've gone and made it worse. One thing for sure, I'm going to drive immaculately: however long it takes, I'm not going to do a repeat of the Trepucó manoeuvre.

At last there is a break in the traffic. He still has not got out of the car. Indicator on, let him see I am looking oh, so carefully and deliberately, and move out, slowly and smoothly, just like I did when I sat my driving test, and after all, what is this but another testing time? Relief! He's not behind me, but maybe he didn't think he'd time to get on my tail. Phew! Utter relief! I can see in my mirror he's turned the other way, heading towards Maó. I communicate this to Iona.

"Well, you were bloody lucky! Don't do that again!"

"No, dear! Certainly not, dear!"

She gives me an old-fashioned look, but I believe every word I say, although I am exaggerating my humility. I nearly paid dearly for my windmill picture, but I got it and feel almost drunk with relief and the thought that I will not have to punish myself by restricting my import business.

With that little difficulty behind us, with peace restored in the car, we're heading for the coast, to a little fishing village recommended by our guidebook called Cala d' Alcaufar. It is, apparently, where the British first landed in 1708. It's not far and there's plenty of parking when we get there.

This is the sort of place I like. There is a small beach and the tide and my luck is in because there are a couple of topless ladies on the beach and no one else. Why would you want to be on a crowded beach when you could have a place like this, practically all to yourself, though naturally, you would probably sit down quite near to the ladies so they weren't offended, didn't feel that you thought they'd caught the plague or something. I cast longing glances at the sand and the sea, boobing, I mean bobbing, with buoys, presumably something to do with the fishing. It would be nice to take some time out and have a dip but we've come here to see what this place is like and explore the south east coast, so that's what we are going to do.

There are some natural stone jetties, sticking like fingers into the sea, but big enough only for one rowing boat each, or two at a pinch. It adds another dimension to the term natural harbour, which this undoubtedly is. The harbour entrance is a narrow gap between the natural, bare rock - just as nature created it, (and the ladies) apart from the incongruous sight of a Mortello tower plonked like a sandcastle on the right hand side.

There are some very nice villas here, with balconies and balustrades in wood and stone, and purple and red bougainvillea clambering up snow-white walls, and terracotta pots with spiky green leaves, and steps, ending in a gate, leading down to the water where, presumably you park your boat. More lottery houses for me to fantasize about, but what really attracts me here are three tiny white cottages built into the cliff face. Each has a single window with green shutters and a green door and both are firmly closed, giving them an abandoned sort of air. The window is cheek by jowl with the door and there could be, but there isn't, a sign, similar to the one in Caernarfon home to the smallest house in Wales: *Menorca's smallest houses* or even: *The smallest houses in Spain.* I'm glad there's not. These are so small, they look more like huts and that's in fact what in all probability they are and the owners must be out to sea, for there is not a single boat in sight.

That's as far as we can go, for access to the villas on top of the cliffs, on this side, at least, is by boat only. We can either retrace our steps, or take this path up to the right, through the village. The sound of the water lapping on the shore sounds so peaceful; the cliffs, a mellow honey, rust-red sort of colour and the un-crowded beach, tempt me to return the way we came, just as the same road, travelled in the opposite direction offers fresh perspectives on sights already seen, and I'm persuaded to return along the beach. Iona, however, prefers to go through the village.

"You just want to ogle those women!"

"I do not! As a matter of fact, I had completely forgotten all about them. In fact I hardly even noticed them in the first place." I can see them now, but at this distance, they are little more than brown specks and, alas, I have not brought my specs with me. And perhaps, I have protested too much, for Iona gives my answer short shrift.

"Huh! Anyway, we're going back through the village. We haven't seen what it's like." None of this, you take the low road and I'll take the high road and I'll meet you back at the car sort of compromise. It's non-negotiable.

As villages go, it is certainly pleasant enough, but there's nothing especially remarkable about it, just whitewashed villas and one small, three-storeyed *hostal*, which apparently, was Menorca's first tourist hotel, built in the 1950's. I knew that going back by the beach would have been better, but if ever I come back to Menorca, this is the sort of place I should like to come to, where the tourism is quiet and understated, where the character of the place seems to have been unaffected by commercialism, where the *hostal* did not turn into a ribbon of high-rise hotels.

There should be a coast road along to our next port of call, but Iona the Navigator can not find it, so it's back the way we came to my annoyance, practically all the way back to Sant Lluís, until we pick up an even more minor road than the one we are on, before, finally, we pick up the road to Binibeca Vell.

Vell means old but Binibeca Vell dates from only 1972. It's a custom-built holiday village, built to look like an old fishing village, and why not, say I? Surely it's better to have a theme, because if you don't have a theme, how you gonna make a dream come true, as Bloody Mary nearly sang – the one in *South Pacific*, not the one with Calais engraved upon her heart - a dream of accommodating hundreds of tourists without destroying the natural beauty of the island – and even enhancing it.

It's a pedestrian precinct, so there's another good thing, but there's plenty of parking in a car park practically empty of cars and also in the broad avenue which approaches it, where we abandon our little car. I'm sure it's safe to do so

– there are a few other cars there, but just in case, I turn it round facing the way we came for a quick getaway in case there are any parking wardens nosing about. That there are so few cars is a good sign and that there are no buses even better, and by the looks of it, it even looks as if the majority of residents are out, perhaps fled from the hordes of tourists, which, ironically, have not come, probably the result of the gods playing another of their little jokes. That's the downside of Binibeca Vell – it's a victim of its own success. You imagine you are coming for a peaceful, relaxing holiday, to get away from it all amidst idyllic surroundings, and what do you find, but bus loads and car loads of tourists who have come to share your idyll.

It's a seemingly random collection of terraced houses with arches and balconies and slender chimney stacks, like miniature minarets. I have my specs with me now and I need them, for although the balconies have brown timbers, everything else is a brilliant white here, sparkling in the sun - even the tiles on the roofs which are gleaming like teeth in a toothpaste advertisement. The slender chimneys with holes near the top do not have any traces of soot, so I imagine their purpose is artistic rather than functional and very good they look too.

We come to a square with wooden benches and tables and furled sunshades. The only living thing in sight is a cluster of purple bougainvillea cascading over a wall. It's an eerie feeling. A deserted village, not a sound to be heard and looking so fresh and new that it's almost as if it's had a spell cast upon it and it's just waiting for us to arrive before it will come out of its trance and somehow spring to life, like Brigadoon.

Now we go down a twisting narrow alley, so narrow that you could hardly get a bicycle down it, never mind a car. Lights, like carriage lanterns, add to the old-world ambience, whilst green shutters, closed here, as they seem to be everywhere else, seem to confirm that no one is at home. On a wall above us, a brass plate reads: **SILENCI SI US PLAU**. Bloody cheek! I never said a word! The brass plaque some people have! Maybe that is why this place is so quiet – something terrible will happen to you, like you'll be turned into stone, transmogrified into one of those chimneys if you utter a sound. And what sort of language is that to use anyway? Can that really be Spanish? It doesn't look like it to me. It doesn't even look like Catalan somehow, either.

I have a feeling as if I've been transported to a different world, where it's like this world, but different in subtle ways, like the characters in Ray Bradbury's *A Sound of Thunder* where the Time Travellers return to a world different in infinitesimal ways but actually fundamentally altered. I couldn't possibly have died could I? For this could be what heaven is like, as if I'd nipped in whilst Peter had nipped out for a packet of crisps, while the pearly gates were away for a touch up of pearlescent paint. I don't remember having a collision as I executed the Trepucó manoeuvre or a heart attack when I saw the cop car or even a stroke when I saw the topless ladies, but perhaps that's what sudden death is like. If that's the case I like it. But I don't really think so. Besides, whilst my shirt is white, my swimming trunks are black and surely if I were dead, I'd be wearing a white nightie, wouldn't I? On the other hand, I have only been half as good as I could have been, especially below the belt and maybe I have to be dead a while before I get to wear all white, before the sinful part fades and gets a whiter shade of black as *Procul Harum* didn't quite put it.

The sky looks impossibly blue – a heavenly blue I'd call it – and it's pierced by a shimmering cross like a dagger which we can see glinting above the roofs of the apartments which have small square windows which would not look out of place in a 17th century Scottish tenement. Access is gained by a flight of steps with a miniature rustic gate at the bottom like the one opposite our apartment whilst rich brown wooden banisters and arches seem to connect one apartment block with another at all three levels.

Through an arch, through the twisting alleys we wander, in increasing wonderment and anticipation at what architectural delights the next bend will reveal, at what marvels the unsung architect has created here, for neither of our guidebooks reveals his (or her) name, but what fun (s)he must have had designing all this and seeing it take shape, as I imagine Clough Williams-Ellis, the designer and architect of Portmeirion in South Wales must similarly have done. And now, through a gap between the apartments, we can see that the cross is appended to a slender two-tiered steeple, for just as Williams-Ellis knew he needed a dome to complement his campanile, the architect here knew he needed a church, or more precisely, a church spire, to add verisimilitude to his village.

In a short time we come to a small square with a single tree, which bizarrely has also had the whitewash treatment, making it look as if it has been exposed to a severe snowstorm, with snow plastered unevenly to the trunk, showing darkly through in places. I suppose you would call where we are now Church Square, or if you wanted to be more pedantic, Steeple Square. For, unlike the children's finger rhyme which has church, steeple, door and people, here there's neither church, nor door, nor people - just the steeple which, with its rectangular open space at the bottom, looks as if it might be a chimney for some sort of superior barbecue.

And that's not too fanciful an idea either, particularly since at the other end, where the second, narrower tier begins, the steeple looks just like the chimneys on the apartments, with four arches to let out the non-existent smoke, unless, perhaps, after every burning, the mad whitewasher who goes about painting the trees, stalks the streets with a bucket of whitewash, checking for dark stains, for signs of soot, turning everything in this ghostly village as white as a snowdrift.

Tucked into a corner, almost invisible against the white wall, there is a white dustbin, (naturally) and in spite of its invisibility, we have not seen a single piece of rubbish, not a scrap of white paper even, is allowed to litter this immaculate place. The mad whitewasher has, mercifully, left the leaves of the tree in Steeple Square their original colour, and coming to a larger, more open space where some cypresses grow, he has wisely not attempted to press his brush into service there either.

At last we emerge from the tangle of close-knit houses and come down to where a broad paved area, amazingly not painted white, ends in a low wall which is, and which also indicates that we have reached where the village ends and where a rocky cove cuts a jagged rent inland. At the other side, a new development is in the process of being built. Skeletal apartment blocks, square and regular, jostle for space in military formation, whilst unseen, but definitely not unheard, a mechanical pecker is chipping away at the rocks to make foundations for even more. If it's like a nail being driven into my head, and it is, it must be intolerable for the residents here – peck, peck, peck, peck all day long, disturbing the silence, eroding their sanity, like Chinese water torture. Perhaps that's why all have fled and I don't blame them.

Actually, if I had to choose, it sounds a whole lot better than the din I have to endure back at the apartment. I think I could get used to that drill, although it's impossible not to hear it without thinking of a visit to the dentist's. It may be painful and may get on your nerves but at least it's regular and you know what to expect and perhaps, in time, you might become accustomed to it and not hear it all. I doubt it though but I wouldn't mind betting that with my neighbours, switching on their fiendish contraption is an automatic reaction and if they hear it at all, it will only be at a subliminal level.

No, this really is a fiendish din. Even the water has retreated in horror, for although they have built a broad ramp down to the water's edge, the water is far out at sea, leaving a couple of fishing boats high and dry. Perhaps they are retired boats, just part of the scenery, like the steeple, for if there's one thing an imitation fishing village needs more than a steeple, it's a real fishing boat or two. There are no other craft about, not a single rowing boat or any pleasure boats as one might have expected in a holiday village like this. Perhaps they too, like the cars, have been banned or much more likely, they have fled from the noise.

We follow the low white wall around the perimeter of the village and come to an attractive bridge which has its parapet and arch neatly picked out in white and across which, Binibeca Vell continues to offer a pleasing prospect, this time with the addition of palm trees and huge terracotta pots crowned with scarlet geraniums and purple bougainvillea tumbling down the walls.

Thus we emerge, by a circuitous route, behind the car park and walking through an avenue of red hibiscus, return to our car which is just as we left it, with no little scrap of white paper attached to the windscreen by the wipers. Our guidebook had warned us that this was just an imitation village, as if we may feel cheated that it was not the real thing – to beware of cheap imitations so to speak, of the present masquerading as the past. But for my money, and once again, I hadn't needed any of it, this was as good a thing as I had seen in Menorca, certainly better than Maó and a rival to Ciutadella, though I'm not sure that I would want to stay here – better to come and admire and go away again. I've a feeling it might be a bit claustrophobic and I certainly wouldn't want hundreds of gawking tourists trooping through the place.

But where are they? And where are all the residents? For, incredibly, in all the time we had been here, strolling through the meandering alleys of this incredibly white village, we had not come across another living soul, nor heard a sound until that awful pecking noise, and even that was an intrusion from across the cove. The population of this place must amount to several hundreds, yet we had not seen a single one, nor a single visitor. Once again that eerie feeling returns, as if we have just been visiting a ghost town.

There's a good road along the coast as far as Es Canutells but there the road seems to end in an *urbanización* and Iona the Navigator is not too sure if we'll be able to pick up the road to our next destination, Cales Coves, again, so we play safe and take the road north to Sant Climent, then turn west again on a road which is as straight as any crow flies, or any Roman road, which it apparently is, until we see the sign to Son Vitamina, from where the book says it is either a brisk half-hour walk to Cales Coves, or it is just about negotiable by car. A half-hour brisk walk probably means three quarters of an hour as far as we are concerned and as the road is sloping gradually down hill, that possibly means a return journey of an hour, if not more, so we're talking about the best part of two hours just to go and come back, not allowing for the amount of time we stay there, depending on what there is to explore.

Cales Coves is a prehistoric necropolis, the largest on the island, with over 100 Bronze Age caves hewn out of the cliff face for the dead - and the living, who lived in the same cave, apparently as their ancestors. We should be able to see how they transformed these caves into what sounds like comfortable dwellings, with windows and interior rooms and even patios. There are also some Roman inscriptions which indicate that the Romans used them, and indeed, says our guidebook, some are still in use today by modern troglodytes who go swimming, naked, in the cove's crystal clear waters. Well, that sounds very interesting and it's good to see that they take their hygiene seriously, even if they do live rough.

The road, never particularly good, soon deteriorates into a rocky road, full of potholes and humps, which means I am reduced to a crawl, weaving round as many of them as I can, and even then we are jolted from one side of the car to the other as I make my way, painstakingly choosing what I think is the smoothest, least bumpy path. It's bad enough to imagine what damage this may be doing to the tyres, which, I expect are not covered by the insurance, and even more alarming, I am not even sure if there is a spare wheel in the boot. I hadn't specifically checked, but I can't recall actually seeing one and I know that a lot of hire companies don't include one for some reason.

But what concentrates my mind more than this alarming prospect is the memory, many years ago, after not long having passed my test, of driving my father's car down my uncle's farm road, as smooth as a billiard table compared to this, to officiate at my cousin's wedding and on my return, discovering there was not a drop of oil in the engine - for a stone had punctured the sump. If that could happen there, it could easily happen here.

There is a car ahead of me which seems to have negotiated the road so far, sending up great clouds of dust, and if he can do it, so could I, but I'm not for continuing any further. We don't even have a mobile phone with which we could contact the hire company, for stupidly, neither of us had thought to bring one with us and even if we had, it would take hours for them to reach us here in this remote spot and I could just imagine their reaction when they saw the state of the road: *You actually took our car down this apology for a road and you seriously ask if the insurance will cover a new engine?*

Forgive me for asking, but are you quite mad, señor or just completely crazy?

In any case, at this speed, walking would be just about as fast, so I pull off to the side and park amongst the olive trees. As we make our way on foot now, I can see that other drivers have had the same idea, for abandoned cars occasionally can be seen sheltering, like ours from the sun, half hidden in the olive groves. And as we reach the last bend, an S which curves sharply downhill, I am sincerely glad that I left the car behind, for water erosion has carved a series of treacherous canyons, to say nothing of leaving a deposit of stones and rocks which would have made driving down it hazardous to say the least, but coming up even worse and something I'd prefer not to negotiate.

The car which was ahead of me has persevered and lies close in to side of the road, covered in a patina of dust, hugging the shade of some overhanging foliage. There's a house down here too, although it looks uninhabited and there's a board which says *Calas Coves* and a notice which says that the site is closed. (Make up your mind, is it *Calas* or *Cales*? You would think that the correct version would be here, at the point of contact, but the map and the guidebooks have it as *Cales*). However it's spelled, we've come all this way, and now they tell us that it's closed! Why didn't they spell it out to us at the top of the road, for God's sake and save us negotiating this horrendous road? How can they close caves anyway? I'm not going to be put off by a little notice like that, not when I've risked tyre and sump to get here.

I can see some caves off to the left, peeping above some dense and impenetrable trees and bushes. According to our book, these are the earliest caves, dating from the 9th century BC. You can tell they are man made, too regular to be natural, but also irregular – some square, some rounded at the top, some close together, some further apart. It looks like an apartment block in Bedrock, home of *The Flintstones.*

Those caves look impossible to reach but there is a dusty brown path leading into the trees at the left, which should ultimately lead us to a cave away round on the left and the only one, either to left or right that we can see. The right is where we would have preferred to go because that is where the younger, the Iron Age caves are supposedly to be found, dating from the fourth century BC and where the Roman inscriptions (graffiti?) are, not to mention where the modern troglodytes hang out. I'd like to see what a modern troglodyte looks like, with or without clothes, but it seems that you *can* close down prehistoric caves after all, for to the right, the sea is in, leaving islands of isolated boulders and there is no discernible path either at this level or higher up, so that looks like a non-starter.

The path, like the road we had just come down, flatters to deceive. It begins broad and wide and in the open, but as we proceed, becomes narrower and at times necessitates bending low to duck beneath overhanging branches, while from the sides, thorny bushes prick and clutch and scratch the skin. I'm beginning to feel like the Prince fighting his way into Sleeping Beauty's castle, instead of a Pleb trying to reach a humble cave. This didn't happen overnight. I wonder how long the caves have been closed because this path practically is.

Off to our right, we are near some boulders which would allow a difficult but less restricted access to the cave. To get to them is scarcely any more difficult than proceeding along the path, so stooping low, knuckles practically scraping along the ground, I burst through and pick my way across the boulders. Iona has turned back.

When I get to the cave, there's nothing to see in the cave itself, as I expected, apart from one wall which is completely black, from floor to ceiling, a Benibeca Vell's whitewasher's worst nightmare (try saying that when you're drunk, or even when you're sober – almost as bad as the sick sixth sheik's sixth sheep's sick) and which could be and probably is, the soot residue of ancient and innumerable fires. However, there is a good view of the cove and the cliff opposite and there's another smaller exit further into the cave, which, like a *boinder*, gives a view further round the cove - a tomb with a view you could say.

Scrambling through this on my hands and knees, it becomes clear that there is another arm to the cove and it is actually splits into two, like a Y. Just inside the other arm, a small sailing ship lies at anchor, its sail unfurled, its prow pointing to a series of caves rising in gradual stages from perhaps some twenty feet above the water level to some forty or fifty feet higher. It's as if there is a corridor inside, linking all these holes in the rock together, perhaps a series of linking caves. These could be the modern caves, the 4th century ones and the 21st century's too. But how do you reach them? Even if I had been able to, it would have involved a walk round both arms of the Y and even then I don't see how I would have been able to actually get into the caves. I made the right decision I think, to come to this side and at least see them from the other side of the water.

From the entrance of the cave I can see the path by which I should have arrived here and since I prefer not to take the same way back if I can possibly avoid it, I take the high road as it looks reasonably clear ahead but before long, I come to a chain link fence which bars my way. It's not the highest of fences, nor the newest - I should say it's been here some time, for if not rusty exactly, like me, it's not exactly in the first flush of youth either. I could easily shin over it I suppose, but I realise that when they said this place was closed, they meant closed, that I am not supposed to be here. Perhaps the reason is to keep the troglodytes out, but I have defied the ban, got in and, for that matter, have been walking here (not to mention Maó after I bought the gin), in a primitive, even simian sort of manner. I had wanted to know what a troglodyte looked like. Perhaps I had the answer all along: all I needed to do was look at myself.

Back where I began, I presently rejoin Iona who has been whiling the time away in the present whilst I have been following in the footsteps of the past.

"Where have you been all this time? What took you so long?" she wants to know. Sitting around in the sun, sunbathing by the sea, has never been her style, even *with* a book and she had not come armed with one as nothing could have forewarned her that she would be abandoned like this, on this rocky shore.

Although it hadn't seemed a long time to me, I think I have a witty rejoinder. "It takes a long time to get back from the 9th century BC."

It's not very witty apparently. She has already had enough of this place and is setting off towards the uninhabited house and the road which is beginning to look as rocky as our marriage. When I'm not driving her to distraction, my driving is scaring her to death, and when we eventually toil back to the car, by which time her face is as pink as her blouse, so it's hard to tell brow from bust, it turns out that my parking is not exactly without fault either - for the second time that day.

Actually, it's not my fault that the car is like an oven. It is just where I left it, but the *unruly Sun*, as John Donne called it, has moved and you could bake a cake in it. We open all the doors to let as much of the heat out as we can before we move off, for even at our snail's pace, if we opened the windows, we'd inhale great lungfuls of dust. They say that you eat a ton of dirt before you die, but there's no point in having it all at once.

I am not relishing the drive back up the road and wish that I hadn't taken it so far, and although there are one or two cars secreted amongst the olive groves, there is no sign of their owners. Perhaps they are tramping the hillside somewhere. Following upon our experience in Binibeca Vell, we could be the only people on the planet. Even the people who were in the car ahead of us, who had been down at the shore when we arrived, I hadn't seen again after I set out on my time travels, and Iona didn't see where they went either, so not much good asking them for help should the worst happen. Peace and quiet, Menorca seems to be able to offer in spades, but typical of the gods, just when you get what you wish for, you wish there were some other people about.

But the gods are on our side this time and we make it back to the paved road without incident, and almost like one of James Bond's martinis, shaken and definitely deterred from taking it anywhere near a road like this again and as my word is my bond, vowing to take my mobile phone with me the next time I go out in the car again as well.

7. A Fish That Talks

It's getting late. If we want to sit on our patio, noisy neighbours permitting, and have an apéritif before we go out again to explore the culinary delights of Ciutadella, and we do, we must make tracks. So we head straight for base on what must be another Roman road towards Alaior and then the C721 which bisects the island across the middle.

I'm not a person who enjoys shopping, but I had noticed a *hipermercado* on our way out this morning and as we have made good time and as the sun is still relatively high and warm and showing no signs of cloud cover, I reckon I can afford to spend some time stocking up on some supplies. Iona is quite happy to stop too as she likes exploring foreign supermarkets, checking out the sort of things which we can't get at home, like *Turrón* and the different varieties of the sort of things we can, like kinds of cheese.

So while she goes walkabout, I go directly to the wine and spirits section. There's a lot of these we can get at home, only at vastly inflated prices – the problem is, which Spanish brandy will I choose? It's so difficult. I've had most of them before. In the end, I choose Soberano as it is more likely to keep me sober; a bottle of Cava for the caves we did not see and in case we have anything to celebrate, like the neighbours next door moving out, or the consummation of Menorca; and a bottle of rosé to reflect my mellow attitude to life or as a compromise apéritif as Iona prefers white whilst I am more of a red man and I'm not just referring to my face. But actually, a nicely chilled rosé is nice if you can sip it in the sun, especially if it is as warm as this, even although it is the middle of October.

We're in luck. There's no sign of the neighbours I notice, as I drive past, looking for a parking place. The nearest is down by the pool. At the apartment next to it, an older couple is sitting outside on the patio, in the shade, enjoying a glass of wine.

"Nice day," I call in the passing.

"Yes, lovely," they agree.

"I see you must have a corkscrew," I add, nodding in the direction of the wine. If they think it's a bit of an obvious and odd remark to make, they are too polite to say so or to let it show on their faces. "I don't know how I'm going to get into this," I plunge on, in explanation, waggling the rosé in front of them. "We don't have a corkscrew in our apartment."

"Oh don't you," says the old-timer. "We've got two, haven't we, Doris? Never leave home without one," he cackles, bringing on a fit of coughing which crackles with the phlegm in his chest.

Doris gets up from the table. Now that her husband has got his coughing under control, I can hear some music which sounds as if it belongs to the forties wafting out the door. If only this were what my neighbours played, I wouldn't mind it half as much if they played it twice as loud as the rubbish they do deave us with.

Doris reappears with a corkscrew which she proffers me.

"Oh, thanks very much. I'll bring it right back."

"No need," says Doris's husband. "That's the flat's. We've got our own."

I thank them very much. If only we had them for our new neighbours!

There's no sign of the neighbours from hell and even better, no sound of their hellish "music". Taking advantage of their absence, we sit out in the front, catching the last of the sun on our terrace. We've hardly begun our apéritifs, gin for Iona and in deference to the fact that I'll soon be driving, a red wine for me, when I spot the enemy coming back. It would be hypocritical to greet them politely when I really want them to drop dead, so I engage in an earnest conversation with Iona, so they, seeing me, might assume that I am too busy to notice them, but my eyes are telling her: *Oh, God, don't look now, but they're coming back!* From her position on the patio, further back in the shade, Iona can't see them. They've been at the pool evidently, for they are carrying lurid towels, (they would) and seem to be able to move without music after all apparently, because there is no sign of the ghetto blaster.

To be fair to them, they don't put the din on right away. No, first they sling their wet towels over the dividing wall so that a third of them are hanging over on our side. For all they knew, Iona could have been sitting there, and if she had been, she might well have received a clout on the face. And, if things had been different, if Iona had been the sun-worshipper, not me, and I had been sitting there instead, it could have been even worse – it would have been me that got the slap in the face with the wet towel.

Bloody cheek! Not content with invading my privacy with their fiendish "music" they have to torment me with their horrible towels too. Actually, one of the towels is a bit smaller, the girl's presumably. It is white with a Greek keys pattern round the edge and T O N in embossed letters in the middle. It's a pretty safe bet that the letters on their side say S H E R A. Well, what else can you expect? I'm just amazed that they would let plonkers like them over the door, let alone *stay* in a swanky place like that, to lower the tone.

I can hear the door being opened. Any minute now: it's just a question of time. But there is a stay of execution. Clop, clop, clop! It's Jane's business-like heels beating a tattoo on the pavement. She has come to find out how our new neighbours are settling in. Actually, she has probably come to see if they've been electrocuted yet, but that's how she puts it. I can hear them clearly, though cannot see them. I am holding my breath – this could be our release, if they have a complaint about this apartment too. Please God, let them say that they get a funny tingling when they use the shower and their hair stands straight up, though his does all the time anyway, cropped down practically to the wood, hedgehog style.

But no! Everything is fine - they like the tingly feeling. It gives them a bit of a zing in the morning, to start the day.

"That's good!" says Jane. "However, I have found another apartment for you in another resort."

My heart leaps up like Wordsworth's did when he beheld the hills of the Lake District but plummets to earth like a stone just a second later.

"Nah! Thanks, but we'll just stay here, pet."

"Just as long as you realise that you stay here at your own risk." He still doesn't get it does he? I don't suppose it's his fault he was born without a brain.

"Nah! We'll just stay here." Which is Geordie patois for: *We like the next-door neighbours. They don't mind us playing our crappy music really, really loudly and we play it just about all of the time and they don't say a thing. We may not have such nice neighbours at our next place, so we'll just stay here, pet.*

Clop! Clop! Clop! It's like the pecker at Benibeca Vell, the sound of Jane's departing footsteps, like nails in my head, like nails in my coffin and it sounds the death knell of any hopes I may have had that I would be rid of this pestilence from next door. Actually, now I come to think of it, I haven't noticed that pestilential smell of tomcat, though anyone looking at my expression right now might well be forgiven for thinking that there was a particularly obnoxious *and* noxious one right under my nose at this moment. And as if to set the seal on it, the "music" starts. We'll not be un-popping the Cava tonight evidently, at least not to celebrate the departure of them next door.

"Right! That's it!" I say louder than necessary, picking up my glass and scraping the table on the tiles noisily as I stand up and push it roughly away. I don't care if they hear me now – I am mad enough for a fight, (a verbal one at least) but at the same time, I am perfectly sure that they won't be able to hear me, not over that racket. In any case, they have probably moved inside, to leave us to enjoy the "music" on our own, leaving the patio empty, leaving the door open, so we can hear it, together with the rest of the immediate neighbourhood.

Not for the first time and now, regrettably, not for the last time, I'm sure, I thank God for the back door. It's not exactly a pretty sight, the view from our back door, and there's no sun but it is roomier, but above all, we can't hear the bloody noise. Without it, I think I *would* have gone mad. That's the danger of a package holiday - like marriage, you just can't tell what baggage comes along with it when you make the original contract.

"Don't eat too many crisps," says Iona, looking up from her stitching, as I pour some more from the bag into the bowl. "You'll be going out for your tea soon."

I don't eat crisps normally – only when I'm on holiday, for a wee change and this admonition from La-Belle-Dame-Sans-Merci comes as a change from *don't drink too much wine,* but I know that will follow later if I try to get another glass. One small one will be all I'll be allowed, if I'm lucky. I'm lucky to have someone to watch over me, as the song goes, like this. In fact, there's just no end to my luck.

It's amazing how quickly it gets dark here and there seems to be a bit of a breeze getting up and I've had one more handful of crisps and one more small glass of wine, so we may as well go now. As we head for the car, I look over my shoulder to the neighbour's patio where the "music" is still holding forth. As I expected, they are inside, with the doors open. Would it be too much to ask them to close their door and keep the din in? Ah, well, we'll be away from them for a couple of hours or so and by that time, hopefully, it will be the girl's bedtime, she will have turned in and the ghetto blaster will be turned off. Or even better, someone else like me, driven mad by the noise, but braver, has asked him to turn it off. If someone has, he should be easy to recognise by the black eye or the dagger protruding from between his shoulder blades.

The problem is, where to park in Ciutadella? Well, not where to park exactly, but how to get there, to the Plaça de Sant Joan which is what they call the finger of land at the far end of the harbour and which I am sure must have been under water once, but where or why they have diverted it, I couldn't possibly begin to imagine. I'm glad that they did though for if we can find our way to it, it would provide convenient parking for us, for from there we should have any number of choice of restaurants within walking distance, along by the harbour front.

It's ironic how when you expect difficulties, it actually turns out to be straight forward and when you think everything will be plain sailing, you end up ship-wrecked. I am sure there are must be shorter ways to the Plaça and that we came to it in an arc, via the Avinguda del Capità Negrete, right along the Avinguda Jaume I El Conqueridor, then left along the Avinguda de la Constitució. But although we can see our destination now, I can't see a way down to it. Not to worry, although we are still far away, we are at the other side of the harbour now and a left turn as soon as we can and then another, should get us where we want to be. And so indeed proves to be the case, and Iona the Navigator was hardly needed.

The breeze we had noticed back at base is not noticeable here. It is very pleasant to stroll down by the waterfront this warm softly-scented evening, with the restaurants lit up and their reflected lights twinkling on the water through the forest of masts, to read the menus, to look at the people. Hmm. This one looks a possibility, I'll bear that in mind... And so does that...Hmm! That looks tasty too...I suppose I should stop looking at the women, chicly dressed for dining out in these classy eating houses and begin studying the menus. The problem is - which restaurant, when there are so many to choose from and I am no good at making decisions at the best of times.

"Why don't we try the other side of the water?" It may sound like a hesitant suggestion, a modest proposal, in the non-Jonathan Swift sense of the expression, where, to solve the problem of the starving Irish, he satirically proposed eating babies or *chillen* as that restaurant in the Commercial Centre calls them, but even before we came, I think that in the back of my mind, I'd like to try *Es Moll*, the one that is recommended in our guidebook, before we make a final decision. Unfortunately, it means walking back all the way we have come, crossing the bridge and all the way down the other side as it happens to be the very last restaurant.

Iona sighs long-sufferingly, not for the first time today.

"Well, all right. I suppose so, but don't make a big production out of it. I want my food - soon."

There's no mistaking the emphasis on the final word - she's spelling it out like the woman in the restaurant last night. That's the thing about Iona: once she has started thinking about food, she starts to salivate so much that if she doesn't have it fast, she begins to drown.

But in fact, it doesn't take long to cross the little bridge and stroll down the other side and check out the restaurants there because it is a prerequisite that we sit outside, and not many restaurants offer alfresco dining on this side.

Es Moll however, fortunately does, with cane armchairs with gay yellow cushions with blue flowers and cane tables with glass tops such as you may find in a conservatory. They are set at the water's edge surrounded by nets and lobster creels. And another attraction, as I had clocked earlier, is that the view is better from this side of the harbour as there is more to see - the lights of the restaurants strung out like a pendant and the floodlit Ajuntament sitting on top of the sheer cliff of the city walls, with further along, the great bulk of the Bastió de sa Font a reminder of the past history of this charming place. It looks quite perfect.

We study the menu. Unfortunately, the *menú del día* is no longer being served, so this could be a bit more pricy than the more expensive-looking restaurants at the other side.

"Well, what do you think?" I ask Iona, with just a hint of reluctance in my voice. I'm not so sure if I like the idea of this place so much now, but Iona has had enough of tramping about and she knows that once we go back to the other side we will have to begin the process of choosing all over again.

"Let's just go here," she says and starts marching off to the nearest available table before I can say: *Yes... but the prices!*

We are the only diners, so every table is available, a detail I point out to Iona, which is perhaps not a good sign – the restaurants across the water, in spite of the competition, are all well patronised, apart from one which, carved deep into the living rock, charges extra for the restricted view. And you can't believe everything you read in the guidebooks after all - just look at what they said about the caves at Cales (Calas) Coves. Caveat emptor. Perhaps this place might not be so great after all.

"It's not too late to move – I don't think they've spotted us yet."

"We're staying," says Iona. The tone means the subject is not up for further discussion. Ah well, we need someone in the family who can make a decision. I just hope she's taken all the factors into consideration. It worries me sometimes that she doesn't always take prices into the equation. Still, it is a very pleasant view.

Ah, here's the menu. We'll undoubtedly have the fish.

"Just look at this!" exclaims Iona, after a moment or two - she always was a fast reader. I am reading the other column, the one with the figures and I am a bit slow as far as figures, in the mathematical sense of the word is concerned. "Baked githead €19:50 Grilled githead €18:50."

"What? Where? Where?"

I can't believe it! But it's true! Just as the supermarkets offer varieties of food we have neither seen nor heard of, the menu here is the same. I don't know what sort of fish the githead is, but I know what it looks like – it's got thick arms and legs, but that's nothing compared to the thickness of its head, and it lives next door to me.

I don't know why it should cost more to bake a githead than grill a githead but I'd really like to grill him: *Why do you play insufferable "music" all day? Doesn't it drive **you** mad, for God's sake? Don't you have any consideration for your neighbours? Has it never crossed your teeny-weeny brain that they may not like your taste in "music" and don't want it rammed down their ears all day? And why have you got a Geordie accent but wear a Man U T-shirt? And, just tell me this - why did you have to come here in the first place? But above all - tell me why you had to change apartments? Do you **like** getting electric shocks, for God's sake or are you just insane?*

"So this is what they do to lager louts in Menorca!" I say to Iona, enlarging on my theme. It was worth coming here, just to read the menu alone.

I have ordered the *vino de casa*. If I had known what it was, I may not have asked for it. The label on the bottle reads *Canals* – a delicious melange of varieties gathered from waterways within the EEC – though it actually says it's 11% and Spanish. It tastes better than it sounds anyway and, contrary to what you might expect, has a nice pale colour.

All the same, we do not choose to eat the githead. It doesn't sound too appetising somehow. Instead I order sole and that's what I get and Iona has hake, but that's not what she wanted. She ordered the rake. She's got sophisticated tastes, which is why she picked me of course, why she likes to explore the *hipermercados* for something different and why she ordered the rake, which, though still disreputable, is undoubtedly a much more upmarket sort of fish than a githead.

Although I know what a githead looks like, I have no clear idea of what a hake looks like and even less of what a rake looks like, but I know this doesn't look remotely like anything I use in the garden nor remotely like anything from Hogarth's famous series of etchings either, but when Iona says that what she has on her plate is a hake and not a rake, I am inclined to believe her.

"I expect it was a mistake – rake for hake," I point out, "like that funny menu we saw in the Commercial Centre."

But Iona is sure that both hake and rake were on the menu.

Whether they are or not, the waiter said, when he put the plate before Iona: *Your hake, miss.* The trouble is that rake and hake sound so similar, that we begin to wonder: *Did we say it clearly enough? Did he? What did we actually hear him say?* That was the moment when we should have asked or sent it back, but we didn't. I guess neither of us are very good complainers, whether it's about rakes or githeads.

It's a blessing I had sole, as I was able to give her half of mine, (which makes us sole mates, I suppose) to help her get over her disappointment.

We pay the bill and leave the waiter a tip. I'd like to leave him another one - to listen more carefully to orders, but there doesn't seem to be much point now. On our way past, we check the menu on the board which we had looked at when we first appraised the menu. Sure enough, there is *both* hake and rake, and the hake is the cheapest on the menu, while the rake is the dearest. I knew Iona paid scant attention to price. God bless waiters who are hard of hearing. I'm glad I did not give him a tip, after all, other than money. In fact, I should have given him a bigger one.

When we eventually return to the apartment, by a slight detour, ironically finding it, like Maó, harder to get out of Ciutadella than to get in, - until, by good fortune, coming across the *hipermercado*, I knew where I was and where to go from there. I never thought shopping could be much use, but it just goes to show you it can be sometimes and perhaps even I have some uses as yet undreamt of.

I am pleased to see that the Githeads are behind closed doors and the bloody "music" is off, but the breeze, which was getting up before we left, is much stronger now. Perhaps it means that the weather is going to change. It wouldn't surprise me if it did. I expect it's a sign. My luck was in tonight with the fish, if Iona's was out, but experience tells me I can't expect it to hold, to rake in much more good fortune, so to speak. If I believed in symbols, (that cock which was crowing yesterday when he should have been having a siesta, certainly wasn't one anyway) I might conclude that this stiffening breeze feels more like the wind of change. It could spell a change in the weather.

As I insert the key into the lock, Iona is yawning and I have a feeling that the Cava will stay in the fridge tonight. Like the weather, I think my luck is already beginning to change. I'll just have to settle for a Soberano.

8. Frozen Music

It's one of the pleasantest times of the day, relaxing on the patio, eating your breakfast in the sunshine with the plop, plop, plop of the seeds from the date tree the only noise. No "music", no barking dog, no crying children, just the twittering of the sparrows and the seeds falling on barren ground. Just as long as that's where they do fall and don't end up in the grounds in your coffee. That's not likely to happen to me though because another of my peculiarities, apparently, is I prefer instant coffee to ground. And by the way, I never ever have it in a Chinese restaurant. When the waiters say to me: *You fu' coffee*, I always do what they say and leave instantly, particularly since they are so nice about it, the way they incline their head deferentially and smile when they are saying it.

Breakfast, when we're self catering, is always the same – orange juice and crusty bread with local honey. Iona of course has had hers long ago and is inside, getting her daily quota of stitches done.

There are a couple of sparrows hopping about, hoping for crumbs, a male and a female, presumably married. I like sparrows. They used to be very common when I was a boy, but you don't see them so much these days. Probably been eaten by bloody cats. I'd better help keep the population up by feeding these two. Hopefully, she's pregnant anyway and eating for five or six, though you wouldn't expect so, not at this time of year. She looks pretty scrawny, but he looks pretty fat, so I throw a bit of crust towards her first. She can't believe her luck. She looks up at the sky as if it were manna from heaven. She nibbles away at it, right where it landed, but when I lob a bit at him, he picks it up and flies off with it. He may be better looking, but he's not so much fun. I toss another bit of bread at his missis, but nearer this time and, showing no fear, she comes to get it, though her bright black eye keeps me under surveillance. The next one I'll try and see if she'll come closer and perhaps by the end of the week, she might even take it from my fingers.

It reminds me of the youth hostel we were staying in New Zealand, where the sparrows actually came inside and even perched on the chairs and tables. They were cute, not like those cheeky kias, (the New Zealand indigenous parrot) at the Franz Joseph Glacier car park which ate the rubber seal round the car windscreens and when you yelled at them: *Oi! Oi! Bugger off! Bugger off!* and made to chase them, waving your arms at them, they just strolled away a few yards in an awkward manner as if their trousers were too tight. You just knew they were waiting for you to turn your back before they had another peck. When we came back, the rubber round the windscreen looked like a lace doily.

There's a scraping of a table from next door and that's the end of my nature study as my pet sparrow flies off. The Githeads have surfaced. No! Not the "music" yet, please God. But it's all right, the girl must still be asleep. Instead, I hear the sound of an aerosol being squirted and presently the air at my side of the wall becomes tainted with the sickly smell of some fragrance or other. My God, are there any of my senses they are not going to assault? They've done them all now, except touch. I hope that means he is not going to bash me so he can get the full set.

This morning, I hadn't been aware of the tomcat smell that had been plaguing us since we came. I had thought it had gone, but the Githeads must be able to smell it, or maybe she's just another of those house-proud sort of people like our neighbours on the other side, our nice neighbours, even if it's not her own house.

"They've let off a bloody stink bomb now," I report to Iona as I carry my dishes in and place them in the sink where I hope they will begin that mysterious process which results in them becoming clean and dried and put away ready for use again. Sometimes the washing-up fairy doesn't do them however and I'm forced to do them myself, fairly frequently, as it happens. "And they scared off my sparrow that I was trying to tame."

"What are you on about now!"

It's more an expression of exasperation than a question, so I just curse: *Githeads!* and go off to the bathroom to do my teeth. I'm really glad we went to that restaurant last night. Calling them Githeads really makes me feel better. I notice that with a mouthful of foam, I can bare my teeth and say *Githeads* without moving my lips. It's not a very practical skill, but after a few of them I feel better.

When I emerge from the bathroom, it is to find that our maid has arrived. Damn! If I hadn't practised my ventriloquism so much we'd have been away by now. Now we don't know what to do – to go and leave her to lock up, if she has a key – or wait until she goes. I suppose we could ask, but the way she smiled at us in a self-effacing way and muttered in Catalan: *Bon dia* suggests she doesn't have much English, if any, and neither of our Spanish is up to the task, even with pantomime. It seems we would do anything to avoid an embarrassing situation, so we both sit outside on the patio, Iona with her stitching and I with the guidebooks, as if that's what we'd intended to do all morning.

We're going to do this side of the island today, the north-west. We're also heading back into the past. First stop is Cala Morell, another Neolithic site. It sounds rather like what we failed to see yesterday, a series of caves dating from the Bronze and Iron Ages with pillars and windows and raised seating areas and chimneys even. Some are said even to have classical-type carvings. If Iona the Navigator can find it, we should be able to cut out the apparently uninteresting north-west corner of the island and cut across to Cala Morell via Sa Torre d'en Quart, the best example of a fortified farmhouse on the island, built as a defence from pirates.

After Cala Morell, the intention is to head right across the north on a narrow coastal road to Fornells which will take us just about two thirds of the way over to the other side of the island and after that we'll decide what we'll do. At least the weather which I had thought was going to change, hasn't.

There it goes! The bloody "music" has started up already! Girl Githead must be up, or the parents have decided she's had enough beauty sleep (she could never get enough of that, poor child) or they have decided they been suffering from "music" deprivation, I mean depravation, long enough. It's nearly 10:30. That will be it on probably for the next twelve hours, unless they go to the pool, which they probably will. Imagine if it did start to rain and they were stuck in the apartment all day, with us next to them! No, too ghastly – like Macbeth's *horrible imaginings.*

Not a moment too soon, the maid is finished. She gives us a slight nod and a weak, embarrassed sort of smile. If it had been Phil's pal I could have understood her embarrassment, if she had recognised me, but it's not. I suppose she's just naturally shy. Anyway, she goes to our good neighbours of whom we have seen neither hide nor hair since I spoke to the lady of the house about the candles and the disinfectant. Presumably they have already left as I don't see their hire car. That's another thing, I'm pretty sure that the Githeads don't have a car, that they just hang about here all day, annoying people. The only culture they'd be interested in on this island, would be the mould on the bathroom wall, and, I imagine, only by Mrs Githead, who would be intent

157

on eradicating it. In any case, you've never seen a githead riding a bike have you? So why should they drive a car? No, driving people crazy is the only kind of driving they are likely to do.

I don't care if the maid does realise now that we have been hanging about waiting for her to finish – the sooner I put some distance between me and the ghastly Githeads the better. The minute she's out of the door, I lock it and we head off towards the car.

Iona the Navigator has done it. Skirting Ciutadella, we have found the little road which will take us to Cala Morell. Confirmation comes in the shape of the Torre d'en Quart, standing lonely sentinel in a field, like a terracotta milk carton. It looks a pint short of a quart to me, short and squat, but it's flat around here, so would have afforded plenty of all round vision of an impending attack. It looks impregnable to me; windowless and with walls which look as if they were at least six feet thick. It looks to me as if the idea was when the pirates came, you made no attempt to fight back, you just holed up in there for as long as it took. The only attack nowadays however, seems likely to come from a grazing herd of unconcerned Friesians, and we head towards Cala Morell through a wooded area, where there are more of those curious bags hanging from the trees that we had seen on the Cami d'es Kane yesterday.

"Those black bags on the trees really bug me," I remark to Iona. "I wonder what they can be for? Do you think they are for collecting bugs?" Although they are not very pretty, they don't really annoy me, not like the Githeads – it's just an excuse to make the joke I'd thought of yesterday but even I thought too weak to waste breath over.

It hasn't improved with the keeping. In fact, it's so weak for a moment I think it hasn't crawled its way into Iona's ears, but eventually she shoots a look in my direction which says: *That's about your most pathetic yet.* I'm inclined to agree with her, puerile might be a better term for it but what's said can't be unsaid and the truth is, I am just a little drunk with too much happiness: happy to be out in the open countryside; happy to be exploring a new island; happy with the prospect of visiting houses 3,000 years old, letting my imagination off the leash; happy that the sun is shining, that I was wrong about the weather; ecstatic that I'm far away from the Githeads - and all this has gone to my head and made me feel just a little reckless and bold enough to make one of my worst jokes in spite of the ban.

Although the object of our trip is primarily to explore the past, before we go there, we stop and look at the present. Cala Morell is a cluster of white villas tumbling down the hill and up the other side of the bay, with a little sandy beach which also serves as a harbour. The tide is out and a dozen or so small fishing boats line the perimeter. The left arm of the harbour is a red rocky finger of land stretching into the sea, eroded into fantastic shapes. It's as if Monument Valley in Arizona, the one that's in all the cowboy films, had been drowned, leaving the spires and pinnacles to project through the water like the periscopes on half-submerged submarines.

And the erosion is still going on, because, right at our feet, the cliff has given way and the double white wall and part of the pavement has gone with it and narrowly missed the backs of the terrace of houses below. There is a bit of tape, like at the finishing line of a race, across the gap. We wouldn't get off with such a meagre deterrent back home. To our right, there is a dirty great crack in the wall which looks like another great chunk is just about to do the same and this time it is not going to miss the houses, but dislodge tons of red earth and bricks on top of their pristine white roofs. Further to the right, there is an expensive-looking villa with a terrace and balconies bedecked with geraniums in terracotta pots and in all probability, a pool round the back, offering a splendid outlook to sea, but my lottery money will not be going on this, or the other ones. Whoever coined the phrase as safe as houses wasn't thinking of these evidently, for the outlook for these houses is not good.

Now we're off to see some houses from the past which have lasted a lot longer than the future of these seems to be. The entrance is through a double pair of those charming Menorcan gates and up some steps which have been cut into the rock and which I suspect are a modern addition, just like the lean ginger cat, as ginger as the earth – if it lay down it would practically be invisible, but which, tail erect, comes towards us meowing a greeting, probably telling us it's a few steps removed from its ancestors which used to roam this area.

Now this is really something. Goethe once called architecture *frozen music* and this is truly harmonious. If yesterday looked like Bedrock, it has nothing on this. It's just as the guidebooks said. Carved into the cliff face, there is a terrace of openings and with none of the uniformity which modern architects of housing schemes seem to deem so desirable. Here are doors of various dimensions, and windows: rectangular, square, and even one shaped like a fifty pence piece, and next to it, a neat rectangle on its end, a door, presumably. But for my money, the one I'd spend my lottery winnings on, is the one with pilasters at each side of the entrance, looking for all the world as if you were about to enter a Greek temple instead of a humble cave.

To allow access to one of the caves, they have built a flight of steps. Inside, it looks much like the cave I was in yesterday, but coming out and clambering into another opening, Iona with some difficulty due to the restrictions of her skirt, which she has to hitch up, we have the feeling of very much being in a house rather than a cave. There are pillars, finely carved, with pediments, so the effect is not so much of being in a house even, but perhaps in the cellars of some fine mansion, or the crypt of some ancient church, for as well as the pillars, they have rounded off the ceiling to give a barrel-roofed, vault-like effect. In another, although the pillars have not been so finely finished at the back of the cave, they have carved a couple of deep arched recesses into the rock to create separate rooms. And roomy this place certainly is. I wonder how many people lived in this settlement, how many to a house, for you can hardly call these sophisticated dwellings - caves.

But this one has to be my favourite. There are pillars dividing it into rooms and by the door, there is even a flat surface in front of the window which might have been a work surface or perhaps just a window seat or a bed with a view across to the houses built in the cliff opposite which now has modern villas plonked on the top.

The guidebook had said there was a chimney, but I expected some crude hole in the roof. This is astonishing! It must be fifteen to twenty feet high and perfectly round with some sort of square coping round the top. You can see the chip marks where the ancient masons chipped away at the rock and inside the chimney, a series of rectangles, too deep and too big and set too far apart to be a mere stepladder, but more likely some sort of larder, going right up to the top. And that's not the only curious thing about it. There is not a single black mark, no trace of the smoke which must have curled up here all those centuries ago.

Going outside, the mystery deepens because on the outside there are these big oval holes carved into the façade, not only of this house but others too. They are roughly all of the same size but at varying heights, and near ground level, a big rectangle, as if a window had been begun but never finished, but far too low down for a window, unless, below our feet, there are more caves and we are standing on the top floor of an apartment block. Other than that, I can't imagine what they could possibly have been used for, and I've a feeling I'm never going to get to the bottom of the mystery either. And the mystery is compounded by more holes above another cave entrance, a series of small holes drilled above the lintel. Perhaps they had an awning of sort here, some sort of protection from the sun? Who knows?

The mystery continues to deepen further, for when we go round the side of the site and climb onto the roof of the cave complex and look down the chimney, I am surprised to see that while there are coping stones at three sides of the chimney top, on the fourth side, instead of the coping stone, there is a stone with a channel, like some sort of drain or where some liquid would have been poured into it, from whence it would have gone down the chimney. But why would you pour something into a chimney and why are there no soot or smoke marks? Perhaps it wasn't a chimney at all, but then, if not, just what on earth was it?

It's just no good, I can't work it out; the guidebooks have no answers and there are no notices to read here like at Trepucó and no one to ask – just some kids who have arrived with their parents, whooping in the caves to test the echoes. Heather and Rosemary are at my feet and have been here for a long time, and like the ginger cat, have an illustrious pedigree, their ancestors first putting roots down here millennia ago, literally. But it's no good asking them - for they are plants and if they know the answer, they're not telling.

From the top we can gaze over the whole complex. What a mix of housing styles! From the troglodyte to traditional villas, to a terrace of tourist apartments with their identical balconies all shuttered up and looking somewhat grim and severe as if disapproving of the site, when in fact, they are the newest style on the block and if there were to be any disapproving going on, it should be at them, especially since they seem to be as uninhabited as the caves. Perhaps they were built by a speculator who mistakenly thought nothing was safer to invest in than houses and who found, like the owner of those houses we had seen on our arrival, that nothing could be further from the truth.

Some may say, like Iona, that once you have seen one cave, you've seen them all, but we have seen that's not the case, that they are as different on the inside as the villas differ from the block of tourist apartments on the outside. There are some caves on the cliff face opposite which I'd like to explore, although they don't look as promising as the ones on this side. For all I know, if this were a Monopoly board, this could be Park Lane and over there could be the Old Kent Road, but I'd hate to go away without investigating, only to discover later that there was something stupendous I'd missed.

"It's all right for you," Iona complains, who, at the last cave, had to sit down on her bottom, dangle her legs over the precipice whilst I tried to put her feet into handy crevices and which afforded me an unrestricted view of her knickers. Ah, that colour today, eh! If I'd been asked to guess, that's what I would have said. They usually are that colour. But she follows me anyway to have a look at the caves on the other side of the ravine.

I pick my way over some rocks to enter the first cave. It has mysterious square holes to the right of the doorway, just a bit higher than the entrance, extending perhaps for ten feet or so along the side of the cliff. It's a bit of a step-up to get into it, but not necessarily a knicker-revealing kind of entrance, but Iona wants to know what it's like before she assays the attempt.

"It's a bit dark," I call back, for unlike the others we have been in, the entrance is the only source of light. "There's a big central pillar..." I pause. "And I think there's bats." I can hear a high-pitched incessant squeaking and although they are not flying about, I think I can make out masses of them clinging to the roof in the far corner.

"Eeek! I don't think that I'll bother!"

If there's one thing Iona can't stand, it's bats. She's got this irrational idea that they will get caught in her hair. She's got the same notion about daddy-longlegs, and she often tells me to get out of her hair as well, but where I stand in the evolutionary scale between bats and crane flies, she's not yet revealed, unlike her knickers.

She'll not bother with any more caves either. The thought of possibly meeting some bats has extinguished any remaining spark of interest she may have had in exploring this necropolis further and she wants to go.

"I'll just have a quick look in these. You go on, I'll catch you up."

I do a lightning tour of the remaining caves, discovering nothing new and when I come down to the entrance again, Iona is sitting on a rock with the ginger cat. It follows us to the gate but when we pass through it, it comes no further. This is its territory apparently. It welcomed us and escorted us off the property, the self-appointed guardian of Cala Morell. Now it must wait for the next visitors and we never even offered him (all ginger cats are male) a titbit. Anyway, he wasn't much good as a guide.

"Right, which way now?"

Iona the Navigator consults the map, turns it upside down and makes her decision.

"Into Cala Morell, then straight on. It looks a straight road."

We stop at the other side of the harbour and look across the water at the cliffs opposite, where we had stood beside the crumbling wall. It looks quite a lot bigger than first impressions, Cala Morell, with a lot more houses hugging the hillside so closely that we had not been able to see them from above. There's the villa I had admired. They've built some sort of patio in the garden but there's not a pool, as it happens. It must be built on top of thirty or forty feet of solid rock but the problem is that a great bite has been taken out of the earth below, as if some earth-eating giant had come along, had a nibble and then moved on. The problem seems to be with the red rock. It is quite striking how the red stops abruptly, a great gash, like a forward slash to where the grey limestone begins. I know it's red because of the iron in it, but for all that, it's not very strong, not so much rock now as turned to crumbling red earth and it's on top of that unfortunately, not the grey limestone, that the houses have been built.

So it's on we go up the hill, heading east but instead of hitting the road to Fornells, which will take us along the top of the island, we seem to be in some sort of *urbanización*. I stop, turn round and go back, assuming that we must have missed a turn somewhere, though we shouldn't need to turn off this road anyway. But I haven't, and can't see where I've gone wrong. There are some roads striking off on both sides, but they are clearly minor roads, merely leading into new housing developments so we turn round again, pass the place where we were before, and continue straight on.

"Keep right on to the end of the road," I sing. I told you I had a song for every occasion. But where the hell is Fornells? There should at least have been a sign. But maybe on an island this small, where everybody (apart from the tourists) knows the way anyway, they've forgotten to put one up here. After all, as Iona the Navigator says, if it's a straight road, all we've got to do is follow it and we should get there. Right?

The housing becomes thinner and thinner and eventually the road just ends at the top of a cliff. They've built a low wall here and a turning circle, so plainly they plan to make a further development here. Further proof, if it were required, is there is another of those infernal peckers chipping away at the rock. The greater spotted (unfortunately) Menorcan rockpecker. I get out to have a look at the cliffs and the sea and the wind literally almost sweeps me off my feet.

"Aren't you coming out?" I have to shout to be heard over the buffeting wind. Iona is still poring over her map.

"No I bloody well am not! It's blowing a gale out there."

What she means is that she's annoyed at her lack of map-reading skills and she's not going to be beaten by some stupid map which can't even show you some stupid road on some stupid little island like this. She gets angrier with inanimate things more than me sometimes, even when I'm really animated, usually when I've been at the Cabernet Sauvignon.

I go over to the wall and step over it. I realise at once that was not a very clever thing to do. It's a sheer drop below, a couple of hundred feet and more to where the sea foams at the rocks at the bottom of the cliff and the way the wind is tugging me, it is blasting in my ears: *I'll huff and I'll puff and over you'll go. I'll huff and I'll puff and down, down you will go. You're a bit heavier than you look for such a short specimen, otherwise I would have had you by now.*

It may look stunning here where Menorca ends and the sea and the sky merge, but I have no desire to be part of that great unity and I suspect I would not be in one piece by the time I got to the bottom either, so I hop over the wall again, smartish, like a smart person, and on the way back to the car, pause a moment to watch the pecker. I'd only heard it across the bay at Binibeca Vell and am curious to see it in action, to see what a machine capable of making such a fiendish din looks like to add to my collection of pestilent noise polluters, to add the mechanical version to the human - well at least something simian which approximates to *Homo sapiens.*

It's painstaking work and would certainly drive me mad if I were the operator, even if I were issued with regulatory earmuffs. To me, it looks more like a miniature crane than a woodpecker, though bird recognition is another one of life's skills in which I am lacking. Yet, having said that, a few years ago on Mallorca, a strange and exotic bird flew into our back garden one afternoon.

"What's that bird?" Iona asked.

"It's a hoopoe," I said definitively. I had never seen one before, not in real life, but I do remember how I know. I had seen it on a postage stamp when, as a boy, collecting them was my passion. I was so keen on them in fact, that I had them in little piles, sorted, organised, in an arcane system which only a pubescent teenager could understand, on every flat surface that my bedroom would accommodate, only somehow, I never quite ever got round to sticking them into the album. I was well warned.

"Tidy those stamps up, David!" my mother said, repeatedly. (She wanted to dust apparently – a futile exercise and a waste of one's life, if ever there was one). Then one day, the ultimatum: *If you don't tidy those stamps up, I'm going to throw the bleeders out the window and the album which they should be in too.* That cut little ice with me: *Huh! She'll never do it!* thought I and, like Shakespeare's schoolboy, went unwillingly to school as usual, for a week, and then had a precious weekend off, but when I came back on a wet and windy Monday it was to find the precious collection dispersed to the four winds and the album lying face down in the garden. It wasn't best planning to go through puberty as my mother was going through the menopause, but my mother married late because of the war and that's just the way it was.

But philately can be a great source of painless and pleasurable means of picking up information and after I had picked up my soggy album from the sodden grass, I resumed my hobby and it's just as well, because that was how I was able to recognise the hoopoe - there's no mistaking that crest, that long beak and especially the black and white bars on the wings, like a zebra with wings.

"A what?" Iona looked at me in amazement.

"It's called a hoopoe." I remember making my tone sound as if I were saying something as obvious as: *It's a sparrow,* trying to keeping the excitement out of my voice at seeing, at least for me, this rare and exotic creature.

"How do you know that?" But the amazement in her voice was soon replaced with the deepest and severest kind of scepticism. "You do not! You're just making that up!"

She was not persuaded by outraged protestations and it was only when she saw, in reception, a bird poster featuring amongst others, our feathered visitor with *Hoopoe* written beneath it, that she believed me and marvelled at my ornithological knowledge, which is why in our house, whenever Iona asks me something to which she doesn't know the answer (which is rare, as like the rest of her ilk, she knows the answer to practically everything) and suspects I don't know either and am just making the answer up to impress her with the depth and breadth of my knowledge, you can hear me utter the immortal words: *Remember the Hoopoe!* And she is convinced, well, sort of.

Anyway, as far as this rare bird is concerned, for a beak, it has a great mechanical chisel which is making heavy weather of carving out a flat base in which to lay the foundations, although it has made good progress, creating a miniature quarry. With rock this hard, it looks a good place to build a house, right enough, far better than that unstable red soil, but who would want to risk being parachuted out to sea every time you took your bloomers off the washing line? Naturally this would not happen to Iona, whose knickers are not nearly voluminous enough, nor made out of silk, like parachutes, to catch any wind.

"Well, have you found it?" I ask ingenuously, blowing, rather than breezing, back into the car. And if I had thought it was going to be less stormy in here, I would have been sadly mistaken.

"No I have not! I just don't understand it. We *must* have missed a road somewhere. Look!"

She shows me on the map where we must be. We must be at Punta Llevant de Cala Morell and we shouldn't be here – we should be on that brown road which comes out of Cala Morell and goes straight, more or less, along the top of the island, to Fornells.

"But we tried that already," I hesitate to suggest.

"Well, we'll just have to look again. Perhaps if you drove more slowly, instead of like a bat out of hell, we might be able to spot it."

Ah, ah! So it's my fault now is it? It's my driving skills to blame again, nothing to do with Iona the Navigator's map reading skills! I told you she had a thing about bats. After all, she has navigated all round the world, in different places, not round the world, please note, which is just as well, or we'd still be going round in circles. Besides, I wouldn't say that 40 kph was going like a bat out of hell exactly, even if I were breaking the speed limit, which I may have been, but how can you tell without any signs?

Whatever the case may be, though I drive as fast as a snail, there is still no sign of *the* road. There's nothing else for it – we'll have to go back all the way we came, all the way back to Ciutadella, and if there's one thing that does drive *me* bats, it's having to return the way we came, especially to get to somewhere else, because it now appears that to get to Fornells, we are going to have to go three quarters of the way round a square: one side we have just done, one we did twice yesterday, (it will be four times by the time we are finished today) and the remaining one, we will have to do twice.

The atmosphere in the car is decidedly gloomy. If Ruskin is watching, he ought to be gnashing his teeth, because what he denounced as The Pathetic Fallacy, where nature is said to reflect the mood of the artist, is patently true in our case, because the sun has gone in, out of sympathy, and the weather is looking decidedly gloomy too.

We had always intended going to the Naveta de's Tudons, the Bronze Age burial chamber, but because it is near where we are living, we thought we would probably leave it till nearer the end. But as we pass it now, on the C721, we notice that there is no bus in the car park and very few cars either. Since we have come all this way back to our starting point, almost, it seems that now would be a good time to visit, as if it had been ordained that we should arrive here at the moment of most opportunity.

The Naveta, looking more like an upturned bread tin than the upturned boat which inspires its name, is clearly visible across the sparse, shrubby ground and there is no more than a handful of people visiting it. There seems no time like the present to visit the past again, if we want to have the place more or less to ourselves, so I pull in to the car park.

Over by the far wall, there is a woman leaning over it, with a man, presumably her husband, standing next to her. She seems to be studying something at the other side extremely closely. Every so often, her bottom jiggles up and down. Perhaps she's a twitcher, twitching with excitement at some rare bird nesting in the grass. (Well maybe they do nest later in Menorca). Menorca is said to be good for bird-watching, (haven't I just seen the greater spotted rockpecker?) but I suspect the answer is more prosaic, for I have seen a bottom twitch just exactly in this manner before.

It happened many years ago when our friend, on our camping tour of the USA, swallowed her tooth which had a nasty spike at the end. Concerned more at what the spike might do to her intestines in its twisty travels if she left it there, rather than the loss of the tooth itself, she went behind a tree and attempted to make herself sick into *my* coffee mug, if you please. (I think it was the nearest receptacle to hand). She thought she was undertaking this operation out of sight and out of sound, but neither turned out to be the case unfortunately - the tree was not thick enough to hide her bum and it was shaking in just this sort of way. If that was intriguing, the accompanying sound effects were an antidote.

We are too far away to hear anything from this woman, but I suspect she is vomiting over the wall. Whether it was something she had eaten or something she had seen in the Naveta or she's merely sick of her husband, it's impossible to say, but he's standing there looking as if he doesn't know what to do, and doing his best to look elsewhere, as well he might.

But it's looking even better for us, for as we follow the path towards the Naveta, we can see that the people who have been visiting before us have now decided to leave. We're going to have the place practically to ourselves which is more than someone with my sort of luck has the right to expect. I know there is one small entrance at one end of the Naveta and that if we had arrived at the same time as a bus tour, we would have had no chance of seeing the interior on our own or without having to queue for hours.

Suddenly, out of the bushes to our right, comes a man fastening his trousers, not just the zip; he has plainly had them all the way down, for he is fastening the waist band and tucking his shirt back in. As we pass, I give him a *buenas tardes* though he is unlikely to be Menorquin. He doesn't seem to be too embarrassed or flustered. Iona and I exchange curious glances. What could he have been up to? Will he be followed by a young lady I wonder? It's not what I would have called an ideal location with people passing on the way to the Naveta all the time, and neither the ground nor the cover seeming conducive to such activities, unless you're a masochist or an exhibitionist.

I look behind after a few minutes and he's still making his solitary way to the car park. That could be a deception of course, she might still be lying low, but I suspect that he's really been answering a call of nature, but not the sort of one men can do standing up. Isn't life strange? We've only been here a couple of minutes and we've already seen two people doing two of the least attractive bodily functions. If you put it in a book, people probably wouldn't believe it was true, would assume that you had a fixation with the scatological.

The Naveta is surrounded by as fine an example of dry-stane dyking as I have ever seen, as fine as the Naveta itself. Yes, this is certainly Goethe's *frozen music* again and certainly not in the Githead sense of the word. No, the equivalent of his music, architecturally speaking, would be something loud and ugly, like the Pompidou Centre in Paris. And when you think of the architectural delights of Binibecca Vell and even Cales Coves yesterday, not to mention the captivating Ciutadella and the tantalisingly mysterious Trepucó - you might conclude, in Goethe's sense of the word, that like the lady in the nursery rhyme, *with bells on her fingers and bells on her toes,* in Menorca, music has been following us wherever we go, and some parts of Mao, excepted, it has a very pleasant aspect indeed.

There is a notice board telling us about the Naveta, that it was used between 1200 and 750 BC. It's a pity that they didn't do that at Cala Morell as our guidebooks are already reasonably well informed on the subject. Like Trepucó, it's another unique Menorcan experience. Navetas are only found in Menorca. There are only about 45 left and this is the finest example of them all and we are the only people in the world visiting it! It's as if we were the only people on the Great Wall of China, or Machu Picchu. Well perhaps not quite the same, for although this claims to be the oldest roofed building in the whole of Spain, it's hardly on the same scale. Our guidebook tells us precisely how big (or small) it is – 14 meters long, 6 wide and 4 high.

It may be the oldest roofed building in Spain, (heavily restored) never mind Menorca, but no one ever lived in it. It is, or rather was, an ossuary, having seen service in the interval as a shelter for the cattle, who were Friesian and glad to get out of the bitter winter wind. It reminds me of the holiday in Brittany, one of our worst for both us and the children, when after visiting countless Calvaries and ossuaries, our son George, aged about eight, tried to tear up the Michelin guide and put it in a bin, thus he thought, putting an end to any further visits.

He'll be glad he's not here this time then. To be honest, we gave our children some pretty crappy holidays, (there I go again in this scatological vein) dragging them round archaeological sites and architectural sights, but to them, piles of boring old stones, whilst their contemporaries were enjoying themselves at aqua parks and beaches, at fun fairs, having fun. We've never quite got rid of the guilt, all these years later.

But that was the past, they're not with us now and this is the Rolls Royce's of Navetas. It had an upper floor where they put the bodies and when they were sufficiently ripe, they moved the bones down to the ground floor. When they excavated - amazingly, not until the 1950's - they found over a hundred bodies, some still with bronze bracelets on their arms, bone buttons and bits of pottery.

In through the little door of a door we crawl – no skirt hitching or knicker-revealing manoeuvre required. This time it is the opposite, it's not so much as a down-on-your -hunkers, as a more of crawl-through-on-your-belly sort of style.

Inside, there is a short narrow passage before it opens out again. It's shaped like a bullet and quite narrow which indicates how thick the walls must be, with a beaten earthen floor, though there is plenty of room to stand up inside. The roof is composed of large flat slabs through which some light comes streaming in between the cracks. This is where the bodies were put to rot, before they brought them down here. It's not all that roomy, so they must have piled them high and that's not all which must have been high. It must have been awful putting a fresh body in to the upper storey or checking to see if any body was ready for removal downstairs and perhaps a bit upsetting for the relatives to see their loved ones reduced to such circumstances, though presumably they made no bones about it since that was their culture.

And it was undoubtedly an improvement on the lifestyle of cave-dwellers who kept the deceased in the cave house: *Mum, can we move granny away from the fire – I can't get any heat.* But at least this custom must have had one advantage: it must have solved the problem of persuading reluctant children to leave the nest: *Stop complaining - there's just no more room, you'll just have to share the bed with poor grandpa. Look at it this way - at least he can't pinch all the skins off you now, now that he's dead.*

When we come out of the Naveta, it is to discover that we've been joined by a young family. There is a child of indeterminate sex in a buggy and a blonde young girl of about six with her two parents. And to think our George thought he was badly off! These people are starting their kids off even earlier. The mother is speaking, which allows me to deduce they are Dutch, but then the father says something – in English. He doesn't deceive me though: he's not English, not even British or from the colonies, or former colonies even, such as America. He's Dutch too and speaking the sort of English that you hear in American movies, so it's a strange mélange of American drawl and guttural Dutch.

Obviously very pushy parents, (especially the one behind the baby buggy) keen to enhance their daughter's education on as many fronts as possible. Actually, quite a good idea, talking to her in both languages which I imagine they have been doing since she was born which should ensure she should acquire both less painfully than she cut her teeth - or else become hopelessly confused between the two so when she's older and goes out on a date, she doesn't know whether she should go Dutch or not.

We stick strictly to the path on the way back to the car (you don't know what you might step on if you step off the beaten track) and not a moment too soon, for a posse of bus passengers is advancing towards us and although the woman with the twitchy botty has gone, I have no inclination to go over to where she had been appearing to peer over the wall at something extremely closely, just in case I see the evidence which would show I was right in my supposition. I may be curious but I feel reasonably confident I don't need to put my deduction to the test.

We're heading for our destination now, straight there, without stopping to view the attractions of Ferreries or Es Mercadal, where, although it is a severe temptation, I resist having a closer look at its windmill, and at long last, we see a sign for Fornells and take the C723.

We're on the right road at last.

9. Of Shoes and Shops

If it's good to see that sign, it's a bad sign that we arrive in Fornells just behind a coach.

I'm in luck though because there is a parking space right on the main street. There's not much of a pavement and when Iona opens the door, she has to beware of passing pedestrians in case she bats their bums and knocks them for six down the street or hits them in the belly and blocks the pavement while they bring up their lunch, like the lady at the Naveta, for it is so narrow that one step more is all it would take to get out of the car and walk straight through the open door of the florist's shop I've parked outside, pretty much like the Qui no Passa in Ciutadella. Pedestrians standing outside the shop with nothing better to do, are watching my manoeuvre as I park equidistantly between the car in front and the one behind, so I'm glad I did it without making a muck of it.

In the little square, the bus is disgorging what looks like hundreds of passengers. It wouldn't be so bad sharing this village with them, but it's lunchtime and they are heading for the cafés which are rapidly filling up. I notice there is an official car park at the other side of the square by the harbour's edge and I begin to feel an uneasiness at the ease I had at finding a parking space. What if the pedestrians who had watched me park were watching me with more than just idle curiosity? Although the street was filled with parked cars, what if they were for the disabled (before Iona hit them with the door) or parking was limited for a certain amount of time or they operate one of those systems where you display a disc to show what time you arrived? For my ease of mind, since we will likely be here for some time, I think I'd rather go and move it and put it in the car park. You can call me paranoid if you wish, but the incident in San Lluís is too fresh in my mind and I don't want another brush with the parking police and even worse, a fine.

Whilst I run back for the car, Iona heads over in the direction of the car park to look for a space as it looks pretty full. When I get there, she is standing in a space looking worried.

"I've had to turn one person away already," she says. "I thought you were never going to get here! This is the only space in the whole place."

Well, I didn't know she was keeping a space for me, but in any case, I had come just as quickly as I could. But I agree, when you are standing keeping a parking space which you've really got no right to, a minute can seem like an hour. Still, it was time worth spent because I don't have to worry about parking anymore and I hadn't had to spend any money to park either, which is just fine.

In the square, it seems all the tables are occupied by Germans, so it sounds. There is a choice of three eateries and there are no free tables at any of them, never mind any in the sun. All we can do is hang about until someone goes and like vultures, we hover nearby. If I hadn't been so paranoid about the parking, this would never have happened – we could have had our pick of tables as we could have beaten most of the bus passengers to the tables before it disgorged.

At last a table becomes free, and my luck is in, for it is right at the front of the canopy which means that Iona can sit in the shade and if I pull my chair forward, and alarm the person at the next table with my friendliness, I can expose to the sun the bits of me which I'm allowed to expose in public.

177

The waiter, (he appears to be the only one) is rushed off his feet. It takes a while before he notices us or even has time to issue the menus, which he produces from his oxter like a conjuror, slipping them on to our table and rushing off to take an order somewhere else without breaking step. We have plenty of time to study the menu and then sit back and take in our surroundings.

From the little we've seen of it, Fornells looks an attractive little place with palm trees and white houses fringing the harbour, full of little boats, a mixture of working boats and pleasure craft, which like Maó, seem to be all in white, apart from one show-off which is blue, while in the distance, blue hills hem in the bay in a ragged ridge, like a page torn from a jotter.

We are still waiting for our order to be taken. If we wait much longer, we'll be fully experienced waiters ourselves. I appreciate the waiter is very busy, and has hardly had time to turn round, let alone look around, which is why, presumably, he takes an order from some people two or three tables away, people who arrived *after* us.

I try to attract his attention, but it's no good - he has scurried inside to place the order and hasn't noticed me. I keep my eyes on the door and the moment he reappears, I not so much beckon him over, but wave my arms like a windmill fending off Don Quixote. Desperate times call for desperate measures. I've decided I am having an anchovy pizza and unfortunately, I'll need a big beer to go with it, as it'll be salty.

Our waiter has pencil in hand, poised above his little notebook. One word from me and it will be busy scribbling hieroglyphs which, after, I imagine, quite a period of time, will translate themselves into food on our table and more importantly, drink. But suddenly there is an imperious voice from behind us.

"Excuse me, but we were here before these people. *A long time* before these people," the speaker adds menacingly.

I shift in my seat to see who is speaking. She's middle-aged, stout, with died red hair and although she is speaking English, the accent is unmistakably German. Her body language is belligerent and no less effective than her English: it's serving notice that she means to be served and *before* us and from the way her brows are knitted together, she is obviously the real, original and best, Frau Ning. She has a female companion with her, a good deal leaner and about the same age, though she has left her hair to grey naturally and which she has scraped back into a long ponytail, just like Mrs Githead. It must be a fashion. And talking of fashion, she is wearing the sort of clothes that were fashionable about 30 years ago and which she must have got from one of my chain stores or much more likely, a jumble sale or car boot sale as these look like the sort of clothes which people dump on the charity shops and they in turn have to take to the dump in big black plastic bags. In America, friends of ours had called such people who looked like this, *granolas*.

This is obviously none other than Frau Ning's good friend, Frau Sy, who hails from Vietnam or thereabouts, whom, no doubt, Frau Ning goes about with because she thinks it makes her look slimmer, younger and better-looking. That's true at least, but I doubt if it means she gets many more offers.

After this unexpected interruption, I turn my attention back to the waiter. "I'll have the anchovy pizza and –"

"Did you not hear me! I said we were here before these *people!*" The emphasis on the last word leaves us in no doubt that Frau Ning is more inclined to consider us some species of louse rather than members of the human race and it us, rather than him whom she holds responsible for jumping the queue. I can understand her point of view, for if she *has* been waiting longer than us, she has indeed been

waiting a long time and if she is in the bus party, she isn't a
free agent. All this time she has been waiting for something
to eat has been eating into the time she has to spend in this
village.

"Excuse me!"

I am not surprised to find that our waiter has abandoned
us for Frau Ning and friend, for as it is written in the waiters'
handbook, is it not better, for heaven's sake to rein in those
that create hell than serve us, as Milton nearly said. He is
already with the Germans, trying to pacify them, ready to
take their order. I don't blame him: that's what I would have
done too. But before he goes into the café to pass it onto the
chef, he comes back to get our order.

"Sorry about that!"

"Don't worry about it. She terrifies me too. Have you
seen the way she is Frau Ning?" But of course it's too
linguistic a joke to expect the waiter to get it, and he's too
harassed to be in the mood for jokes in any case.

I don't know which of the two orders will be prepared
first, but if I were the waiter, I wouldn't dare to bring ours
before theirs. In fact, I hope, for our sake, he *does* bring
theirs first. I keep my back firmly towards them. There is
a strange pricking feeling between my shoulder blades and
I can feel my ears burning. But how was I to know I was
jumping the queue before them?

I daren't turn round. It's time to devote my attention to
something else, to be so engrossed that I can pretend that I
am totally unaware of the little embarrassing incident which
has just occurred, just in case Frau Ning, catching me eye,
launches an attack. But what? If I were religious, I could
pray for divine inspiration, but alas, I'm not. Wait a minute!
Isn't there a hymn which goes something like: *I to the hills
will raise mine eyes/From whence doth come mine aid*?
That's as good an idea as any.

I stare into the distance, in A.E. Housman's phrase, at *those blue remembered hills* at the other side of the bay when we first arrived. But that's funny, they're not there any more! I may be a Man from Banff, not a Shropshire Lad, but they were definitely there when we arrived. But there's no mystery. It's easy to see why they are no longer there – there is a nasty-looking storm cloud coming our way – fast.

"I don't like the look of that much," I remark to Iona, and I pull my chair in under the awning, though bizarrely, the sun is just as bright and intense here as ever.

When it comes, just a few minutes' later, it's with an intensity even fiercer than I had expected. I suppose you'd call it a squall – great sheets of rain which, within seconds, bulge the awning ominously and send a cascade of water over the edge to splash off the pavement in a two-foot high ricochet. The people like us in the front row leap to their feet and jostle for standing room further back, under shelter. Unfortunately, this manoeuvre brings us into closer contact with our Germans, but it doesn't matter - everyone is too interested in the rain to notice each other much.

It stops as suddenly as it came and we can resume our seats. Unfortunately they are a bit damp, to put it mildly, and the table is soaking, but the waiter wipes the tables and we tip our chairs to get rid of the worst of the water, leaving our bums to absorb the rest. Hopefully, when people see the damp stains later they will not leap to the wrong conclusion. It's one thing being mistaken for a Gerry on the continent, but quite another thing to be taken for an incontinent geriatric.

By the time we have finished our meal, thankfully presented after the German ladies' and thereby preventing another stormy outburst, the blue hills are visible again, the sea which was grey is blue again, and the blue boat is bobbing peacefully at anchor as if nothing had happened and amazingly, as we walk up the red paved slope of the pedestrian precinct away from the harbour but parallel with the bay, the street appears as dry as if it had never rained for months and as empty of people as if the cafés had not been teeming with patrons. Perhaps the Germans have gone down to the harbour to rejoin their tour. In any event, we have the whole of this street to ourselves.

Not a shopping street this, which might also explain the dearth of pedestrians, but a residential street of pleasing but unremarkable white houses with some huge terracotta bowls containing, what is to me at least, unidentifiable greenery rather than colourful flowers, and strung out in a line across either end. I suspect that their purpose is more practical, as bollards, blocking off the street to vehicular traffic rather than an effort to beautify the street. But as bollards, I must say they both look and are, pretty effective.

We're just going for a stroll really but with a purpose, heading for the Castell Sant Antoni which once stood guard over the harbour. On the way, we stumble across the church, like the street we have just come down, charming enough without being especially remarkable with the bougainvillea climbing up one corner a purple splash of colour against the white, and before very long, we come to the Castell.

It is in an extremely dilapidated condition – just a few arches, and on top of them, what our son George could rightfully describe as just a pile of stones. It was built in the 17th century, to protect the natives from the Arabs and the Turks, was refurbished by the British and modelled after Castell Sant Felip at the entrance to Maó. And indeed, like Maó, Fornells has a splendid natural harbour, almost as long as the one in Maó but not quite so deep, apparently, with two craggy headlands poking out to sea, like the pincers on a lobster.

An appropriate comparison, for if Maó's claim to fame is its harbour, Fornells is its fish food, in particular its spiny lobster stew – *caldereta de llagosta* with onions, peppers and tomatoes. It doesn't come cheap at €60 – about £40. The king, apparently, gets in his yacht and drops into Fornells from time to time, just to eat the lobster, which I suppose he can afford to do. It's ironic really, because once this was a poor man's meal, eaten by the fishermen, their catch too precious for the cash it brought for them to eat themselves and this is what they ate instead as lobster was considered too infra dig to grace a nobleman's table. Probably too much bother and too much like hard work to dig out the flesh by those not used to doing any work at all.

Back at the harbour front, there is a restaurant called *La Llagosta* with a bright red spiny lobster well out of its depth, climbing the wall. Could this be where the king dines? It wouldn't be far to walk anyway, straight out of the yacht. If he could get it parked at the door, it would be just like me with the car at my original parking place on the main street. I stick my head in the door out of curiosity, to see what a restaurant fit for a king looks like. Hmm. I don't think this looks like it. It looks pleasant enough, like everything else in this village, but the Ritz it is not. It doesn't look posh enough for a king, not unless he came incognito, dressed like a peasant like me and was prepared to put up with people moaning about him jumping the queue.

Suddenly, the awning over *La Llagosta* begins to flap and snap like a wet blanket on a washing line and the palm trees are tossing their branches like the manes of wild horses who have just been lassoed and are tossing their heads, trying to escape. Looking over to the hills, there's an evil black cloud hanging over them and blowing this way. We'd better get back to the car before we're caught in another deluge.

We make it back all right and sit in the car as it drums six-inch nails into the roof, effectively pinning us down. There is no point in driving in this. It probably won't last long anyway – it's too violent for that. The car is becoming steamed up though.

"Someone is breathing in here," I remark.

Iona, who has heard it before, many, many times, says nothing but doesn't take the hint and still continues to breathe – and mist up the windows.

When it stops lashing down and merely spitting, after I have demisted the car from someone's breath, we set off back the way we came, towards Es Mercadal. There's no alternative, unless you want to take an alternative route to Maó, but whether you do or not, you must begin the same way, by going out of town first. Whilst it had been raining, we'd improved the shining hour (I don't think) by studying the map and we decided we would take the Maó road to begin with, then head across to Menorca's third city of Alaior, if Iona the Navigator has better luck in finding the little yellow road than she had in finding the little brown road earlier, that is.

But in fact we're going nowhere. A white van has blocked the road, parked outside a souvenir shop. Actually if it hadn't been for the time spent demisting the windows, we would have missed this obstacle, for the young driver has just arrived, leapt out, flung the back doors open and disappeared with a pile of boxes into the shop. We sit and wait. I am such a patient person. It's just as well as I am getting a lot of practice waiting these days. If this were France or Italy, the place would be reverberating with a cacophony of car horns. And to think *I* bothered about possibly being illegally parked!

But when we finally get moving, when we reach the end of the bay, and take the green road to Maó, on a whim, because it also is a green, therefore good road, we decide to follow it to Son Parc, where, with a bit of luck - and good navigation, we should be able to pick up the brown coastal road to Arenal d'en Castell, then head towards Na Macaret where we should pick up another green road which rejoins the road to Maó, then we'll follow, follow, follow the yellow (on the map) road to Alaior. It will take us round in a square and should provide an interesting diversion and not that much of a detour.

We can't find Son Parc. Or perhaps we have been in it all this time and didn't realise it, for after streets and streets and roundabout after roundabout, eventually we see a sign, not to Son Parc though, and have ended up in Arenal d'en Castell, so the sign says. And although it has stopped raining, the weather has failed to clear up. However one mystery is cleared up – why wherever we go, we have the place to ourselves, for *this* is where all the tourists in Menorca are. Row upon row, rank upon rank of identical holiday apartments face out to sea with a couple of massive hotels standing over them like severe parents looking disapprovingly down on small children. This must be the capital of Tourist Land. It is a far cry from Binibeca Vell, or the first tourist hotel we had seen in Cala d'Alcaufar.

The location has been chosen for the splendid beach, but it too is deserted now and all the tourists have taken cover in their little whitewashed boxes. It looks a nightmare sort of a place to me. Finding your apartment again amongst so many identical ones could take up the best part of the day and the rest you spend on the beach, though it is so large, I imagine even with all the people here, you'd still be able to find a place without your neighbour knocking your eye out with her bare bosoms every time she changed position on her beach towel or sunbed, though with so many people here you'd be sure to get an eyeful, so it's not all bad I suppose.

I'm sure the Githeads would like it here. It's a pity they are not and although I would hate to be here, I'm glad that I am now because if this weather has reached Ciutadella, they too will have been forced inside and will be playing their infernal tapes.

From here, the road is signposted to Maó so we have no difficulty getting out of the place and in due course, cross the main road and head towards Alaior. After a while, we turn on to the Cami d'en Kane for a short distance and at the cemetery, turn right towards the sprawling town, dominated by its imposing fortress of a church, Santa Eulàlia, on the hill.

Alaoir's speciality is cheese which they unselfishly call Queso Mahón, after Maó, from where it was exported in the olden days. It's made primarily of cow's milk, but with a touch of ewe's which gives it its distinctive flavour. It comes in four stages of maturation – *tierno* (young); *semi-curado* (semi-mature); *curado* (mature) or *añejo* (very mature – God help us). It was Nelson's favourite cheese apparently, but the book doesn't say which variety.

Alaoir's other export was people. Apparently in the 18th century, a vast number of people left for the British Colonies and founded a town in Florida which they called St Augustine, and if you look up the phone book, you'll see it contains a lot of Menorcan names, apparently. I didn't know that then, which, as it happens, was where our friend lost her tooth with the spike and tried to sick it up into my coffee mug. Well, if you *really* want to know, if you *insist*, but at the risk of sounding as if I am obsessed with bodily-functions, she was not successful and had to search for it daily, lower down, so to speak. Eventually, in the fullness of time, she found it, but how she could ever put it back in her mouth is what I want to know, because, gentle reader, that's exactly what she did. (She did wash it first though).

We must stop and get some cheese Iona says and she's quite right because when you're drinking the wine of the country, what better than some cheese to go with it? There's meant to be a couple of factory shops which are signposted, but if that's the case, neither I nor Iona the Navigator can see them. Furthermore, as we weave our way through the narrow streets, it's impossible to find a parking space, nor do we see a sign to a designated car park, never mind the cheese factories.

The sky, which was grey, is now taking on the hue of an ugly purple bruise and I take it as a sign that we are not meant to stop here, even if we do find a place to park, wandering about looking for cheese shops, not if we want to end up like drowned rats. Iona is disappointed but I'm inwardly rejoicing as the book says the cheeses are expensive, though cheaper than we'll find anywhere else. Besides I don't want the car to be stunk out. I wonder, in fact, if that is what is causing the smell back at the apartment. Perhaps it's not the drains at all; someone has bought an *añejo*.

No, a slice from a supermarket will do me. Like the *roast chillen* at the restaurant we'd seen on our first night, I find you can get easily cheesed off, so to speak, with a whole one and on the way back from Cala Morell, I had spotted a new *hipermercado* which I'd like to visit for the purposes of expanding my own import industry.

So we don't stop at Alaoir after all and head for home, which means that we head for Es Mercadal. Anyone who comes to Menorca, must come to Es Mercadal (unless it is the king in his yacht) – even the Githeads must have passed through here on the way from the airport. It lies at the centre of the island, midway between Maó and Ciutadella and at the T junction of the only other major road in Menorca, the one we had just taken, which runs north to Fornells. As its name implies, it's a market town, most famously for *abarcas*, sandals whose soles are made from re-cycled tyres and *amargas* and *carquiñols*, types of almond biscuit.

Ever keen to support the local economy, Iona wants to stop, which we would have done anyway, but whether she'll run to spending money on re-cycled tyres remains to be seen, but since she's never tired of spending money, she might well invest in sandals, if she can find a pair which look good and have a low mileage.

But in fact, Es Mercadal has a greater claim to fame than these products. It was here that the British were given the pretext to invade Menorca during the war of the Spanish Succession (1701-1714) when the Menorcans declared in favour of the Archduke Charles of Austria, pretender to the Spanish throne. The British had come to help. Although their candidate did not carry the day (the Bourbon claimant became Felipe V) but at the Treaty of Utrecht, the British negotiated retention of Menorca. Now they had the whole island instead of just the harbour at Maó, which they had been using, with Spanish permission, since the early 17th century.

But before you come into the town from this direction, there is an attraction, though I would call it a repellent. You can't miss it, nor are you meant to. It goes under the guise of having a museum in the old flourmill, but actually it is a tourist trap. You can have all the parking you like; in fact, there's a couple of buses here now: *We are stopping at this point of cultural interest. (Remember and spend freely. Remember my commission.)* and there is a large playground for children and a small, not very interesting museum, but a vast shopping area, regrettably.

I leave Iona to shop and poke about on my own. The place is so full of goods: textiles, pottery, ceramics, leather and glass, not to mention people, that there is scarcely room to move and a great danger that I may bring some priceless article crashing to the floor in smithereens. Best get out of here before it happens and make space for the serious shoppers, but as I am leaving, I am stopped in my tracks. Surely I recognise that voice: *Excuse me, but I was here first.*

I turn to look at the counter behind me. It's a bit of a mêlée with a harassed shop assistant being assaulted by a line of women, all brandishing euro notes, their would-be purchases lying on the counter before them, and amongst them, Frau Ning from the café in Fornells, with inevitably, her symbiotic friend, Frau Sy, by her side. And from her tone, it is clear that Frau Ning is almost beside herself with indignation and pent-up anger. Not so incredible that she should be here I suppose, but unbelievable that I should hear her complaining about the same thing again – unless she makes a habit of it, and by the looks of it, she probably does.

I don't stop to see how the assistant deals with it this time. They are probably all on the same bus, so what's the rush, unless she's in a hurry to snap up more bargains before the bus moves on to the next tourist trap. These coach tours bring the worst out in people. Anyway, I get off lightly. All Iona has bought is a light blue sun hat which will squash up into a corner of the suitcase and come out again wrinkle-free, but by the looks of the sky, she'll not be using it today.

I may not be a fan of the flourmill, but as I said before, there is a very nice windmill in Es Mercadel and like the tourist trap, you can't help but see it as you bypass the town on the C721, and now we stop to look at it at closer quarters. It's just like the one in Sant Lluís, but while that is now an agricultural museum, this has been transformed into a restaurant, although with its skeletal sails and wires connecting them to each other as well as to a pole which projects horizontally from where the sails meet in the centre, it would not look out of place at Jodrell Bank.

As we walk down the main street, the Carrer Major, it becomes apparent that it's another ghost town. Actually it's siesta time, though perhaps this little place is sleepy at the best of times. The shops are closed and the green shutters are shut on the immaculate white houses with their terracotta pots of scarlet geraniums standing sentry at the doors and occasionally hanging from brackets on the walls.

What a shame Iona will not be able to buy any biscuits. I remember her buying some almond biscuits in Italy called *Dead Men's Bones*. I think it was the name which intrigued as much as the almonds and it was not one of Iona's better buys. They *could* have been made of dead men's bones for all the taste they had but they *should* have been called *Dentists' Delight* for the damage they did to our teeth.

The other point of interest here is a huge artificial waterway, with only a trickle of water in it now, despite the rain we've had, perhaps *because* of the rain we have had. Normally it may be completely dry but if in spate, wide enough to be mistaken for a canal. I suspect it is something to do with that man Kane again. Apparently he built a reservoir here, adding water to the list of things he did to improve the island and this being the mid-point of the island, it would be a good place to store water for his troops marching up and down the Cami between Ciutadella and Maó. So this channel is not a canal but a conduit from the reservoir, containing not the wine I had in the restaurant the other day, but pure unadulterated water. Well, water anyway and not even that nowadays, evidently.

Well I got off lightly in Es Mercadal, but I'm not yet out of the woods. The next town is Ferreries, Menorca's highest town (a giddy 150 meters). The sort of place with as many r's in it that for a dyslexic like me as far as foreign places are concerned, not only looks like Ferraris, but sounds like one revving before a race and is a lot easier to say. Actually, it owes its name to the Catalan for *blacksmith*, and nestles below the island's second highest mountain, S'Enclusa, which translates as The Anvil. It was famous in former times for making iron door hinges of all things, but I bet it was where Kane's troops had their horses re-shod. But now the shoes are not made of iron, but fine quality leather and they're not for horses.

And this is one of the two places where they are made - a factory outlet shop. This place has expensive written all over it, from the glass and chrome and marble foyer to the lift which whisks us up to the shop. It's not the sort of shoe shop evidently where we will be able to buy the re-cycled tyre sandals, not unless they come from a Jaguar or a Ferrari, more like. And it's just not shoes, but boots and hats and handbags, and coats and jackets. If they can make it out of leather, then you can buy it here.

I look at the price tag on the first jacket on the nearest rail. They can't be serious can they? Nobody would pay *that* for this would they? I certainly wouldn't. And it's not just sour grapes, because as Nina Simone's song nearly goes, I don't care much for clothes. Apart from the price, I don't like the style. Admittedly, I probably am not the best dressed man in Scotland despite Iona's attempts to do something about that, but I know what I like and as far as clothes go, the cheaper they are, the more I like them - within limits. I draw the line at looking like a *granola*.

In fact, as I look round here, there's not much here that I *do* like. I suppose this place is like the cheese factory, expensive, but cheaper than you'll find in the shops. I just wonder why, if you're rich enough to be able to afford the articles in this shop in the first place, why would you bother with a discount at all? Still, this place smells a lot better than the cheese factory, I bet and I'm not referring to the smell of money either. Here at least, you can inhale the heavenly scent of leather for free, in contrast to the cheese factory where you would block your nose off, breathe through your mouth and taste the cheese for free.

I don't think there's much to detain us here. In fact, we have been here two minutes already. It's not that I'm worried about Iona buying anything – she's as shocked at the prices as much as me, as much as the pink of these thigh-length ladies' boots with the stiletto heels is a shocking pink. Bloody hell! How did I miss these, why didn't I see then right away, for now that I have, I cannot tear my eyes away from them in disbelief. Presumably whoever buys these, apart from having more money than sense, considers them to be the height of sartorial good taste and talking of height, these would add so much to your height you'd be in danger of getting altitude sickness. Or perhaps the prospective owner just wants people to notice her, which they most certainly would and consider her to be an outrageous show-off to boot.

When we emerge unscathed from the leather outlet, it is to find the landscape bathed in an apocalyptic black light.

"It looks like reindeer," I comment unnecessarily to Iona as we make for Ferreries town, for the shoe and leather outlets are on the outskirts of the town and you can't miss them, (but which you should, unless you can trust your wife not to bankrupt you or like the prospective owner of the pink boots, you are incredibly well-heeled). It does look very much like rain - and plenty of it.

Apart from the shops, Ferreries has other attractions listed in the guidebook, but I'm not so sure about that. There is the town hall, but there always is, and the church, which there always is, this time dedicated to Sant Bartomeu which would be a new saint for me admittedly, and the Museu de la Natura, a natural history and ethnographic museum, of which the latter is of more interest to me, and Iona, naturally. Well, if it's going to rain, we may as well visit it. It probably doesn't cost very much. It might even be free in which case it will be an even better museum and anything is better than going back to the apartment and listening to the Githeads' insufferable din.

In a place so small, it's not difficult to find the Museu, in spite of the one-way system and only on the second attempt we find it and approaching it from up the hill, park opposite. But before we can get out the heavens open. If we thought it was a squall in Fornells, this is nothing other than appalling. Within seconds the windows are misted up and the Museu only becomes visible through the glass, as some sort of ghostly mirage.

"Will you stop breathing," I say. "I can't see if the museum is open or not." This is not so unreasonable as it sounds as it is on Iona's side of the car that the windows are misted up, the side nearest the Museu.

The rain is ricocheting off the road, *stottin' aff the pavement,* as we say in Scotland. It may be a small, cheap car but it has electric windows. I switch on the ignition and lower the window on Iona's side.

"What the hell do you think you are doing?"

A bucketful of rain has been picked up by the wind and been hurled in a broadside at the car unfortunately just as I lowered the window, and drenched Iona in a shower of the wettest rain I've seen outside Scotland. To tell the truth, I think that anytime I had picked would have had the same result – great sheets of white water are sweeping down the road, rendering the Museu completely invisible now, a mere twenty yards away.

"Oops! Sorry!" I shoot the window up as Iona screws the water out of her eyes. My apology might have been more convincing if I weren't trying so hard to stop laughing.

Fortunately looks can't kill, so I go on breathing – and misting up the car. We wait, hoping it will go off. I clear a porthole in the windscreen with my sleeve and peer through it.

"You know, I don't think that place is open anyway."

Iona clears a space in her window and peers through the glass. "I think you're right," she says. "Besides, I am not going out in that. I'm wet enough already," she adds pointedly and I have to bite my lip.

To tell you the truth, I'm not that bothered about going to the museum, I'd rather go shopping. It's true, you heard me right. I don't mind shopping if it's for the right sort of things, which is why I am now the proud possessor of: 1 litre of Bacardi; 1 litre of vodka; 1 litre of Drambuie; 1 litre of Cointreau; and three bottles of Vat 69. That'll do for now. We have come to this *hipermercado*, the one I had found earlier today, and the good news is, it looks cheaper than the first, but I'll need to compare prices first and get the rest later.

Iona does some shopping too. She has bought some biscuits and a tube of Nestlé's condensed milk which she squeezes straight into her mouth from the tube. I think that is pure indulgence and disapprove, but some sort of instinct tells me this is not the right time to say so. The whole thing comes to €83, about £55 and would have been even less if Iona hadn't wasted money on her purchases. That's not a bad price for all that booze, I reckon.

Fortunately, it has stopped raining when we cart our purchases from the car into the apartment. The Githeads are sitting under cover on their patio, and wonders will never cease – their ghetto blaster is not on. Perhaps even they have been satiated, for by the look of the ground it has been pelting down here too and no doubt they have been listening to it for hours. It predisposes me to be grateful and friendly. After all, it's not his fault he was born with the brain of a gnat, not that it matters as I do not intend to have a deep, meaningful conversation with him, just mutter a greeting to the nutter.

"Hello."

No answer. Perhaps it's because I have already passed out of sight behind the dividing wall before he could answer, or perhaps he can't believe his ears or perhaps he had no intention of speaking to me in the first place. Perhaps they had heard me complain after all, or perhaps he's got more sensitivity than I gave him credit for and he's picked up my antipathy towards them and him in particular. Anyway, I don't care, just as long as that infernal ghetto blaster remains silent.

"I don't believe it!" I rage at Iona. "The bastard is doing it deliberately, I'll swear he is!"

For we haven't been back five minutes when it starts again. I know he'll not have been able to hear me from where I am arranging my purchases on the table in the centre of the lounge/dining room and especially not over his din. I stomp over to the sliding door and make sure I slam it as noisily as I can. That deadens the noise, but I can still hear it. Thank God for the back door and thank God I don't have him for a neighbour permanently, back home. I'd have had to move – if I could get him to be quiet long enough to sell the house. No wonder there are murders. It would be murder living next to him.

10. Food For Kings and Thought

Ciutadella by night, down by the harbour, is even better than during the day. From here, with the floodlights of the Ajuntament and restaurants reflected in the water, the whole scene seems bathed in a golden light. There's no point in going across to the side we were at last night, so we're just going to look for somewhere on this side - but where?

It's good that the proprietors or maître d's don't bother you here, or not much, apart from an invitation to come inside, accompanied with a gesture at an empty table, unlike Egypt, where even to hesitate is fatal, so you can reply: *We're just looking, thanks* and we're left alone to study the menu, looking for a *menú del día* which appeals.

There are two restaurants which offer one for €12 – about £8 – not bad for a three course meal. But which one? I don't know and Iona is leaving it up to me. She does this so if it turns out to be a disaster, I can't blame anyone else but myself. But now she is hopping from one foot to the other.

"Oh, for heaven's sake, make up your mind!" Patience is not one of her virtues when she's hungry. "I've got stomach cramps."

"Oh, all right then, we'll go to the other one," I say with some impatience myself. I hate being rushed when there are important decisions to be made.

The waiter is pleased to see us, recognises us for sure, his smile saying: *I knew you'd be back, once you had realised this is the best restaurant in town. I could have told you, but you wouldn't have believed me.*

"We'll have the *menú del día*," I tell him, even before we sit down.

He inclines his head fractionally and brings us two fat padded folders and pads away again. This looks like what we want. We ignore the table d' hôte. There's a page with a three course meal on it and it's the main course which settles it, we don't need to look any further – crayfish casserole, or poor man's *caldereta de llagosta*. The king may pay €60 for his, but I can have it as part of a three course meal, for a fifth of the price. The king should follow me about - but then he doesn't need to.

A meal fit for a king deserves a wine better than the house wine and I have chosen a *blanc de blancs* which should go very nicely with my starter and the stew. But when the wine comes, I am disappointed to discover it is warm. That's not a good sign. It comes with a bucket of iced water though. Of course I should have complained to the waiter when he hovered about while I tested it but I'm afraid he'll say: *Are you blind? What do you think the bloody bucket's for – to plunge your red face in?* So I say nothing except the wine tastes fine and he pours out a couple of glasses and plunges the bottle into the ice bucket instead and goes away.

For starters, I have mussels in fisherman's sauce and Iona has fish soup. My sauce looks suspiciously like her soup. I beg a taste. Just as I thought - it is. Perhaps this is another bad sign, but it tastes good enough and they have brought me a plate for the discarded shells and a soupspoon (appropriately enough apparently) for the sauce, unlike in Skye, where I last had mussels and where I had to manage without either.

We're waiting for the main event now. It's very ambient to sit at the waterside and watch the people go past and sip the wine which has, amazingly, cooled down. Still not as cold as I'd like it, but I am glad I didn't complain as I feel sure that had I done so, the waiter would have said: *Bucket!* - or something that sounded like that anyway.

Most of the people ambling past are tourists like ourselves, couples on the prowl seeking a watering hole, but here's something different, a skateboarder rumbling past. He's wearing a T-shirt, camouflage shorts held up by a thick studded belt from which a pair of metal hoops, like handcuffs, is jangling. He's got a goatee beard, shoulder-length hair and an Alsatian trotting along beside him. He's swigging from a bottle of Amstel. You see some interesting people when you're just sitting doing nothing. But I wonder what he's doing. Is he merely just walking the dog, or is he, perhaps, an undercover cop, like the one I met in Florence last year, only I'm sure he only said he was so he could rob me of my passport. But if this bloke is an undercover cop, he has blown his cover, letting his handcuffs dangle out like that, to say nothing of the dog. As a master of disguise, he's not much cop, that's for sure.

Ah, here's the main course coming now, only it's not. It's the waiter with dentist's implements. There's a pair of pliers, that'll be for the extractions and some sort of tool with a hook, which will be for howking out the fillings. I am on the point of wittily remarking to the waiter: *I thought this was a restaurant, not a dentist's* but I think better of it. It's better, I think on reflection, to pretend that I am used to this sort of thing, but I am looking at them with a sort of mixed horror and anticipation – horror because I don't know how I'll manage to use them and anticipation because if this is not a sign that we're going to be getting what the king eats, then I don't know what is.

Iona is looking similarly worried. I say nothing but raise my eyebrows as if to say: *Well, we'll just have to see what happens next.* A quick glance round at the other diners is enough to show that we are on our own – no one else seems to have chosen the same as us. Perhaps we have made a mistake.

As soon as it arrives in two great steaming cauldrons with a bowl each for discarded bits, I realise that it has been a mistake after all. If I'd seen it first, I would never have chosen it. Pieces of claw and shells and some unidentifiable pieces of marine life are swimming around, dead hopefully, in a sauce which looks suspiciously like the soup Iona had had and the sauce I had with my mussels. One taste of the sauce is all I need to confirm that this is indeed the case. It's a nice enough sauce, but they certainly know how to stretch it out.

I fish out a red claw. Oh well, here goes. Crunch! Crunch! I bite into the claw, with the pliers, naturally, not my teeth. Splinter! I can see some flesh, gleaming white, like unexposed skin surrounded by a severe case of sunburn. I take the thing that the dentist uses to scrape tartar off your teeth with or which he uses to poke about in your cavities. There's not a lot of flesh and it's a very fiddly process to get it out. I suppose with practice, you can howk it out in bigger chunks that I am able to do, but it's like me, a bit reluctant to come out of its shell. *Nature, red in tooth and claw* Tennyson said. The claw is certainly red, but getting my teeth into it doesn't come naturally. It's going to be a long, slow - not to say messy - business.

Our fingers are sticky, having been covered in sauce, which the napkin fails to remove completely. I am lucky. I have the ice bucket beside me and I dabble my hands in it. At the other side of the table, La-Belle-Dame-Sans-Merci is giving me a glower, in a manner of speaking, as if to say my manners are so abominable, she's ashamed to be seen with me. I don't know why she's doing that. It's not as if I am the king with appearances to keep up. I look like a pleb and I am. Besides, nobody knows me here. And it's not as if it's a crime, having sticky fingers - as if the management are going to stop the skateboarding cop (if he is) with his Alsatian side-kick and say: *Officer, arrest that man! We caught him red-handed with his fingers in the bucket!* I don't care if anyone did see me. La-Belle-Dame-Sans-Merci may wish to wash her hands of me, but I dry my hands on the napkin, sticky no more. I call that mission accomplished and I don't care if some people do think it's bad manners – they should have brought me a bowl of water with a bit of lemon in it and then I wouldn't have had to use the ice bucket.

Well, that wasn't the best main course I've ever had in my life. The king is welcome to it. I'm just glad that I am not paying the sort of prices he does, and it confirms my philosophy that the higher your expectation of something, the more disappointing it turns out to be in reality.

The sweet is *Crèma Catalina*, a Menorcan speciality, apparently. It comes in a shallow terracotta ramekin about four inches in diameter and it's blisteringly hot. I look at it in dismay. When it cools down enough to taste, it's just as I suspected. It doesn't taste of the soup or the mussel sauce or the *caldereta de llagosta,* but it does taste suspiciously like crème caramel. Never a sweet lover at the best of times, (neither of those things actually) this is one of my most hated. I push it over to Iona, as if I'd been poisoned. She's looking at it hungrily, as well she might, for although our main courses had come in big cauldrons, it was more shell than substance. Crème caramel on the other hand, is one of her passions. If only she had her tube of Nestlé's Condensed Milk with her to squeeze on the top, her happiness would have been complete, for now she has two, mine as well as hers.

Well, at least it didn't cost too much. I console myself with this thought as we wait for the bill. At least my pudding wasn't wasted and it was a bit of an experience I suppose, but not one I intend to repeat. It just shows I was never cut out for the sophisticated life.

As I pick up the bill and look at it, there's a tremendous crash of thunder and a moment later, the sky is splintered by an amazing display of forked lightning running laterally across the sky, from end to end. Iona, who had her back to it, has not seen it, but could scarcely not have missed the effect, just as she scarcely could not ignore the thunderous look on my face. In fact for a moment, I thought that I may have been responsible for the cataclysmic events in the heavens.

"What's wrong?"

I show Iona the bill. €83. 60. "How can this be?" I ask her. Two twelve's are twenty-four - even I could do that without making a mistake, and although the wine was dearer than we would normally have had, it certainly didn't cost €60. Why, you could eat like a king for that price! It's been written down as €24 each. They must have made a mistake, written two 24's instead of two 12's.

Iona agrees. The *menú del día* was definitely €12. There's only one thing for it – to ask the waiter. He comes in response to my beckoning on smooth, well-oiled legs, seeming to glide, rather than walk between the tables. Although he must know from the way that Iona and I have been exchanging the bill and our puzzled looks, that there must be a problem, if he's worried, he doesn't look it. He has an air of a man who knows that there has been no mistake on his part, at least.

"The bill," I show him. "Surely there must be some mistake? Two *menús del día*. €24 together, not each."

"No, no! Not *menú del día* – special menu."

"Special menu?"

"Yes, you had special menu - €24. Look, €24." He shows me where it has been itemised on the bill.

"Yes I know it *says* €24, but we had two *menús del día,* at €12 each." Already I feel as if we were going round in circles.

The waiter is unruffled. "As I said, sir, you had special menu, not *menú del día."*

"No we had *menú del día.* I told you when we came in, *menú del día* and that's what we had, with crayfish casserole as the main course."

"That's right sir." He is infinitely patient. "Crayfish casserole, more expensive, is on the special menu." Then, as to leave no scintilla of misunderstanding, to make sure he has permeated this customer's thick cranium, he adds, unnecessarily, in my view, "More expensive dish, so on special menu. Never on *menú del día.* Too expensive."

I think I am getting his drift, but I am not convinced. What we had looked like a *menú del día*, three courses, and there was nothing else which did.

"Could you show me?"

Completely unruffled, he floats off and returns a moment later with the menu which he has opened at the place. There it is - SPECIAL MENU and it is what we've had. Across the page is – MENÚ del DÍA and it is not what we had. There are no prices. I can see right away what has happened.

"There was no *menú del día* in the menu you gave us!" I protest. But what am I to do? Go through all the menus until I find it, the one with the missing page? If it's not in the stack not being used at the moment, go round the tables and ask: *Do you mind if I look at your menu a moment?*- to be told - *No bugger off, get one of your own.* That would make me look even more of an idiot than the idiot I feel now.

The waiter shakes his head, lifts his shoulders, absolving himself of all responsibility: *Nothing to do with me mate if you are too stupid to read a menu.*

We check the menu on the board outside as we leave. Right enough, there it is. Special menu €24. Menú del día €12. Well, I've paid the price for my carelessness. By far the most expensive meal we have had this holiday and ironically, by far the worst, as far as I am concerned, and Iona too, for not even two puddings could make up for the main course. Of course I know whose fault it really is. It's all Iona's fault – if she hadn't rushed me into a decision, this would never have happened. If she hadn't been so eager for food right there and then, I would have checked the menu before we sat down. As it is, it was *my* decision to come here, *my* bad luck that *menú del día* page was missing from the menu, *my* bad luck that the prices of the special menu and the *menú del día* were also missing.

The lightning gives another flash – great jagged fingers forking across the sky, the kind I love to see, none of that sheet rubbish, illuminating all around in one incandescent flash and - one elephant - two elephants - three elephants - four elephants - then *loud and long the thunder bellows,* just as Tam O' Shanter heard it, all those nights and centuries ago.

Somehow I have taken a wrong road and we find ourselves on a coastal road; the sort of road which had eluded us all day, which we now find by accident. It's not the same coastal road which we had been looking for admittedly, but once again, the truth of another of one of my little philosophies has been proven to be right: if you can't find something – stop looking. It will find you when you are looking for something else.

We've stopped near an interesting-looking floodlit building. Beside it there is a statue to David Glasgow Farragut (1801 – 1870). (You would have thought with a name like that he would have changed it by deed poll – to Aberdeen, for example). He's holding a telescope, but feeling the weight of the heavy end in his left hand as if he were thinking of clobbering someone over the nut with it as if it were a baseball bat.

According to the legend on the pedestal, his claim to fame is that he was the first admiral of the United States Navy. That's interesting, because when we lived in

Kirkcudbrightshire, we lived near the birthplace of John Paul Jones which is how I come to know *he* founded the American Navy and you would have thought that if you'd invented a Navy you would have made yourself the first admiral. After all, when we were kids, if it was your football, you got first pick of the players and were captain of your team and if, by some chance, your team was losing, you'd pick up the ball and say you had to go home for your tea or your mother would kill you. So, if David Glasgow Farragut really were the first admiral, I think it was pretty admirable of John Paul Jones to let him be. He did have a dance named after him though. Probably because his Navy led the British a merry dance.

The floodlit building is the 17th century Castell Sant Nicolau. It has elaborate pilasters and three coats of arms and its date, 1682, carved in a cartouche emblazoned over the front door – indeed the only door, which once would have had a drawbridge, but now has a fixed bridge over a dry moat. It's not much of a castle really, more a squat sort of watchtower with a couple of turrets, one above the other, standing guard over the entrance to the harbour at the end of the rocky promontory. At the other side of the inlet, a light is flashing like a strobe, but behind it, Nature's flashing light outdoes it a million fold and a million times more spectacularly. Three elephants this time. By the looks of it there's going to be a tremendous storm tonight.

Facing it (and the admiral) is a huge modern hotel. It must have hundreds of rooms, thousands of guests. It seems to stretch on for miles before ending in a short curve like a hockey stick. Perhaps Admiral Farragut has had a bellyful of looking at this thing, could see it far enough and that's why he has drawn his telescope out to its limit, intending to club it to death or perhaps challenge it to a game of hockey, but his body language is all too aggressive. I don't think he likes this newcomer one little bit.

I have to agree with him. There's no comparison between the old and the new, facing each other across the boulevard. It's like comparing Sleeping Beauty's Castle, (only not so ornate) with Cumbernauld's Shopping Centre, recently voted Scotland's most architecturally reprehensible. And from it comes the sound of mirth and dancing, just as Tam O' Shanter heard it coming from Kirk Alloway on his journey home and as if to confirm the resemblance, the lightning flashes behind the hotel, followed by two elephants of earth-shaking thunder. They are certainly stomping about up there - and getting closer. At least my wife isn't waiting at home for me, like Tam's, *nursing her wrath to keep it warm.* She's sitting in the car. At any moment she's expecting it to plump down and having been drenched once today already, as she pointedly reminded me, she's not taking any chances, so she's not coming out to admire the admiral.

I think she has a point. I bring my musing on architecture and admirals and poetry to an end and return to the car where I tell her about Admiral Farragut being the first admiral.

"You know, there's something funny about that," I tell her.

I don't have many skills but one thing I am, even if I say so myself, is I am a mine of useless information, which means of course that I am still not much of a use unless you want me on your team for *Trivial Pursuit* and that doesn't happen often. In fact, I play that even less than I have sex and that is saying something. Nor is it the sort of game you can play by yourself, though my son George thinks I have read all the cards which is why I know so many of the answers.

It so happens that I know John Paul Jones' birth date precisely. I don't imagine a lot of people do, but I do, coincidentally because I happened to notice that he was born exactly two days and two hundred years before me. That's the only reason I remember it. And that tells me that JPJ was what some people call old, if not dead even, (because I don't actually happen to know his death date) before Mr Farragut became first admiral.

Iona looks at me in disbelief, as if I'd just made one of my worst jokes. In fact, that is what she says - "Are you joking? Tell me you are joking. Can you really not see?" Her tone is expressing as much incredulity as the look, so I am beginning to feel I have made a monumental fool of myself over this statue.

"See what?"

What is she getting on about? I am mystified.

"Can you *really* not see why Farragut was first admiral?"

"Well, all I was saying –"

"Spare me the puns. I heard them the first time. Look, thicko – presumably you've heard of a rear admiral…Farragut was a *first* admiral."

Ah! Light invades the brain, just like when you are driving through a tunnel it seems very dark until you realise you have got your sunspecs on and when you take them off, suddenly you are able to see much more clearly. I can see it now! Right enough I know that on ships there is such a thing as a first mate, so why should there not be such a thing as a first admiral? All the same though… .

"A bloody stupid way of putting it on his pedestal if you ask me. I mean anybody who didn't know about John Paul Jones would automatically think Farragut was the first admiral *ever*, wouldn't they?"

Whether she agrees with that, or whether she still thinks I am just a complete idiot, she has no time to reply for just then the heavens open and down it comes. The elephants have landed. Or at least the rain drumming on the roof of the car sounds like they are stampeding across it. The windscreen wipers can hardly cope – at double speed. Because of it, like my brain, I make slow speed back to base.

And talking of baseness, you can't get much closer to lowering your spirits after a romantic night out at a posh restaurant, than the thought of coming back to live next door to the Githeads, but fortunately, when we get back, they are not sitting outside, thus we avoid an obvious ignoring of each other or a hypocritical acknowledgement of each other's existence. It's not surprising they are not sitting out, for although the rain has stopped, the atmosphere is very damp, not conducive to being outdoors. I didn't expect there to be any noise at this time, and there isn't. Miss Githead will be partaking of her much needed beauty sleep.

It's so damp, it feels like Scotland. What better than to get wet and warmed on the inside with the product of Scotland, while sitting outside, watching Nature's pyrotechnics? Iona and I both like thunderstorms, so we sit out the back, Iona with a hot chocolate and I with a Drambuie and a hot chocolate also as La-Belle-Dame-Sans-Merci says I must. She thinks it's a bit of an antidote. The Drambuie had to be opened anyway because it will need to be decanted. An empty Drambuie bottle is very heavy, never mind a full one. This will help keep the weight of the substitute bottle down, but not by much if I know the drinks police.

I'd better not have too much anyway. Tonight might be the night that I will be called upon to produce my own brand of pyrotechnics. I'd better be prepared; we don't want any damp squibs. But although she likes thunderstorms, they tend to give her a bit of a headache. I have a feeling, like a rocket, I may be let off tonight and tonight, like our *caldereta de llagosta*, will turn out to be a damp squib after all.

11. Southward Ho!

Iona is driving. I am in the back seat with an ex-girlfriend who is showing legs up to her neck. I know we are going shopping but I don't know for what except she is all made up for the trip and looking very desirable; the girlfriend I mean, not Iona. I'd like to make wild passionate love to her but I know it's a bit rude to do that behind your wife's back, especially when she is driving as she might look in the rear view mirror and cause an accident. At the moment I am keeping myself under control but now my ex is giving me a come-hither look and moving closer, causing her skirt to ride up even higher. I am close to losing control (let's hope that Iona doesn't) and giving in to temptation. She is moving nearer and I am coming closer ...

Then I woke up. There was a bloody big bang which rattled the window and the door and interrupted my dream just when it was beginning to get interesting. I would have loved to have known what happened next. Would I have loved or not? What would Iona have done or said if I did? Probably she would said something like: *You're welcome to him —you can keep him* or *Put him down, you don't know where he's been.*

If it hadn't been for that enormous peal of thunder, I would have found out, but then probably I wouldn't have remembered it. From the sound of it, it must have been right overhead. The biggest, fattest elephant in the world landing right on top of the roof. Then it started to pour, coming down in torrents. Not since Noah, I think, has it rained like this.

I am too tired to get up and see, but by the sounds of it there's a drain being emptied, an endless cascade, sloshing onto the pavement at the other side of our patio. It must be the effluent from the terrace above which must be awash. Add to that the sound of the rain hissing and belting onto the road, and sleep is impossible. Besides, I need the toilet. I creep out of bed and across the pitch-black room, trying not to wake Iona but I know for sure that she'll be awake because she wakes at the drop of a hatpin. Although I can't see her, I know in the satiny dark she's just pretending to be asleep.

It has been a dreadful night. At 11:30 the Githeads started moving the furniture about. It seemed to go on for hours, whilst I quietly fumed. Then, incredibly, the people up above us followed suit. Is it all a plot calculated to drive me mad - that the Githeads have made friends with the people above us and have arranged they'll keep me awake from 11:30 to midnight, then the upstairs will take over at midnight? But I suspect I am merely being paranoid. More likely it's new people who have just arrived and they are moving the beds about to suit their requirements. But what on earth could the Githeads be up to?

I stumble back to bed and try to sleep, and I suppose I did eventually, but I had no more dreams and after lying awake for ages and further sleep being impossible, at 9:12 precisely, I swing my legs out of bed and decide I may as well get up. This is the last day of the car and at least this early start means we can make full use of it.

Iona is already at her sewing and is amazed to see me, but she doesn't say anything. We don't greet each other lovingly, especially not in the mornings.

"Couldn't bloody sleep last night. I'm as tired as an elephant," I mutter as I step onto the front patio to survey the day. I always think that elephants look tired and wrinkled, as if they can scarcely put one foot before the other, just like me in the mornings. The sky is as grey as an elephant too, as well it might considering all the stomping about they did in heaven last night. It's not looking good. The ground looks saturated; the whole atmosphere seems almost to drip with moisture held in suspension.

"There's *ensaimada* for breakfast," calls Iona from inside.

"What's that?"

"It's over by the sink."

There's a paper bag and I extract something shaped into a spiral like a Cumberland sausage and dusted with icing sugar. It looks like the sort of thing you buy from a joke shop if you've got a particularly puerile and scatological mind. I look at it doubtfully.

"What did you say this was?"

"*Ensaimada*. It's delicious." She doesn't look up, doesn't miss a stitch. She'd put on her cagoule and trudged up to the baker's as usual this morning, despite the weather, whilst I was trying to get back to sleep. I hope the Women's Union doesn't get to hear about this.

Hmm. It's obviously something Spanish and a treat in store for me. In the meantime, I shuffle off to have my shower. The floor of the bathroom is soaking wet. Maybe I should just roll around on the floor instead of getting in the shower and save water. But there's no need to do that. It looks as if a year's supply fell yesterday and by the looks of it, it's not finished yet. And that smell is back again I think.

"Do you think that smell is back?" I ask Iona, passing out to the patio with my coffee and *ensaimada*.

"No, I don't think so."

Hmm. I don't have a good sense of smell. If she can't smell it, then no doubt it wasn't there at all. For as we nearly hear the song: *When you're smelling, when you're smelling, the whole world smells with you.*

Out on the patio, Mr and Mrs Sparrow are pecking up the seeds from the date tree. The ground is black with them, brought down by the rain. They look exactly like peppercorns, much, much more than Peter Piper could possibly pick if Peter Piper did pick up peppercorns. I'll maybe take some home and plant them and keep them in the conservatory. I don't expect they'll grow though. I didn't get many dates when I was younger and expect to get even less now. Anyway, no need to waste my *ensaimada* on the sparrows. Iona is right. It does taste better than it looks and anyway, it makes a change.

It's too early for the "music" but there's another pestilence devised by the cunning Githeads. They have lit up. It's not bothered me before. It must be something to do with the damp atmosphere but the smoke seems to creep over to our side of the wall, then, spent out, lingers and hovers on the air. I can't stand the smell of cigarette smoke, but that's not as bad as what happens next. He begins coughing as if he were going to bring up his breakfast, except this is probably it, how he starts each and every day. *Anything you can do, I can do better*, thus runs the song, and now Mrs Githead is taking up the refrain.

Right that's it, I've had it up to here. First they pollute my *ensaimada* with their obnoxious smoke and now they've assaulted my ears with their coughing. I wish they were dead. If only their coughings were coffins, I wouldn't have had to endure this. And so they *will* be reduced to that one day, after they've bled the NHS dry, but that no doubt will be many years from now. I get up, come inside and slam the door.

Iona looks up, astonished. "What's the matter?"

"It's like a bloody bronchial hospital out there."

Before she can answer, if ever she had any intention of so doing, I'll never know, because a flash of lightning electrifies the room and stops me in my tracks, listening for the thunder. It follows almost immediately; booming and rumbling on and on as if God hadn't eaten for days and His tummy's rumbling. Now He's spitting in protest. The rain is coming down in spears.

"Wow!" I rush to the back patio – nothing to do with the Githeads – there's more sky out there, more chance of seeing some forked lightning - and more rain, as I can see that my supposition of last night is correct and that rain is indeed pouring from a spout on the floor above in a never-ending flow.

After a few minutes Iona joins me. She's added a stitch or two in the time and thus has saved nine, presumably. After five minutes, it becomes obvious that this is not just going to be a sudden downpour, that it's going to be on for some time. I go and get my postcards whilst Iona fetches her sewing. Ironic. You get up early to make an early start and find yourself confined to base. There is laughter in heaven – the gods have done it again.

Even when I have finished my postcards, the rain hasn't. There's no end to Iona's sewing so it's just as well the rain wasn't waiting for her to finish before it stopped. I may as well put on warmer clothes, change out of my swimming trunks and T-shirt which bears the legend THE LIVER IS EVIL AND MUST BE PUNISHED. It was given to me by a friend but I've had my liver tested and it's in extremely good nick and it's my best friend considering all the punishment I've given it, so I don't think it's evil at all. In fact, I think it is rather good, and I should leave it to science when I die, but that doesn't stop me giving it further punishment, just to make sure it stays good, a bit like the hell-fire preachers of yesteryear or like the Free Church minister at my uncle's funeral who painted such a graphic depiction of the grave and what awaits you if you are bad, that the young grandchildren were reduced to hysterical wrecks. It just goes to show you that the best things in life are not always Free after all.

I take off my swimming trunks and put on my boxer shorts with the pink copulating rabbits instead, also another article of apparel given to me by a friend, a female friend. (If only all my friends were as generous, I wouldn't have to buy any clothes at all). And if the liver T-shirt was meant to be an encouragement to keep on drinking, is there a message there for me to read in the shorts? Actually, now I come to think of it, my liver is actually only my second favourite organ, as Woody Allen once said, only he was referring to his brain and La-Belle-Dame-Sans-Merci often asks me where mine is, so I presume I probably don't have one any more. So, sorry, liver, but man cannot live by liver alone and you are relegated to number two favourite organ.

It's getting tiresome hanging about here and we're getting cabin fever. Even Iona has had enough of sewing for the moment. We may as well go and hope where we're going is going to be fairer. It's better than hanging about here, even although we are not being bugged by the Githeads. Besides, I am paying for the car and it is just sitting out there and although we have seen most of what we want to see on this small island, there's still more to see and who knows, we may stumble upon something really interesting. We certainly won't here - unless it's on the slippery bathroom floor. We have to get out.

"What are you doing *now*?"

Do I detect a tone of impatience in the trouble and strife? She's all dressed up and ready to go but I am still dithering about and it's plainly irritating her.

"Can't find my bloody sunspecs. They're hiding from me." I am shifting things, looking beneath and behind things where they couldn't possibly be but when all other possibilities have been exhausted, there's nowhere else to look.

"Sunspecs! What do you want sunspecs for on a day like this? Come on, let's go." La-Belle-Dame-Sans-Merci is more annoyed with the weather than me – I think.

Amazingly, as we dash for the car, there is no noise from the Githeads and no sign of them either. Their patio door is closed, allowing them to get double the effect from their cigarette smoke, breathing in each other's exhalations in the fetid atmosphere. The ghetto blaster is playing *Killing her Softly*, specially dedicated to Miss Githead from her fond parents, only I can't hear it because they don't play anything half so tuneful.

The road at the end of the complex is flooded. We plough through it, churning up brown water. By the time we get to the outskirts of Ciutadella, the rain has practically stopped, but here too, the road is flooded – we can see it pouring *up* the drains, instead of down. A woman, struggling along the pavement, her head bent against the rain, is drenched by a car coming in the opposite direction whose wheels send up a shower of dirty brown water. In my mirror, I can see her, stopped dead, legs and arms spread out like a starfish gasping for breath, standing there dripping, too shocked at the moment to hurl insults in the wake of the car.

"Pooh! What's that smell?" says Iona, looking at me suspiciously, wrinkling up her nose.

She's right, for as we plough our own furrow in the opposite direction, a foul stench has invaded the car. No doubt it's much worse outside, unfiltered by the metal and glass skin of our car, but there is no doubt in my mind that the brown pigment in this floodwater is not entirely due to the rain.

"It's nothing to do with me, if that's what you're thinking. The sewers have burst." I hope that the woman pedestrian had her mouth closed when that car drenched her.

*

214

We've decided to go to the prehistoric village of Torre d'en Gaumés, which means crossing the island to Alaior then following the road to Son Bou on the south coast. It's killing two birds with one stone because there is a 5th century Christian basilica there. It also has the longest beach on the island, but that will be deserted today unfortunately, unless the weather bucks up, but that doesn't look in the least likely.

However, when we get to Torre d'en Gaumés, it *is* threatening to clear up. Instead of grey elephants lumbering across the sky, the clouds are woolly white sheep scudding across a patchwork blue field. There is a car park with one or two cars and a hut which sells tickets unfortunately, the first site we've had to pay for, so presumably this has a bit more to see. Or it might be for the car park, which looks new. It hardly amounts to the equivalent of a pound each – less than many parking charges back home.

Torre d'en Gaumés has been occupied for centuries. They reckon it began about 1400 BC and lasted till the Romans in 123 AD. There's a path roped off leading up the hill and stones, stones everywhere. There are three massive *talayots* on our left, still incredibly high despite their collapsed and ruinous appearance, but no match for the Romans evidently and another to the right, though that may just be a huge heap of stones.

Behind one of the *talayots* is a decapitated *taula.* There's the massive headstone, conveniently lying on its back so you can see the groove into which the notch on top of the upright has been carved out, but which is serving as a water trough or bird-bath today. In the gap between the *taula* and the perimeter wall apparently, they found a grave and in it, amongst other things, a little statue of Imhotep, the celebrated Egyptian architect, but worshipped here as a god. Incidentally, it also shows how they got about a bit, even in those days, even if they didn't have trains and planes, but merely boats.

Further on there is a bijou residence with an extension in the cliff with a south-facing, hole-in-the-wall for a door, complete with a patio area, would you believe, and according to the little notice board outside, it even had running water. As we had seen before, the ancients in Menorca were very attached to their dead relations, but it looks by the time this house was built, (a few decayeds later undoubtedly) the deceased were relegated to the extension from where they could still make their presence felt to the survivors, especially if they had a good sense of smell, but in a less powerful way. Or, on the other hand, this may not be typical: this might have been a rich family who could afford this superior accommodation up on the penthouse heights and who therefore could remove the useless relations to the extension. It's dangerous to draw conclusions from one example.

It's actually the same principle that I hypothesise to Iona: only poor people sleep together. We all know since Michael Fagan who broke into the queen's bedroom for no other purpose than to declare his admiration from close-up, to sit on the mattress and have a chat with her, (he didn't want sex to rear its ugly head between them and spoil a perfect subservience) that Phillip was in the spare room and the balance of probability was that she did not have a headache, nor was he snoring, nor had he been banned from the bed for some other solecism perpetrated under the blankets, but that this was a regular occurrence, simply because they are rich enough to have separate rooms.

Now that's exactly how I see it. They're like us, though not in the same class, obviously. Why should we spoil a perfect subservience by me sleeping with the boss? In my view, we shouldn't mix business with pleasure. We're not rich, but we've got a spare room since the children left.

We shouldn't behave like poor people, cramming ourselves into the same bed like we do, when we could have separate rooms, never mind separate beds. Besides, sleeping together could lead to unhealthy, horrible things, such things that a queen would never do, (at least not more than four times).

As a matter of fact, considering how the ancients here held on to their dead, I think I could well have been an ancient Menorcan once upon a time, in a former life, as opposed to being merely ancient as I am now, as I hate to throw anything out. The garage is about as far as it gets, though sometimes I have had to rescue items from the bin which La-Belle-Dame-Sans-Merci has ruthlessly thrown out with complete disregard to future possible usefulness, though admittedly it might take years before this use becomes apparent.

I creep into the cave whilst Iona keeps *cave* outside, though I take it entrance is permitted and allowed under the meagre price we paid for the entrance fee (or parking). There's a grave all right, but only one and room for one body only. It's definitely only built for one occupant at a time: *If we put granny in there, Mum, where's granda going to go? - Granda's just bones now, don't you know. - But where's granda's bones going to go, Mum? - Why don't you stop asking stupid questions and leave me alone? Can't you see I'm trying to make some stock?*

Yes, I can see the grave all right but where's this channel which brought water in here and made it one of the most desirable des res's in town? Can't find it. I'd never have made an archaeologist if I can't even see what they're telling me is right in front of my eyes. Of course one has to assume that what the board outside says is the truth but like estate agents' descriptors, perhaps it's a somewhat imaginative, not to say, creative interpretation of the facts: *When you said running water I did not assume you meant down the walls and this grave is a dead loss – I'd never get my mother-in-law in there, never mind my wife.*

217

Down the hill there is an intriguing system of holes guarded by ankle-high chromium rails, cunningly placed just at the right height for tripping over and plunging into the depths below. According to the helpful notice board, this is a system of water cisterns. Well, well, well, what do you know? I imagine they *would* have had to store water, since it does not rain very much in these parts – so they say.

We walk over and peer into the void of the nearest one. Dry as a bone. Amazing. After all this rain, you would have thought that at least some of this downpour would have collected at the bottom. Perhaps this limestone being so porous, it has soaked right through. So how did they keep it in the olden days and how did they get it to that cave up the hill? Maybe if they were clever enough to have leak-proof cisterns, they were clever enough to devise a system of pumping water up there, to the cave, even if it took donkeys - and a long time.

Ah, ah! Here's something interesting. There's something down there, but it's not water. It's a pair of sunglasses. Now there's a remarkable thing! Lose one, find one. Just what I need. Obviously someone leaning over, looking for rainwater no doubt, has a slippery nose and ears like jug handles and failed to stop his glasses from falling into the abyss. They look a pretty expensive pair too, much better than I would buy, or at least more flashy, with gold trimming. Not my taste actually, but they're free, so I am prepared to live with them.

The only problem is – can I reach them? The tantalising thing is that they look just about reachable, which is exactly what the original owner must have thought, unless of course they are prescription glasses, in which case he may not have been able to see them at all. I could easily get down there – but could I get out? It's shaped pretty much like a beehive. I would need to have a strong helping hand from above and I doubt if I'd be able to get a good helping foothold to get out. Has Iona got the strength in her arms to haul me out of here? Would she even try, or would she leave me down there and collect the life insurance? I reckon I'd be a lot more use dead. I am weighing up the possibilities, when she speaks.

"No! Don't even think about it."

"What?"

"You know."

It's remarkable. I haven't even said anything. I was merely looking, looking at the bottom of the well, but she knows *me* too well. It may be looking increasingly sunny above but it looks dark for me if I go down there. If I can find no support for my feet, I know I can not depend upon any support from above. I'll just have to leave them. Like the fox and the grapes in Aesop's fable, I turn away from them consoling myself with the thought they're probably prescription glasses which would be unlikely to suit me and anyway I don't like the look of them.

We head on down the hill where the water from these cisterns would have flowed to the more modern houses, (all mod cons) stone-built, detached, abandoning the troglodyte dwelling in the cliff, and arrive at what is called the hypostyle.

The hypostyle is a tortoise sort of building. It doesn't look much from the top, barely distinguishable from all the other heaps and piles of stones which litter this site, but it is deceiving, for although the roof is barely above ground level, there is more of it, much more, under the ground. It is, in fact, by far the most complete building we have seen in the whole complex. The roof is made of enormous slabs supported by elegant, yet roughly hewn pillars which taper towards the bottom, giving the edifice an airy, diminutive cathedral sort of a feeling, standing as I am now at its centre with the sunlight streaming through the gaps between the slabs. They think it was used for storage, some sort of warehouse, and it was attached to a house. Probably that's where the janitor lived with his wife and son whom they called Rocky. But I don't believe it. If you ask me (and nobody is) it looks far too posh a building to be a mere warehouse, but what do I know?

It's a pretty big site this. There must have been hundreds of houses here at one time, tens of thousands of people who must have lived (and died) here when you think that this piece of ground was occupied for more than a thousand years. Now they've all gone and the houses are in ruins and this place has not been occupied for almost as long as it *was* occupied. It makes you think. Makes you realise how puny is our own brief stay on earth. And mine, my time left, is going to be truncated if I don't get a move on. Iona is far in the distance as I have stayed behind musing over the ruins of this collapsed dwelling. She may not find it amusing to be kept waiting, especially if it starts raining again and she can't get into the car for shelter as I have the keys.

But the skies remain blue as we head for Son Bou. Compared to this place, we are heading far into the future, though only to the 5th century. There's no mistaking the Christian basilica we have come to see, not because of the basilica itself, but because of the wall they have built round its ruins, the coping of the honey-coloured stone having been painted an eye-catching white. I wish I had my sunspecs with me – or someone else's, but as long as I don't have them, the sun is guaranteed to shine, so on reflection, I think I've got the best of the deal.

There's more stones in the wall, I imagine, than what's left of the basilica, just stumps like ground-down molars showing above the sand, but no doubt sufficient for the archaeologists to get their teeth into. There are three naves apparently and there's meant to be a huge font carved out of a single piece of stone. Well, that's what our guidebook says, but I can't see it. You'd think that I'd be able to see a thing like that wouldn't you? Unless it has been removed to some museum or other, which I suppose is possible, but the book is relatively recent, so perhaps it's just another example of my archaeological myopia.

I can see an apse however, and those stones could be what's left of the nave, though I wouldn't have known without the guidebook's helpful hint, but that's about it. Hardly worth coming all this way really, for that. I'm not even a church-goer. No, the real attraction of Son Bou is its beach, reputedly Menorca's longest at nearly 3kms, so long that although normally very crowded there is room enough for all – so the guidebook says. But today you could count the number of people on it, dressed more for a hike across the moors than for the beach, their clothes whipped by a stiff breeze which is driving an endless series of white chargers before it until they smash themselves to smithereens on the shore.

It's possibly always windy in this spot. Was this how the basilica was discovered I wonder - one stormy night, the sand being blown off it, in the same way that the Neolithic village of Scara Brae in Orkney gave up its secrets? How long the basilica lay hidden under the sand, I don't know, but it was only re-discovered in 1953. It's an ill wind, as they say.

Behind the basilica there are more cliffs and it comes as no surprise to find that they are perforated with more tombs - but here's something new. There's a house actually *built* deep into the cliff here, so deep it looks like a pupil, not the ones I used to teach, but an eye peering out through heavy lids – and people are actually living there. In fact, now I've thought of the image, it is unnerving and looks somewhat sinister. The house itself looks attractive enough. It's like a little cottage with walls inspired by the colour of the beach, a green door and two windows with the frames neatly picked out in white. It doesn't have any shutters, but who needs them here, when those natural shutters could come down in the blinking of an eye, so to speak, and seal you off from the world, never mind the sunshine. Out in the countryside, this may be a most desirable residence, but here? It must be claustrophobic in there, not to say pitch dark. Do they have electricity I wonder?

But that's not what makes it really sinister: it's the thought that underneath the floorboards of that house lie God knows how many bodies, well, at least, used to. I imagine they removed the bones or, more probably, swept out the dust when the new occupants gave it a spring clean. It's like building a house in a cemetery and we all know about the Amityville horror. Living here would be enough to give you nightmares.

But it's far from being the only horror in this place. Whereas the horrors of the cottage in the cliff are more a product of my imagination than actuality, even if you were poked in the eye with a blunt stick, you literally could not fail to recognise the monstrosity of the development along the littoral.

Huge skyscrapers dominate the landscape. Like enormous playing cards belonging to some devilish gigantic hand of poker, they stand end on to the sea, just as the cottages in Crovie where I used to live, not to mention all the other fishing villages of what used to be known as Banffshire (but regrettably and unforgivably, now called Aberdeenshire) stand gable-end on to the element that gave the inhabitants their living, but which they knew was capable of a much more sinister side and was the reason they presented it with the smallest target area possible.

Oh, you can have a sea view all right, as long as the see is not spelt with an *a*. I think I must be right about a storm uncovering the basilica. Had these monstrosities of collective tourist centre accommodations been built with the surface of biggest area presented to the prevailing wind, that is to say, facing the sea, in severe conditions they might well have toppled like a house of cards, and what a pity they weren't, just as long as no one was in them of course.

So, as they stand, you can either have a view of the cliffs (if you play your cards right) and like the hotel we stayed in Cairo which advertises every room with a Nile view, here too, you might be able to get a glimpse of the sea as long as you are prepared to commit death-defying contortions from the insecurity of your balcony railings. If, however, you have a bad hand and are destined to spend your week, or even worse, a fortnight, on the other side of the card, then you can have a very fine view of the balconies on the card across the way. Of course, depending on who is sunbathing on the balconies, it might turn out to be a very superior view indeed, but if you have the sort of luck that I have, that won't happen.

It would require more chargers than there are in the whole of this sea, to drag me to spend an hour in one of these places, never mind a holiday. If I'd thought Son Parc ghastly, this is reminiscent of something out of Stalinist Russia. By contrast, away up in the cliff behind these hotels, and you could scarcely imagine anything more different, there is a tiny white house built into the cliff with an overhang so hung-over it could be me on a Sunday morning. And although even tinier than that other troglodyte dwelling - it has only one tiny window which stares poker-faced at the thousands opposite - it nevertheless somehow contrives to look far less claustrophobic, whilst for charm and appeal, it beats the large windowed apartment blocks hands down.

That's all there is to Son Bou and a big boo it gets from me too as far as I'm concerned.

"We've gotta get out of this place," I serenade Iona as we make our way back to the car. I had merely thought it before, before I executed the Trepucó manoeuvre, you may remember, but this time I give full voice to it and even although I cannot sing a note in tune, and, to recall another of Aesop's fables, unlike the crow with the cheese, I could never be convinced to the contrary - that in fact, my voice sounds exactly like a crow's (which is not that surprising actually, since my maternal grandmother was a Crow and to whom they say, I bear a striking resemblance) - there's no need for Iona to look at me as if I were some sort of low life, as if I were some sort of animal, though that is exactly what I was trying to sound like, like Eric Burden of *The Animals* whose iconic sixties hit I am parodying.

But perhaps she doesn't regard this place with quite the same amount of distaste as I do. In any case, we are leaving this hell of a place behind and searching for architectural heaven, hopefully, in Es Migjorn Gran, the road to which we have often passed on our transits across the island en route to somewhere else but which now *is* somewhere else to go after here.

According to our guide, it is a traditional little village and gets its curious name from the dominant geographical feature, the low limestone plateau on which it stands, the *migjorn,* while *gran* means big. Only there *are* no big places here, on the south of the island, though in fairness, this could claim to be the biggest town on the limestone block, and thus they are entitled to call it big if they want, if as they seem to think, size matters so much.

We could imagine ourselves the only people on the planet if it were not for the occasional burst of riotous laughter from behind firmly closed green shutters as we leisurely wend our way down the Carrer Major. Only a paranoid would imagine that they are laughing at him, especially since presumably if we can't see them, then they can't see us. But perhaps the shutters work like net curtains so that those inside can see *out*, but passers-by can't see *in*. It sounds the sort of laughter that you hear in a pub after a few rounds and after someone has told a moderately amusing joke, and it's disconcerting as we pass down this pleasingly sinuous street of gaily-painted houses, the traditional white being interspersed here and there with peach, apricot, ochres, and blues of various hues with occasional scarlet hibiscuses forming a brilliant splash of colour like recently spilled blood against whitewashed walls - to hear this hilarious laughter emanating from yet another ordinary-seeming house with green shutters. Could they possibly be laughing at us, or more likely me? Could it be that my The Liver is Evil and Must be Punished T shirt has provoked the inhabitants of this remote and un-touristy place (but who nevertheless have excellent English) to peals of uncontrollable mirth? Or is it something more fundamental to do with my dress sense in general?

I ask Iona who knows everything.

"Don't be so paranoid."

Leaving the unnerving laughter behind, we come in a few people-less minutes to the church of Sant Cristòfol, an attractively simple building with the mouldings on its portico and steeple picked out in yellow. Even here, the hub of the village, we have it to ourselves. This is more like it. This is the real Menorca, a matter of a few miles away from Son Bou but a million miles away in atmosphere.

Fortunately for us, the car is not too far away for the sky has become apocalyptically dark again and the atmosphere is pregnant with rain. Iona is already hauling on her cagoule as the first drops, like cannon balls finding their range in the opening salvo of some assault from heaven upon the wicked beneath, do their best to make me holier by drilling holes in my cranium. She's wasting her time, I tell her. That flimsy garment will never keep her dry if these harbingers of deluge turn into a full-flooded downpour. I decide to leg it and leave Iona who can run about as fast as a three-legged tortoise, but not quite that fast, to her fate.

"Thanks very much," she says as, a few minutes later, she scrambles into the car. She is wet all right, but the tone is dry. She's not thanking me for having the door unlocked and ready for her; she's criticising me for making it in the dry whilst she sloshed here in the wet. I've made a mistake – I should have kept her company and got as wet as her. It's only fair after all.

As I drive off, with the heating full on and the steam beginning to rise off Iona's cagoule, the question is – what to do now? It's too early to go back, to spend the afternoon, especially after this morning's incarceration, being deaved by the Githeads. No, that would never do. But what else can we do? Where else can we go?

12. The Hill is Alive with Sound

There's only one possibility, one which we had not really seriously considered before. There seemed better, more interesting things to do with our limited time than visit this place which is why we had passed it several times before but, like Es Mignjor Gran, never taken the detour. But now, since we are relatively near, it seems the best, if not the only option, though to go there on this day of all days, is not the day one would choose if one intended to go there for the view. For we are heading for Es Mercadal and then just a short distance to Monte Toro, the highest point on the island, not incredibly high at 1,148 feet, but from which, on a clear day, they say, you can see the entire island, but clearly not on a day like today which makes this diversion sound like an exercise in futility, if it were not an avoidance from the Githeads.

It's a twisting turning road up that hill to where the clouds conceal the church at the top. As I round one of these vertiginous bends, I have to make a sudden swerve to avoid a car unexpectedly on my side, on the wrong side of the road. It's not coming towards me though. In fact, it's not going anywhere – it's well and truly in the ditch. This is mother of all ditches, a concrete V shaped culvert three feet deep and obviously built to cope with copious amounts of rainwater rushing down the mountain. The car looks undamaged, though the undercarriage might have sustained lacerations, but to haul it out of that canyon would require mechanical assistance. Presumably the driver had taken the corner too fast and now he's going to have to wait for the car to be retrieved, and even if he's lucky and there's no damage, it's going to take hours.

It looks like a hire car, which is confirmed by the prominent sticker on the windscreen, and I wonder if the driver had paid for the excess waiver? Bad news for him if he didn't – not only a loss in time, but in money too. If it had been me, I'd be feeling as sick as the proverbial parrot by now. It's a salutary lesson on how accidents can arise out of the most trivial incidents and when you least expect them, that on this small and apparently traffic-friendly island, accidents can still happen - and do.

There's plenty of car parking at the top, but amazingly, even on a day like this, the place is hoaching. Busloads of tourists have been transported up here because they've come not just for the view, but to visit the convent and church which they just happen to have built here, at the island's highest point. And no doubt, their tour had been pre-booked, weeks, if not months, before departure, just as, a couple of years ago, we had paid for our bus trip to the top of Mount Dalsnibba in Norway, the one which gives you that eyrie feeling as you look down on the summits of the mountains and glaciers hemming in the Geirangerfjord- it's in all the brochures - where a toy ship lies at anchor in a ragged blue sleeve of water.

If we had been there only a week ago, indeed, any day in the last nine weeks, all we would have seen would have been the mist at the other side of the window pane, (no refunds, no cancellation for poor weather conditions) for it had been raining day in and day out, so our guide said, for the past two months and more, and this was the first day in all that time that it had stopped raining and there were clear blue skies, moreover. Imagine that! Not the rain - that happens to us all the time in Scotland - no, that I had arrived on the first sunny day in nine weeks!

Well, so here busloads, not to mention independent travellers like us, are gathered at this highest point in all Menorca. Not that much nearer to heaven considering its meagre height though we are certainly up in the clouds with the church drifting in and out of the veils of mist like some celestial striptease act.

The church dates from the 17th century Iona reads from the guidebook, and contains a statue of a black Madonna with the infant Jesus in her arms and a bull at her feet. Ah, hah! I think, more evidence of this bull worship cult being incorporated into the Christian faith, as the name of the mountain suggests.

Well yes and no. In fact, the name of the place almost certainly derives from the Moorish *Al Thor* which means *high place* but according to legend, there *was* a mysterious bull which lead people to a cleft in the rock where there was a statue of the Virgin. Amazing enough, but we are lead to believe also it had, apparently, carved it itself with its horns! I don't know how they knew that though, unless it had signed it of course: Jackson Bullock. Naturally this would have been an early work from his surrealist period before he went on to his abstract expressionist style.

Anyway, ever since then, this has been a place of pilgrimage, most noticeable now in the enormous modern white convent (appearing and disappearing like a mirage depending on the whimsical thickness of the cloud) which has been grafted most incongruously onto the remains of the castle, of which nothing now remains but one square keep of ancient brown stone and from whose ruinous walls, at all levels, sprouts an incredible amount of foliage as if their very roots, rather than the Spanish equivalent of Historic Monuments, were responsible for keeping this ancient monument from falling down.

On an enormous pedestal, welcoming us with open arms so that the whole figure forms a cross, is an equally enormous statue of Christ, a sort of mini version of the gigantic Christ the Redeemer which overlooks Rio de Janeiro. It's actually a war memorial to commemorate a conflict between Spain and Morocco in the 1920's. Hmm. I wonder if that could possibly be the same one which ended up with the Spanish having two enclaves in Morocco which they still have to this day and about which they conveniently seem to have an attack of amnesia each time they demand the return of Gibraltar?

Whether or not this is the case, although this Christ has not such a splendid view as His Brazilian counterpart, He has a pretty good view nonetheless, or He would have if He had a revolving pedestal and who is to say He hasn't – after all stranger things have happened on this mountain, have they not?

Strangely enough, we have a pretty good view ourselves, despite the weather. We can see practically the whole island, coast to coast, especially from north to south. Closest and most obviously, at our feet lies Es Mercadal, the village spread out in its entirety, an irregular shape of whitewashed houses set amidst a sea of green. It's amazing - like being in a plane, a feeling re-enforced by the clouds swirling about the turrets of the convent. Here and there, plumes of what looks like smoke are spiralling up and out of the verdant hillside around the village and from somewhere below, probably in the village itself, an invisible dog is yapping, yapping, yapping, the sound as clear as a bell though it must, in actual fact, be miles away

Further in the distance, that town has to be Fornells: that narrow gap, that lagoon, that natural harbour is unmistakable and further round, that must be Son Parc and the point we went to yesterday though there wasn't much point to it in the end.

Nor is there much point in trying to identify any other landmarks, as our geography of the island is just about as hazy as the visibility, so we turn our attention to the immediate vicinity. Walking through an arch, we find ourselves in a very pleasing courtyard indeed, with a well as its focal point and a particularly twisted olive (as many of that species are) and bougainvillea climbing the walls. The door to the church, small and dark, lies straight ahead but to enter it, first we must fight our way through a portico filled with terracotta pots, themselves filled to capacity with greenery clambering to escape their confines.

It is an anti-climax, if not a depressing experience, to leave that cool green place behind and come instead to the dark interior of the church. It's like leaving the Garden of Eden behind, and to be reminded that religion (and life) is a serious matter. But for all its sobriety, this is no Calvinist sanctuary as one glimpse of the altar reveals.

Here is the venerated black Madonna with her child in her arms and the bull at her feet – La Verge del Toro – the focus of the festival which they hold annually on the first Sunday in May. She sits in an altar built, apparently, in 1943. Why this recent addition, the guidebook doesn't say, but no doubt it was another victim of the Civil war but it's hard to imagine that anyone thought this fussy, over-elaborate carving an improvement on the old. And if it is, then that which it replaced must have been truly horrendous.

There's nothing else in the church to detain us for long. In fact, I long to be out of it and see the light. Blinking like moles, we re-emerge into the courtyard. To our left, just outside the church, there is an opportunity to buy souvenirs of your visit. I just knew there would be such a place somehow and that we would be destined to visit it.

It's just a small place with a small old woman standing behind the counter but its staggering. We are confronted by shelves stacked wall to wall, floor to ceiling, with a myriad of tacky souvenirs – and no spaces to show where a gaudy Virgin or a red Sacred Heart or a gold cross, (with or without a wee man on it) or a figure of Christ with a gold and silver star bursting from behind His head, or a saint with a halo supported by a nasty spike driven into the vertebra between his shoulder blades - has gone to a good home. It is an assault on the senses. For sheer awfulness, no one can touch it: we are blinded by the glittering gaudiness of it, struck dumb by the sheer scale of it. And as for good taste, it's quite unknown in this shop. And as you might expect, there are plenty of bulls in this china shop also, though I suspect, they are just plaster.

The old woman looks at us suspiciously, says nothing, with not even the slightest incline of the head to acknowledge our presence, constantly on guard for pick-pockets tempted beyond endurance by the abundance of delights on display. This is probably the most under-worked sales-person in Spain. It's hard to imagine the till jingling here with the sound of the punters' money changing hands. She's probably not made a sale in weeks.

For politeness' sake, I pick up the nearest Verge del Toro (there are scores more like her) and look at her bottom, if you pardon the expression. She was probably made in China or Hong Kong, though it doesn't say so. €3.50. You must be joking! Even before I picked her up, (though I am not used to picking up women in shops, though I believe supermarkets are a source nowadays) you can see she has been so badly painted that the black dots meant to represent the pupils of her eyes have missed the centre and have been relegated to the corners. Painted by a poor pupil presumably. And likewise the mouth. When Mary was applying the lipstick, she did so without a mirror, apparently, because she has partly missed it and smeared it across her cheek. Still, it's interesting, because before I came here, I never knew that Mary wore lipstick and I didn't know that about the bull either. That's what I like about foreign travel – you end up learning the most amazing facts.

The old woman is looking at me closely: *Don't even think about pocketing that – I'm watching you!* Or maybe this is the closest she has been to a sale all day, perhaps all week, and her eyes are gleaming with the thought of activity and meeting her monthly target of four, but she is thinking: *Er...how do I work that till again? I hope he doesn't want to pay Visa.*

She needn't have bothered worrying. "It's lovely," I tell her, "but I'm afraid it's just a little bit expensive for me."

She doesn't look as if she believes me or perhaps she doesn't speak my language, but in anybody's language, there is nothing here anybody could remotely want to buy unless their taste was all in their mouths. I have to let her down gently. I pretend to look at some other *objets d'art* as if with the object of buying one but they are all equally objectionable and I give her a sympathetic look and a smile as I head towards the door which says: *Not today, Josephine.* I am sure she must be called Josephine. Maybe I think that because that's what the badge pinned to her flat chest says.

It's all the same to her. She looks at me stoically, impassively. She's been here before; she is in no-sale retail. That is her job. She has learned not to get her hopes up. She is a philosopher after my own heart - that way she'll never be disappointed and like the person who has sex once a year, (though I doubt if Josephine has it as often as that) it's all the more special when it happens, for the infrequency. It's just a long time to wait, that's the snag.

From somewhere off to the left, and given that all our senses (apart from smell) have recently been assaulted and are lying senseless in the courtyard, it makes sense that it should be hearing which is the first to recover, since it was the least beaten up. There is some sort of subliminal sound which I had noticed on our passage through the courtyard, but having been more focused on the church and the magnetic pull of the greenery straight ahead, I had pushed it unconsciously to the back of my mind. Now, opening the door of this white-washed building, what Phil Spector would call a *wall of sound*, sweeps over us and instead of sweeping us back, sweeps us in as if we had just caught it on the ebb.

From straight ahead there is the sound of clattering dishes and the cacophony of countless conversations – obviously the refectory. To the left, there is a shop – this time a real shop. You can stand at the top on a mezzanine and see it stretching far into the distance with goods of all description packed from floor to above head height on both sides with a corridor down each side, packed with people looking for souvenirs: pottery, plastic, plaster, china, clothes, clutter and confusion – it's all here for the discerning and especially, (they hope), the not so-discerning punter, for at a quick glance, although there do appear to be some quality goods here, the bulk of it is not. Nevertheless, there has to be something here for all tastes, to persuade you to part with your euros – even me, because they do sell wines and spirits, except I'm not so daft that I would buy them here. No wonder Josephine looked so glum. The awfulness of her merchandise aside, it is plain that she could not possibly compete with the variety and scale of this.

To say that we wander down one of those aisles would not be true. Rather we squeeze our way past the tide of people who would have been on the beaches had it been a fine day, but considering the inclemency of the weather, have been washed up here on the island's highest point and have been caught in arguably, the island's biggest tourist trap.

But it's not the sight of all the products in this Aladdin's cave which produces the most reaction but the sound of the shoppers sloughing off the slough of despondency in an ecstasy of shopping. From one extreme to the other, from the bathos of this morning's ban from the beaches to the climax of this climb to the convent, they are forgetting their miseries in this serendipitous discovery of shopping heaven and giving full voice to it like children opening their presents on Christmas Day.

But surely they expected this at the highest point of the island? For it is a truth universally acknowledged that a tourist in search of the furthest north, south, east and west, highest or lowest part of a country or island, must be in want of refreshment or a shopping experience, preferably of the tackiest but most expensive kind. Which is why we had not really wanted to come here in the first place as we had suspected it would be a tourist trap. And to think we had thought it had been the Church Shoppe!

But from the sound of it, they thought they had come up here for the view and cannot believe their luck in stumbling upon this. The ceiling is very low. Perhaps when this was a monastery this was the cellar and then when it ceased to be and they wondered what could they possibly do with it, some enterprising bright spark came along and thought and a little voice inside his head said: *Why not see what we can sell her?* And so they sold everything and anything in this prime location, primarily geared towards the female of the species and have never looked back since, especially on rainy days and Sundays which never gets them down as *The Carpenters* almost put it, as the tills ring even more merrily on those days, I bet.

It may be noisy in here, but rising above them all and reverberating round the walls of this confined space, I happen by bad luck to be next to the loudest of them all, though, you might have thought she was speaking to someone on the mezzanine instead of the person right next to her: *Come here and look at this, Maisie*, this to her daughter presumably, looking at pottery just a few feet away, and then to the other end of the room where her husband is shopping for wine and spirits, just about all there is here to interest the male of the species unless you want to buy a leather jacket and *abarcas* to match: *Hey Malky, ye wee alky, pit that bottle doon!* The reprimand is meant to be in jest, for she follows up this witticism with a paroxysm of hoarse laughter which develops into a fit of coughing that is the trade mark of the lungs of a forty a day person. Malky gives her a broad grin but puts the bottle back. Quite right, Malky. She may be joking but with shoulders and biceps that size, I'd play safe too and by the way, save yourself a few euros and get it in the supermarket.

No, that's quite amusing really, but it is the way she thinks that her opinion on what has caught her eye here amidst all the infinite variety should be broadcast to all and sundry. I can still hear her now although I have moved onto the mezzanine: *Oh, is that no pure dead brilliant, Maisie? So it is, is it no?*

In an instant comes the answer. Like mother, like daughter, we can all hear her reply. Roaring like a bull seems to be the favoured method of conversation in their household, so we all know what Maisie knew about her mother – that her taste was as abominable as the Snowman from the Himalayas. When Henry James wrote that novel, *What Maisie Knew,* he could never have anticipated that half the population of Menorca would share in her knowledge: *Away tae yer bed, maw. It's a load o' crap.* Don't say Maisie herself didn't tell you if ever you get around to that book, and if you want my advice, I wouldn't bother if I were you. (Sorry about that Henry or should I say, Mr James, but I'm sorry to say if you can't do better than think of two Christian names for your name, it doesn't say much about the extent of your imagination, does it?)

It's coffee time and Iona, never one to miss an opportunity to take her drug should she smell it in the vicinity, can smell it now and suggests we have a coffee. Whenever she makes a suggestive remark, I always respond positively.

In the restaurant it is scarcely less noisy, but this is more a general hubbub than due to one specific individual, the sort of noise you hear in a school canteen, except worse even than that and God knows, that is bad enough. It's hard on the ears, this Babel of multi-lingual sound amplified by the low barrel-roofed ceiling, the hard tables and hard benches, and bouncing off the walls and windows, unrelieved by the presence of any soft furnishings, and the cacophony complimented by the clatter of dishes from some unseen and some apparently chaotic kitchen behind the scenes. So unlike how it must have sounded all those years ago when this was the refectory for the monks. If, in some ghostly perambulation, they happened to wander in here now checking out the refectory as they knew it, for a little snack, how they would be gob-smacked by the ghastly noise from these hordes of infidels.

And what would they make of the clientèle itself? What would our perambulatory monk make of this bloke for instance, wearing the English football top whose beer belly belies his partaking of any sport except in the most sedentary of manners, slouched on the settee, the only exercise being the bending of the elbow of his beer arm and the pressing of his thumb on the remote control button; the one with the ugly wife and, like Prunella and Phil, the philandering boss of the apartments, with the similarly stunning teenage daughter. How did that happen? He's no oil painting himself. It's curious how nature re-addresses the balance.

Oh, no, here comes Maisie and her mother in search of refreshment with the father tagging along like an accessory. I didn't see her first – I heard her. Nor will whatever she's going to eat do more than muffle her flow, for I'm sure Maisie's mum will spray it rather than say it for talking is like breathing to her and being a woman, she can multi-task and can eat, talk and breathe all at the same time. I bet she even talks in her sleep.

I can't wait to be out of this hell-hole before she starts. There is a terrace off to the left. I gulp my coffee and make my escape, but even here, the tiles treacherous with the recent rain, the sound percolates through and assaults the ears and dulls the appreciation the eyes might have had of the view. In any case, you have to look over and ignore, if you can, the unsightly radio antennae belonging to the military which rather takes the edge off the view of the northern coast which seems to appear more and more out of the mist as we watch, for by now Iona has joined me.

But we can't stop and stare, we must go and enjoy ourselves elsewhere. Well at least go back to base and listen to the Githeads coughing their lungs out which is preferable at least to their bloody "music", though no doubt, we'll be treated to that too.

And talking of music, this epicentre of noise in all Menorca has one final card up its sleeve, one final chord up my eardrums. As we leave the restaurant, from the open door of a room in the courtyard, up some steps to our left, there is a sudden eruption of sound. It sounds orchestrated, a choir of some sort singing a hymn, probably a choir of zealots on tour. We do not stop to listen. Although this sounds as if it might be the most tuneful music, no, the *only* tuneful music, I've heard so far on this entire trip, I can't face any more thank you very much, and turning my back on the delights of this free musical extravaganza, we head back to the car.

It's back down the twisty-twiny road. Slowly, slowly does it. I don't want to end up in the ditch like the Clio we saw on the way up. That dangerously-deep, treacherously V shaped verge is on the right, a bend coming up, the merest touch of the brakes just to make sure I negotiate it safely and suddenly I am in a skid and heading towards that chasm, grimly holding onto the wheel, spinning it away from that seemingly inevitable disastrous destination, yet also pulling back on it like a pilot on a joystick, trying to rise above a mountain, but nevertheless heading towards the abyss and there is nothing, in spite of my training on the snow-slick roads of Banffshire, that I can do about it, but curse my decision not to take the extra insurance, wonder how I'll contact the hire company, how long we'll be stuck here and what exercises the mind most, how much is this going to cost me as I rip the undercarriage out of this vehicle? All this passes through my mind, like a drowning man's life is said to, as we head towards the ditch.

We skid to a stop within a foot short of it. The road, with its surface of finely ground gravel, is greasy on account of the rain and I can see how the unfortunate driver of the Clio had ended up, all too easily, in the ditch. He had, in all probability, not been driving fast at all. If I had been going, I imagine, just one mile per hour faster, that could have been me too.

Iona and I look at each other, wordlessly expressing our relief and disbelief that that which had seemed so inevitable had not in fact happened, that we had escaped by the skin of our teeth. We had been lucky this time. Perhaps next time I *will* get the extra insurance.

13. Last Excursions

George Mallory, before his ill-fated death on Mt Everest, was often asked why he wanted to climb it and always gave the same reply: *Because it's there.* Thus we decide to go to Cala Santa Galdana because it's on the way home, and because it's there. We've no other reason to go there unless it is to waste time before we must go back to the Githeads or because it is a reputedly famous beauty spot, but marred now by the growth of high-rise hotels. It's out of Ferreries, just a few kilometres to the south, on the coast. That's the good thing about Menorca - nothing is ever very far away from anything.

When we get there, squeezing into what seems to be the last parking space, next to a park with one of the most interesting sculptures I have ever seen - a big, brightly painted red tap with water gushing out of it at force. It's obviously been left full on by some careless individual. But where's the water coming from? There's a pipe leading into it right enough, but it only goes back a couple of feet before being plugged off at the end so the water is not being fed from there. But what's even more amazing – it appears to be completely unsupported, just hovering in the air. How the hell did they do that?

It takes a bit of time, me being a bit slow on the uptake as far as matters of a technological nature are concerned (and not just technological, Iona would say) but I reckon the answer has to be that there's a pole up the spout which is concealed by the curtain of water which is apparently coming out of the tap, but which in fact is being forced up under pressure from below. It's the only logical explanation. If the object of the artist was to catch the eye of the beholder, he certainly did that with me, though there's little of beauty in it, it has to be admitted.

It doesn't matter about the tap being left on though for the firmament above, especially above the Puig del Torro from whence we have just come, is looking murderously black and what's more, it looks as if it is heading our way. I don't like the look of it. Best not to stray too far from the car. And already the harbingers of the deluge are beginning to fall: *Raindrops keep fallin' on my head, they keep fallin'.* It's the song for this occasion. It's done nothing but rain practically all day, and never mind my head, it's getting on my nerves.

We sprint for the car. Well, at least I do, so I can open the door for Iona, who follows as best she can. I have a feeling of *déjà vu* somehow, but this time, she actually makes it before the deluge. Like the tap in the park, that tap in heaven has been turned on, with a vengeance. Most of it seems to be falling on our car. We could be in a car-wash. Within minutes, we can scarcely see out of the windscreen it is so misted up.

"Someone's breathing in here." Another feeling of *déjà vu.* I've a feeling I've said this before, not so long ago.

No response necessary or expected. Once, in those far off, golden olden days, the steamed up windows used to be the result of heavy breathing. Now it's got something to do with the equilibrium between external and internal temperatures. Actually, now I come to think of it, the temperature inside my car must have been higher than that of the external temperature in Banffshire, even in high summer, so I reckon all I was doing was merely breathing heavily after all.

At last it stops and we can step out onto the sodden ground. Fine weather for ducks right enough and here are a couple, one with bright red legs like Wellingtons and the other with yellow ones, only just as bright, ploutering about in the mud, their tails wagging like dogs. There's a small girl too, having the time of her life, stomping her feet in the puddles and chortling as the water splashes up her legs and her dress. If she had a tail, I'm sure she'd be wagging it. The mother, watching resignedly from a bench nearby, has long since given up any hope of restraining her and saving the dress. It's good to see that some people are happy with the weather at least.

Ahead of us is the marina, and judging by the forest of masts, no boats have set sail today and there is a boardwalk, dark and glistening with rain, around the perimeter. There's a group of people coming towards us – a teenage boy pushing a small child in a push-chair and a man with frizzy white hair and a woman with the opposite – long black and straight. Opposites attract right enough.

"Oh, hello," says Iona as you would to someone you meet by accident walking down your local high street, except this is Menorca and not really what might be described as Menorca's most visited location either. Incredible! Does she really know someone *everywhere* we go? On our last excursion, in Skye, we walked into a pub for a meal and whom should she meet, but someone she knew! It turned out to be a colleague, though being a peripatetic teacher as Iona is, I suppose does shorten the odds a bit.

"Hello!" they respond, not without a certain degree of surprise.

Iona introduces me. Actually it's not so strange and not so much of a coincidence after all. They are also colleagues of hers, and as with the people we had met in Skye, are like us, here on holiday, along with half of Central Scotland, apart from the ones who are in Mallorca or the Canaries of course. And not so surprising that they should be in Menorca either, as her boss has a second home here and holds court to the great and the good who happen to come here for the October break.

That's what the conversation leads to next, how they had been there last night and drank like fishes and, according to Matt, no-one there was below the rank of rector (apart from him – but that's OK as he is in the embryonic stage of that species). Hmm, I am thinking, Iona must have forgotten to mention to her boss that we were also coming here or had forgotten to give him our address in Menorca. Or perhaps she was worried that I would disgrace her by not keeping my end up by drinking as much as the others. Yes, I expect that is what it was, that's why we weren't invited.

The conversation moves on to where we are staying; where they are staying; where the King holds court (my question the sole contribution to the conversation) and with whom we flew; and from which airport. This is taking a worrying turn. What if they ask how much our flight was? I would never do that unless I was certain that I had got an unbeatable deal, which is why of course they *would* ask, so they could enjoy their holiday more in the certain knowledge that they had got a better bargain. It's a high-risk strategy of course. You might get a surprise and it could be enough to ruin your holiday.

But actually, it's just a way of introducing the subject: they only want to tell us about what happened on their flight. It seemed they were detained for hours on account of a kid who would not board the aircraft. I suppose you can't carry it kicking and screaming on board, strap it in and take off, can you? The other passengers would complain about the din. They didn't know why he refused but what they *did* know was they had to sit on the plane whilst the negotiations were going on. What do you say to a kid who chooses this moment to discover it has a fear of flying? Presumably that was the reason, rather than bloody-mindedness. Then, when after some time, the talks collapsed, all the luggage had to be taken off and the unfortunate family had to identify their luggage and remove theirs before it was loaded on again.

Naturally we commiserate. Bad for them, but how much worse for the family who have lost their entire holiday, never mind the money. I doubt very much if their insurance would cover this eventuality: *You want your money back because your kid refused to get on the plane? You must be kidding!*

We say goodbye and move on. We pass under a stylish bridge which spans the entrance channel to the marina. We can go no further round, but we can go up and we follow a path over the cliffs. Looking back, we can see the beach, the sunbeds and their umbrellas in serried ranks, not needed today. There's one or two people strolling along it and a mother paddling with her small child. Apart from that, it's deserted. All the people who are in the high-rise hotels behind the beach must be in their rooms. Probably the only person more miserable at the present in the whole of Cala Santa Galdana is the man who has the sunbed business. It's not much compensation for the family with the *refusnik* kid, but at least they are not missing the sunshine.

Perhaps it because I've got an aversion to going back to the apartment, or perhaps it's because it's the last day of the car, but as we hit the main road and I see a sign to Castell Santa Agueda, I decide to take it. Besides, it has stopped raining and that's another sign that we should take this road. We've taken just about every other road on this island, so why not this, why should it be left out? Besides, it is a place of historical interest and also the second highest point on the island. We've just done the highest, so why not the second highest? (Or is it the third as the other guidebook alleges?). Anyway, it's only 853 feet and there's a Roman path up to the summit, the best preserved in Menorca where the Romans built a citadel in the second century BC. Who could ask for anything more? Well, after the Romans, it was used by the Moors and was in fact, where they made their final stand against the Reconquest of Alphonso III in 1287 and in Maó we had seen what happened to them after that, to those whose families would not, or could not, ransom them. So there's a couple of good reasons to visit it for a start.

As we park where the guidebook says, at the abandoned schoolhouse, Iona's not so sure if this is one of my better ideas. The sun may be out, but the bushes are dripping wet and the Castell appears high above us, craggy limestone peaks rising out of dense green vegetation like a coxcomb, and from here probably looking more like a Castell than there is Castell left up there to see, for actually the main point of the excursion is for the view and in my view, possibly not worth the candle on a day like today, especially when we had just been to the highest point and had seen as much as was possible to see from there. And now that the ascent looks rather more strenuous than I had imagined and that according to the guidebook it's an hour's march, I'm not so sure that it's a good idea either, but I can hardly say so - at least, not yet.

Iona dons the cagoule somewhat grumpily and off we set. The trouble is that the path, which at first was smooth and easy, (ah, these Romans, they knew how to build paths as well as roads) not only seems to be leading us away from our destination, but also becoming more like the rocky road to ruin than a ruined Roman path.

"Are you sure this is the right way?" says the disgruntled wife, slipping in her sandals on the rocky surface for possibly the twentieth time, though I wasn't counting. "This looks more like a dry river bed than a Roman path to me."

She has a point, though it's actually not quite dry, not after the deluges we've had today - it could scarcely be that, but it's hardly a raging torrent either. But more worrying, it looks absolutely nothing like the picture in the guidebook, but maybe it will further on, if we persevere.

"Has to be," I say laconically. I wish she would say she's had enough and that she's turning back.

But with the perverseness of a cat, she stumbles on and I follow behind thinking just how like a river bed this is, well at least a stream and if it is, it's certainly not going to take us to where we want to go and God knows where it *is* taking us and each further step is another step we have to take on the way back. When, oh when, is she going to give in?

But then, as if by divine intervention, it starts to rain.

"Thank you, God," I say internally.

"Look, I really don't think this is right." La-Belle-Dame-Sans-Merci is scowling at the rocky path and squinting balefully at the rain from underneath the hood of her cagoule. The rain is the final straw and the lady is for turning at last.

"Oh, I don't know. I think it might clear up, might not amount to much."

"Huh! Well you go on if you want. I'm going back to the car." The lady sounds iron in her resolve. "Where are the keys?" Her outstretched hand is already demanding them.

For a mad moment, I think about pretending that I've lost them, just to see what sort of reaction that produces but there's something about the body language that tells me that it's not a good idea. Besides, I have never knowingly bugged anyone.

She can't sit in the car by herself for a couple of hours whilst I clamber up a rocky river bed to see a ruckle of stones and a view that you can't see for the rain and mist, so I magnanimously say I'll come with her.

But I'm not done with the sight-seeing yet. There is one thing more I want to see before we hand the car back. It's the quarry, sign-posted as Líthica on a puce sign that you could scarcely miss. We've kept it till last because it's not far from where we are staying, but not within walking distance and which, like Es Migjorn Gran, we've passed everyday on our way to somewhere else.

But first I must get some petrol. Get a full tank and bring it back full. That was the agreement and a much better one than the system where you have to bring it back empty. That's not good for Iona's nerves as we coast down hills, the needle on red, nursing it back from the back of beyond, just so I don't make a present of petrol to the hire company. It's not that I'm parsimonious, I just don't like to waste money (if you know what I mean).

It's lashing down again as I pull into the petrol station. That doesn't bother me as it's undercover but buying petrol is not always such a straight forward business as it is back home. I can't remember when the last time was that I was served by an attendant in the UK, but on the continent it can be confusing: sometimes you just serve yourself and sometimes someone materialises by your elbow just as you are taking off the filler cap and at other times you do that and wait and nothing happens. You look to see what the other motorists are doing. Are they filling up themselves or are they waiting to be served? And sometimes there are no other motorists and no one comes to serve you, so do you stand around like a lemon or do you serve yourself and as soon as you do that, will some beefy guy with biceps like blown up like tractor tyres with skulls tattooed on them come menacingly towards you, demanding to know what in all of fairyland you are doing with his hose in your hand?

This time it's a situation I've not come up with before and it's no less the worrying. As soon as I step onto the forecourt, an electronic sort of voice is addressing me in Spanish. I have absolutely no idea what it is saying. It could be: *Please wait whilst we finish our magazine and come to serve you* or *We've got better things to do than come and serve you, you lazy git, so serve yourself and hurry up while you're at it.*

I am the only customer, so there are no clues to be had there, so I hang about, taking a long time to unscrew the filler cap in order to give the attendant, if there is one, time to appear and when he doesn't, I decide it's time to help myself. I lift the nozzle off its nest, setting the invisible speaker off into fresh flurry of Spanish. What's it going on about now? Maybe it's telling me to begin fuelling. Thanks, but I knew that already. I'm not a complete fool.

I fill up until it clicks off, then put in another squirt for the petrol I'll use tonight – and no one has appeared in human or even semi-anthropoid form to tell me to get my hands off his equipment. The pump has started yammering again: *Now, in case you are a moron, hang the hose back up on the hook, close your filler cap and in case you were thinking of driving off without paying, we've got your number.*

476. That's the number of kilometres I've done in these three days. And €23.49 is how much it has cost. I can't complain at that. It sounds good value for having covered just about every inch of this island and going where we wanted to go, meandering wheresoever and whenever we wanted, just Iona and me, me and her. And we haven't had any accidents, so I've saved on the extra insurance also. Good decision I made not to get it.

I put the petrol on the plastic and pay to real people, not a disembodied voice in the kiosk. Pay later and it all adds points towards the discount on my next holiday. The best of both worlds.

The sign to the Líthica may be easy to see, but it's not so easy to find the place itself. I doubt if we could have missed another sign like that but somehow we have and we've ended up outside a massive building in the warm honey-coloured stone which is evidence that it had come from the quarry we're looking for. There's a vast empty circular area and a colonnaded passage. And in the wall of the passage, unless I'm much mistaken, filed side by side, one on top of the other, are the dear departed. Filed pending a decision. Most souls will already have departed for their permanent location, the remains remaining behind in this curious arrangement that the continentals seem to prefer of keeping their dead above the ground.

Well, that was dead interesting, but it is the hole in the ground from which all that stone comes that we want to see - or at least I do. Maybe I'm so used to digging holes for myself that I want to see the holes that other people dig. From the picture in the guidebook it looks pretty impressive, a man-made canyon 30 meters deep, with cliffs as straight and smooth and perpendicular as a ruler on its end. And, if only they had been running horizontally instead of vertically, the chisel marks would have looked like the measurements. I'm not especially keen on quarries as a rule, but this is different.

We find it all right on the return journey. There's the pukey puce sign. Pity they didn't sign it the other way. That would have been helpful. Although it's been closed as a quarry for some time, they opened it as a tourist attraction and have great plans for developing it. And now that we've found it, wouldn't you know - it's closed! Typical. Nevertheless, I park the car and get out to see what I can see. Fortunately, what keeps me out is a chain-link fence like a string vest and I can see through the holes. It's better than nothing but all I can really do is look across, not down, and down there, at the bottom, is where you would really have to be to see the enormous scale of this hole in the ground. I doubt if we will come back tomorrow without the car and it doesn't seem to be on the bus route. This island may be shaped like a thick sort of boomerang, but I suspect that this is one part of Menorca that we will not come back to. Ah well, we've done just about everything else.

There's one more thing to do, actually, whilst I still have the car. I must go shopping and get the rest of the goods for my import business. Far too heavy and too far to carry without the car. Been there, done that. I flip the indicator.

"Where are you going?' From the tone, I know it does not bode well. She knows perfectly well where I am going. Even if she does not recognise the route, she can't fail to have spotted the sign, though in fact it is only a little one, a rectangle, sharpened at one end to a point, with white lettering on a blue background and no bigger than it needs to be to accommodate the letters, just like Mozart's famous riposte, when accused of using too many notes replied: *Just as many as are needed.* And amazing that her hawk-like eyes could pick that up, but not the sign to the Líthica, especially, now that I can risk throwing a look across the car at her, she is looking at me stonily, her eyes as hard as granite.

"*Hipermercado.* Need to get a few things."

"Oh no, you're not."

"Not what?" I'm already at the junction, and having indicated, for safety's sake, must proceed with the manoeuvre, though I wouldn't bet on my safety when we get back to the apartment if I were to continue to my intended destination.

"Going to get any more booze. You've got half the booze in Menorca as it is. Have you forgotten the gin you got at the distillery?" There's no doubt about it, it is my Chinese wife, Scow Ling who is speaking and if I could see her back, I know it would have more bristles than Humphrey the Hedgehog hairbrush, her sometime bottom-smacker, getter-up-in-the-morning tool. And as if I could forget the lengths my arms went to, to liberate that gin from the Xoriguer distillery!

"Booze!" I laugh, as if the idea had never entered my head. I hope it doesn't sound as much in sorrow to her as it sounds hollow to me. "No! No! Whatever gave you that idea? (As soon as I said it, I knew I had protested too much). "No, no! I thought you might like some *Turrón* or something…"

My voice trails off. I may be in control of the car, but that's about all. And to think that I once thought I was in control of this marriage. She probably let me be boss for a while, then launched a coup d'état. Funny thing is, I never noticed. Which tells you she is either incredibly cunning or I am incredibly stupid, but I can't work out which.

She doesn't want any more *Turrón;* she doesn't want any more Nestlé's Condensed Milk which she can squirt directly into her mouth (thank God for that at least); no more cheese; she just wants to go straight back to the apartment, thank you very much. I have a feeling that somehow or other, I am not really going to succeed in this import business. Knowing it is pointless, that she'll never see the logic of the economics of the more you buy, the more you save, I see no point in trying to reason with her and instead, execute a three point turn which is better than facing my own execution. I'll just have to make do with what I've got.

And so now we must return to the apartment. Can't put it off any longer. We must go back and hear the Githeads. Although it has stopped raining at last, there is absolutely no chance that they will be at the pool bronzing their tattoos. They are bound to be in their apartment as they don't go anywhere.

And so it proves. They are enclosed in their apartment with the door closed. That's one good thing about the weather I suppose. Even although it has stopped raining, it's so damp and humid that sitting outside is so unpleasant, you just want to close your door and shut it out. I try it for a few moments as it's a Githead-free zone but after a few minutes, I give it up. I can practically feel the damp permeating my bones, just like it does in Scotland. It makes me think of the remedy for that, the whisky which we take medicinally, to keep out the cold and I think of all the other spirits which I need to bottle before we go home. May as well do it now.

I line it up, with the rest of my purchases, on the table. *Jings, is that no' a bonny sicht!* That line from *Lady and the Tramp* where the Scottie dog (how curious he should be an Aberdonian) surveys his hidden treasure of bones, seems apposite here. Despite the limitations imposed by the drinks police, not a bad haul. I've saved pounds but I'm going to have to buy a fizzy drink as I don't have enough empty bottles for the Drambuie, not unless I drink a bit more of it, that is. If I drink enough of it tonight, I can save a bit by not having to buy a fizzy drink. Hmm. That sounds like a good idea.

*

The *Café Balear* is at the far end of the harbour, near the car park. We've not really looked for a restaurant in this area before. For a start, there are no tables outside and it's a bit dark down at this end – all the restaurants and the lights are further on, not to mention the water which is why we were attracted down there, but we have been there and done that and after last night's experience, that part of the harbour has lost some of its gloss.

The *menú del día* looks appealing and it's also cheap. It appeals to me. Through the plate glass window, we can see that it also looks very pleasant inside with pink linen tablecloths and polished glasses and paintings lining the walls as well fishing artefacts, but not too many, just enough to create the idea that fish is the speciality of the house. Besides, it is so damp, to eat in is better than out tonight, so we may as well go in. Our decision: there is no maître d, lying in wait, ushering us in.

As usual, we have the fish – and we both have the same: salmon salad for starters, followed by bream. The wine is nicely chilled and is placed in an ice bucket at my elbow. As an old married couple and having been together all day, there's not much to talk about, so we take in our surroundings instead.

We scan the paintings on the walls. The nearest is a Van Gogh sort of thing, a view of the harbour with swirling waters like the stars in *Starry Night*. I like it a lot apart from a seagull coming in to land, so out of proportion, it looks like Concorde with its nose cone dipped for landing. I get up and have a closer look. It is not a Torrent, the Menorcan Van Gogh. It's not that I am terribly well educated on paintings. It's just that I can read and that's not the signature in the bottom right-hand corner.

But it must be educate your child week in Menorca. At the next table there is an Irish couple with their young child in a high chair and beside which, there is something which looks like a lunar-landing vehicle, but which I presume is merely his push chair. He's getting his education but in a much more intrusive manner than the child at the Naveta d'es Tudons who was being exposed simultaneously to Dutch and English. His parents are aiming so high with his education, that not only have they put him in a high chair, but they've called him Eammon as well. I've no idea what age he is. Two probably, below the age of speech certainly, but he is being taught his words and whatever else he may have eaten (or spilled on the floor), he is being force-fed knowledge. Everything he looks at, everything his eyes flicker on for an instant, he is told what it is: *That's a fork, Eammon, no dirty, don't stick it up your nose; that's Concorde, Eammon, coming in to land in the harbour; that's an alcoholic, Eammon, see his red face.*

At least he should pick his name up pretty quickly. If it is not a relief to Iona, then it certainly is for me to see that Eammon is about to be brought back to earth, being transferred from his high chair to his lunar buggy. But poor Eammon - he hasn't an earthly of escaping the education which will pursue him until his fond parents, especially his mother, who bore him, bores him to sleep with a surfeit of knowledge. When he's a bit older, she'll probably make him take up stamp collecting as a hobby, except she will call it philately and for a goodnight story she'll probably read him the questions and answers from *Trivial Pursuit.*

We have the traditional almond cake as out just desserts as it is included in the menu and then it's time to go. It's the best meal we've had so far, one of the cheapest, (not that that's got anything to do with anything) working at out £10 a head, not bad for a three course meal with wine, with the best service and the best wine we've had all week. We might well come back here tomorrow. Even if we don't have the car, we could take the bus in.

I have to park the car for the last time, down the street, out of sight of the front door of the apartment. Well, it's been a good little car. Thank you, car, for taking us around all over the island and not ditching us, especially when I think of some of the nasty roads I made you take.

My instructions are to put the key under the carpet at the driver's seat, with the car locked of course, so I have to hold the handle up as I close the door. It gives a metallic clang as it shuts, and at the same time I let go the handle. Which is the precise moment when I realise that that's my sunspecs and the sunscreen on the shelf, but even more vitally, my phone. It doesn't matter so much about the other two. By the looks of the weather, we're not going to be needing the first two anyway, but my phone is a different matter. What if my mistress wins the lottery this week and invites me to run away with her and takes my non-reply as a refusal? She'll assume that I don't want to be a kept man, living a life of luxury on a sun-drenched island. It's not so much missing the boat that worries me, but missing the cruise liner sailing off into the sunset. Never mind those dreams I seem to be having these days - this really is the stuff of nightmares.

Perhaps not all the doors are locked. I know it's a vain hope, but perhaps I've left one unlocked. I haven't. Oh well, I may catch the rep tomorrow when he comes to pick up the car and in case he comes early, I leave a message under the windscreen wiper telling him I've left some belongings in the car and where to find me. I hope nobody tries to break into it to get at my precious sun cream – or sails off into the sunset with my phone.

14. City of Culture

It never rains but it pours. The rain continues throughout the night and the overflow from the terrace above sounds like a toilet when the valve in the cistern is stuck in the open position, but the morning at least is dry, even if it is not sunny.

The adult Githeads are up but not the offspring so we have peace while we eat our breakfast unless you call it a duet for two smokers with coughs and smoke effects by one of these modern composers by someone like Stockhausen. On account of the rain, Iona has not slept well and is behind schedule and for once we are breakfasting together on the front patio like a normal married couple. I would and could have taken her to the bakery, as the car is still here. The smart thing to do would have been to have kept the key and given it to the rep when he arrived. But how was I to know that he still would not be here at 10? Of course, had I kept the key, he would have been here at 7 am, if not earlier.

What was that? It sounds like a volley of distant rifle fire, but it's coming from next door and although it has something to with air, it certainly didn't sound as if it had come from an air rifle, more like a Gatling gun. Wordlessly, Iona and I look at each other. We know what it was. I just hope there's no smell.

Now she sees my point about the Githeads. Call *me* intolerant! She snatches up her plate and her mug of coffee and stomps off inside. Thank God, she did not shout out some insulting remark over her shoulder and the wall like: *You're the biggest boor in Menorca* because I'm the one he

256

would have come out and bashed. She's quite capable of doing something like that. Anyway, what right has she to get so aerated about Mr Githead's flatulence (presumably he, not she, was the perpetrator) when his lovely wife doesn't seem to mind?

There's still no sign of the man coming for the car when we leave the apartment. I have had to replace the soggy mess that was last night's notice with one that says to please leave my belongings (whatever they are), at the bar. I just trust that that will be all right. I don't bother to ask. Actually, I'm too afraid that Prunella will be there and say no because she's in a bad mood with Phil and we'll be forced to hang about the apartment all day.

We are going to Ciutadella. Better than hanging about here and best to go before Miss Githead raises her lovely head from the pillow which is the signal to begin the "music". In fact, we *have* to go before the music starts because we are going to listen to the free concert in the Cathedral we had seen advertised the other day. It's not a day for hanging about the pool anyway.

We are the only people at the stop and in good time, which is just as well as the bus is early again, as it was the first time we took it. It leaves right away and doesn't make another single stop the entire length of the journey. There's not many people aboard – a Dutch couple with two small children, both wearing specs; a black youth; a plain girl on her own; and a nondescript couple. It's more like taking a taxi than a bus and we find ourselves deposited in the Plaça d'es Born at 11.01, exactly one minute after we were due to have departed. Since the bus journey normally takes thirty minutes, though only twenty on this occasion, this is a very interesting experience of time travel but unfortunately means we have time on our hands and since we have already explored the town, that means shopping - but only of the window variety, hopefully.

There's a leather shop near the Cathedral and we go in. Iona would like a leather jacket, well she'd like to have a look anyway but it doesn't look as if she's going to be able to do that very easily. I hate it when assistants come to do their job and assist you, when all you really want to do is browse and maybe buy something if the price is low enough. But instead of just being able to browse and look at the prices, the assistant insists she wants to show us various styles.

Iona doesn't like this hard sell either. She looks at some jackets in a casual sort of way and studies the prices, and so do I. Not too bad, considering. From what I remember, a lot cheaper than the leather outlet in Ferreries anyway which is meant to be a place where you get them at bargain prices.

"They're not real leather," Iona whispers to me.

"No! Are you sure?" If it looks like, smells like, and feels like leather, I'm rather inclined to believe that it *is* leather, but then, what do I know about clothes?

"Yes." Then, aloud to the assistant, Iona says, "No thank you. I don't like anything here."

The assistant looks thunder-struck. You'd think that no one had ever refused to buy something from her before, or she can't believe that Iona really doesn't like *anything* here, with more colours to choose from than Joseph's Technicolored coat and with more styles than a cross-country ramble. Then she looks angry and as if she is about to say something, but is biting her tongue. Perhaps she heard Iona's whisper and they really *are* leather after all. It's usually me who opens my mouth and puts my foot in it, but it's not a refreshing change – it's just as embarrassing and I'm ashamed to be associated with this solecism. Like a coward, I move away and start heading for the door, leaving Iona to wallow in her own embarrassment. It's been a bit of an epiphany. So this is what it feels like to be in the company of someone who embarrasses you by association. I see now why La-Belle-Dame-Sans-Merci gives me such a hard time when she gets me alone after I've committed some of my faux pas, like on our Italian Journey last year.

I never wanted to be in that stupid shop in the first place. It just goes to show you this is the sort of thing that happens when you get to a place early. I hate that and I hate shopping and I hope I won't hate the music in the Cathedral too much either. I've had quite enough "music" this holiday, thank you very much. If it had been up to me, I wouldn't have bothered, even if it is free as I am not much a fan of the organ, it has to be said.

It looks as if not a lot of other people have bothered either. As soon as the tide of worshippers exits, we enter, and rattle about the place like a couple of peas in a barrel, but gradually, some more people filter in. There must be about 30 of us sitting in the pews when a young man, dressed in jeans and a T shirt, appears in the organ loft, high up to our right. He takes a bow to no applause and disappears from sight.

Shortly afterwards, the whole cathedral reverberates to the sound of *Diferencias sobre las vacas by* someone called A de Cabezon. What a strange title for a piece of music! *Upon the differences between cows.* How do you get inspired by such a subject – on the differences between Friesans and Herefords! Unless it's cows in the metaphorical and pejorative sense of the expression and he's referring to ladies he knows, perhaps ex-girl friends who dumped him. I know it's called this because we were given a programme when we came in and there were four items on it and this is the first. I have never heard of this composer before, but I have heard of the other three: J S Bach, J Pachelbel and Anónim.

It's not that the cow piece is bad, I don't think, (I'm sure the organist will have milked it for all it is worth, getting each last note out of it) but when it ends, there is silence. I would call it an embarrassing silence. What's the protocol about applause in a Cathedral? Surely it's not sinful to applaud in a church is it – even if it is a Cathedral? Surely the organist deserves some recognition the way he is pulling out all the stops to entertain us. There he is up there, on his own, hidden from view, pedalling away like mad, his fingers thumping down on the keyboard and getting absolutely nowhere. What if he's wondering since there was no response that we think his playing was so bad, that we'd all tiptoed out? Actually, no need to tiptoe, the way the very rafters were dirling like Kirk Alloway's were the night Tam O' Shanter happened to ride by. I decide that when the Bach is finished, I am going to clap anyway. I'm already in trouble for other sins, so this venial one can't make much difference, surely, although as a good Calvinist, I know that going to church is A Very Serious Matter Indeed and to clap a performance in a church as if it were a place of entertainment could be A Very Bad Thing.

To my relief, I am not struck down dead and even better, after a few seconds' suspense, while nothing happens, others follow my example, hesitantly at first. It would have been just too embarrassing if no one else had clapped. A clap of thunder and lightning bolt of divine displeasure would have been preferable to all those people staring at me and thinking: *Who's that bampot?*

In my view, or should that be, to my ears, The Pachelbel is better by far than the other two. His *Canon* is one of the pieces I would take to my desert island, so I am already a fan but unfortunately this was not it. Perhaps the others agree with me, but I think that now that we know it's all right to clap, it's just we do so with more vigour. And at the end of the piece by anonymous, the organist pops into view again like a jack-in-the box, to receive our applause and disappears again as if conjured away, though I think it's fair to say, however good his playing was, I doubt if we were entirely spellbound. No encores then. Too faint an applause no doubt. And taking our queue, we thirty or so who had shared this common experience for those thirty minutes or so, disappear much less dramatically into the Plaça de la Catedral where we go our separate ways. It's unlikely we'll ever meet again for the rest of our lives, however long that may be, and if we did, it's unlikely we'd realise our lives had crossed for this brief interlude.

Well, that wasn't too bad after all. I heard another work from Pachelbel's canon and I certainly can't complain about the price. So what's next? Well, after the music, why not the art, since we seem to be on a cultural bent? The Museu del Pintor Torrent is just round the bend on the Carrer Sant Rafel, number 11. We know where it is because we'd passed it on our reconnaissance tour of Ciutadella, but being a Sunday, it was closed.

Torrent's a local lad, born in 1904 and only recently having gone to the great studio in the sky in 1990. He's known as the Menorcan Van Gogh and that's enough for me to want to visit his museum. I've been to where Van Gogh was living in St Rémy, Provence, where, amongst other things, he painted *Irises* and *Starry Night*. He shot himself not long after that. Hindsight is a wonderful thing but it's clear from *Starry Night* just how disturbed his mind was. If Torrent's work is like Vincent's, perhaps it's more than just his house which is round the bend.

What a great place Ciutadella is! This museum is free too. It's a nice little museum, the kind I like, which feels manageable, which doesn't overwhelm you so your feet don't feel like leaden weights before you even start. Here you can see the development of Torrent's work, from some pretty ordinary efforts when he was beginning, through to his last, Expressionist style. I would express it as hellish, but what do I know about art, except what I like and I like his Van Gogh period and think it's a pity he ever gave that up. Perhaps he was trying to find his own style. However, in view of his sobriquet, perhaps that's what the critics like best about him too and what he really should have stuck to.

Well, that was good. So good we even leave a donation. So what next? There can only be one place – the Museu Municipal, not far from here, in the Bastió de Sa Font, which also had been closed on Sunday when we were exploring the town. It's not free, but on the other hand, it's not exactly going to break the bank either.

I get my pouch out and rake in the section where I keep the coins.

"Two please," I say to the cashier as I do so, because I am man and can multi-task.

"Are you a pensioner?" she asks.

I give her a hard look. Is she serious? Do I really look that old? Well, actually I suppose I am a pensioner. Am I not drawing a meagre amount of teacher's pension every month? I expect she means am I an old age pensioner, but if I look like one, I may as well behave like one and take advantage of the benefits.

"Yes."

"Half price. And your wife? Is she a pensioner?"

What?!! Maybe because she is frowning at me saying I'm a pensioner when I'm not really in the strict sense of the word, Iona's brow has more lines than normal, but all the same, it's a bit of an insult as she has many years yet before that milestone and it's the first time she's been mistaken for a wrinkly, to the best of my knowledge. Nevertheless, it's true her hair, although it has not been exposed to a great deal of it lately, has been bleached by the sun and I hadn't got round to dyeing it before we left. That is another use I have, but I do it for myself as much as her, so I suppose it doesn't really count.

"No! No!" I hope I am keeping the surprise, not to say the amusement out of my voice. I find this notion of being married to a pensioner rather funny, even although I look like one myself apparently. Perhaps this lady has bad eyesight.

"No photography allowed. Please leave your cameras here."

"And can my wife take her stick in with her?"

"Excuse me?"

"It doesn't matter. Just a little joke."

If she were frowning before, she is my German wife, Frau Ning now. She doesn't have a great appreciation of my jokes these days, as you may have already noticed.

As we move from the foyer where there is a display of lurid porcelain, into the actual museum, I ask, "What did you make of that?"

"Huh!" We are not amused obviously, but whether the greater sinner is me for defrauding the museum or the cashier for the insult, I can't tell and deem it better not to pursue the matter.

It's a long, barrel-vaulted room, with a big square window in the ceiling the only source of natural light, augmented by a rail of electric lights round the sides and illuminated glass cases. This room contains Menorcan history in a nutshell, from the Talayotic period, through the Romans, to the Moors. It's the Talayotic period which interests me the most though. As well as seeing the pottery and hunting weapons, what I'd especially like to see is the collection of gruesome skulls which they are supposed to have here showing how these "primitive" people amazingly had trepanning skills, nearly three thousand years ago.

We have the place to ourselves as we move from case to case, leisurely looking at beakers and pots and jewellery. Then there is a noise behind us. It's a woman and her son, aged about eight, coming into the museum. Goodbye peace and quiet. It seems there are some people who just can't do anything quietly. You'd think that she was walking into her own house, that no one else was here whom she might possibly disturb, taking over the place as if she owned it.

God help us, it *is* educate your child week! In the most grating, piping west-coast Scottish accent, fond and doting mother proceeds to tell Jamie what he's to look at. She doesn't bother to lower her voice, so we get the benefit too: *This is a beaker from the earlier Talayotic period, Jamie, about 1400 BC and here's one from the later period, about 120 BC. Now can you see any differences?* Pregnant pause... *What does BC mean, mummy?*

Next a long, involved explanation of Christianity, then: *Can you see this spear, Jamie? What do you think they used that for?*

I swear if I got my hands on it, I'd show him an unconventional use for it - on his mother.

"Primary teacher," says Iona, only she whispers it. Why did she do that? Why didn't she speak up and say: *Look, it's the school holidays, all right? If you must insist on force-feeding your brat information, would you please do it QUIETLY?*

But of course, Iona and I and are too polite and well bred for that whilst the only breeding she's got is Jamie and his siblings - if any, God forbid! I'm sure she's right though. This painful woman has primary school teacher written all over her, if ever I heard one, so to speak. We may have given our children cultural holidays when they were young but I swear we never turned it into a public lecture.

And so she goes on until I'm fit to curse or scream, which is what I imagine these poor people did when they were having their frontal lobotomies without anaesthetic. I have found the case with the skulls. I don't think they look gruesome at all, just skulls with holes in them – the round, ragged holes where the surgeon cut through the bone to reach the brain. Amazing! I wonder why they needed them, but I know some people who could do with them today - and not very far away either.

Well, apart from that irritating woman, that was pretty interesting, helping to flesh out the lives of the people whose monuments and dwellings, or remains of them, we'd visited. Well, that's our culture over for today. I'm not much of a culture vulture but I reckon I've picked the bones clean of what Ciutadella has to offer in the way of music, art and archaeology. And talking of food, now that we've provided food for the mind, but what about proper food?

Since we liked the *Café Balear* so much, perhaps we'll go there again tonight, but this time we'll have to come by bus of course, but we may be lucky again and the bus could in fact be our own personal taxi at public transport prices. We check the menu out and would you believe it – the *menú del día* is different! And yes, we think we could just about manage to find something to eat on it! What a place! Ciutadella suits me all right, right down to the ground! It's either free to get into places or they give you a discount because they take pity on how old you look, and in the evening you can get a slap up meal for less than £10 and they keep changing the menu just in case there is nothing to suit you the evening before. Wonderful! I wonder if they give discounts for pensioners at the *Café Balear*?

My sunny outlook is mirrored by the weather. Suddenly the sun has appeared and the grey and black skies are giving way to the much more preferable colour of blue. What's gone wrong? Are the gods having a day off or are they merely picking on some other poor mortal? Without the car, I was wondering how we would put in the livelong day, but now we can lounge by the pool whilst I work on my tan. Good news for me, but not so good for Iona who just goes red. I've been the driver but now my duty's done and now the car is back, well at least not being used by us any more. I've done what I set out to do, raise my appreciation of Menorcan culture - now it's time to get some rays, charge up my batteries with warm sunshine which will hopefully see me through the dismal Scottish winter.

But first I need to buy some stamps. The main post office is on the Plaça d'es Born. It's a barn of a place, like a railway station, with counters the whole length and not very busy, fortunately. Does it matter which one we go to? Oh well, we'll soon find out. I pick number four as I think it is my lucky number and present myself before the middle-aged man with the glasses behind the plate glass.

He blinks at me owlishly.

"Ticket."

What does he mean – ticket? This isn't the railway station is it?

"No, I'd like six stamps please for Europe and three for the United States."

He shakes his head.

"Ticket."

His English is not very extensive obviously or maybe he's just naturally phlegmatic. No reason why he should be able to speak at least schoolboy English when he's working in the main post office in the second city of this tourist paradise for the British. Every reason why I should have at least learned the Spanish for *stamp,* but I haven't.

"No, no. Not ticket. Stamp for postcards." I wish I had brought them with me so I could show him. Instead I have to mime licking a stamp, though Spanish stamps seem to be self-adhesive these days, before pressing it down on an imaginary postcard with my thumb.

He looks at me through the glass, darkly, and sighs heavily. He's plainly exasperated. Thank God there's not a big queue behind us. He levers himself up from his chair and indicates something beyond the glass, to my left.

"Ticket." He repeats again. I am beginning to feel as if I am in a Pinter play.

I strain to see what he's pointing at, but just then someone comes along and takes a ticket from a dispenser, like they do at the delicatessen counter in some supermarkets.

"Ah! Ticket!"

He nods and smiles at me: *At last you've got it, you moron.*

I rip the ticket out of the dispenser. 24. Can that really be all the customers they've had today? A light flashes above the desk where I had just been standing. That's the ticket! We're in business at last. I give him the precious ticket. He takes it wordlessly and sells me my stamps. What a palaver! Why couldn't he have served me just the same without it? It's not as if there was a queue for God's sake! Sometimes I just can't see the logic in certain things.

It's not far from the post office to the bus stop. We study the bus timetable. Can you credit it, the last bus is at 8:30! What's the logic in that? That's even worse than in Rome last year when the last bus was at 9, at the height of summer! Well, that's the *Café Balear* out then. We could get a bus in, but what's the point when we'd have to get a taxi back, probably for the price of a meal at least? Typical! You find the best restaurant in Menorca and then you can't go to it. I'm glad to see that my luck hasn't changed entirely. I was beginning to get worried about that.

It's amazing how you remember people when you've totally forgotten about them until you happen to see them again. The Dutch family with the kids wearing glasses are catching the same bus back as us and I even remember the non descript couple, perhaps memorable for their very ordinariness, and a British family – a man with anchors on his forearms, like Popeye; his wife, also with some sort of tattoo on her shoulder; their two kids, not yet with tattoos and the two grandparents, a silver-haired man in a singlet and his equally silver-haired wife with a perm and Hapsburg jaw. Imagine coming on holiday *en famille* like that and doing everything together apparently.

It's amazing how people's ideas of having a good holiday differ. I don't suppose there's much you can do about taking your wife on holiday or the kids, (though we soon cured ours of going on holiday with us, just as soon as they were old enough to go away on their own) but I would draw the line at taking her mother and father with me. I tried that once – or rather it was forced upon me. My mother-in-law came with Iona and me on holiday once. Actually, it was our honeymoon. No, I'm not kidding, it really was! Well, actually, she came after the second week and I suppose we did feel like seeing people again by then anyway. That's when the honeymoon period of our marriage ended I suppose.

Back at the apartment, after a brief detour at the Spar, primarily in order to purchase a bottle in which to decant the Drambuie, (I didn't feel much in the mood for it last night – besides, the drinks police was out in force, forcing me to not have any) but also to pick up something for lunch. Incredibly, the car is exactly where I left it. Oh well, that's good – I might catch the rep yet and retrieve my possessions. It looks like I'm going to need the sunglasses and the specs anyway. Of course that's why the sun is shining. I don't suppose anybody realises it, but it's thanks to me, this change in the weather for the better.

Amazingly and mercifully, although the Githeads are at home, there is no "music". Perhaps Miss Githead is having a siesta or perhaps they have run out of batteries. If that is the case, please God that all Menorca has run out of them too and we will have silence, not "music" wherever they go. Or even better, the infernal machine has been worn out. Whatever the reason, it means that we can sit out at the much more pleasant front in the sunshine, though because of the trees, it is dappled and not likely to do much for my tan. Just as long as the sun does not go in before I get round to the pool, which, knowing my luck, is quite likely to happen.

Although I can't see them, my nice neighbour on the left is in conversation with my not so nice neighbour on the right. I can't help but overhear. Mr Nice Neighbour is saying that on his travels yesterday, he saw a car which had skidded into a wall because of the rain. Don't I know it! It's my chance to butt in and make friendly overtures, but I keep my head down and don't say anything.

Mr Githead asks him how much he paid for his car, which just goes to show you that there is some good in everybody and everybody has their use, even Mr Githead. This is the kind of question I'd like to have asked myself, only I haven't got the brass neck, or I haven't had the opportunity to work the conversation round to it. €112 plus €8 for the extra insurance, a day presumably.

It's good to hear he paid more than me, especially with the extra insurance, but then he had a day more and by the looks of it, I could have had another day for free too, but of course, I couldn't possibly have predicted that.

The orange-flavoured cake Iona bought for our sweet is rather dry (probably past its sell-by date) but I helpfully suggest that if we were to douse it in Cointreau, it would be much improved. And indeed, after a liberal application of the orange nectar, this proves to be the case. I am just amazed that Iona agreed to such a measure. Well, not the measure I poured in exactly, I mean the idea in principle.

"I think I'll have a Soberano with my coffee," I say a little later, by way of testing the waters and to my further wonderment, La-Belle-Dame-Sans-Merci makes no demur. *Curiouser and curiouser,* as Alice said. The sun is nowhere near over the yardarm yet. It's not like Iona to let me start drinking at this time of the day, but mine not to reason why. I don't even have to trot out the reason I'd prepared if I'd been asked why – to leave room for expansion in the lemonade bottle. Maybe that's why they call it Soberano so wives think it is not very alcoholic. It might fool some, but not mine, not for an instant. I can only put it down to she's just acting rather strangely and, given what they say about women's logic, that's the most logical answer I can come up with.

By the time the coffee and brandy is finished, there is still no sign of the man coming for the car. We could have been to the Líthica and God knows where else besides if I hadn't locked the key in the car. Iona says she'll stay and come along later, so I go off to the pool at last, sans sun cream, sans sunspecs, sans anything but a towel and a book. The sun is still shining and there is a pile of hay blocking our front door though as I have been busy making some by having seconds of the pudding, though I am not normally a sweet person, and my drink pouring skills seem indeed to be failing, for, just as the gin in the hip flask on the plane came out with a sudden glug, so too did the Soberano. It's not my fault. For some reason the Spanish insist on putting some stupid plastic gizmo in the neck of bottles of alcohol and it either doesn't come out at all, or comes out in a dribble, or unfortunately, in my case, with a sudden rush, so you find you've got a treble before you realise it and turn the flow off. I have a terrible time with these bottles. I suppose I need more practice.

It's remarkably quiet at the pool. We had met Ghetto Blaster Woman going the other way as we came back from the Spar, so I wasn't expecting to see her and The Wild Bunch and right enough, they're not here and the Githeads of course are still at the apartment. I was hoping however, to see the maid and possibly Phil to see how the romance was going but it would have been too much to have hoped to have caught them again, especially in this public area. Perhaps they have run away together, or he's helping her to make the beds somewhere.

In due course, along comes Iona. I can tell that she's not in a good mood from the way she throws her book and towel on the sunbed. It can hardly be me she's mad at unless it's a sin of omission, though of course, I did omit to extract the sun cream from the car. And it's certainly not because of my proximity to any nubile young ladies, for they are not here either. No, it's not me but the Githeads who are the source of the displeasure.

"They've started up their bloody "music" and they're smoking and coughing their lungs up and now they're complaining about the smell and they've lit stinky candles to try to get rid of it."

Probably they got that idea from next door on our other side.

"Maybe she should tell her husband to stop it!" I say, jokingly, remembering his trumpet voluntary this morning.

It's true, the smell had seemed to go away but it *was* back again this morning and though I hadn't noticed it at lunchtime, it could easily have come back, especially if it weren't so strong, so weak is my sense of smell. Then, in sudden panic, but trying to keep it out of my voice, I add, "You didn't say anything did you?"

She could easily have flared up. She's like that. She can endure something, apparently with infinite patience, not letting it trouble her, then something will happen, like the lighting of the stinky candles, and she'll suddenly snap and she doesn't care whom she takes on.

"No, but I bloody well felt like it!"

Phew! The atmosphere is strained enough between the Githeads and us already, a sort of silent hostility, a cold war, without it boiling over into actual unpleasantness. I can't imagine Mr Githead saying: *Oh, is my "music" upsetting you? Why didn't you say so before, old chap, I'd have been delighted to have switched it off.* Still, I bet she made a big production of slamming the door shut and stomping off down the path, which even the dim wit of the Githeads would have been able to read as signs she wasn't best pleased with them. I would have liked to have asked her if this is what she did, but I am too scared that she'll snap at me for asking too many bloody questions, so I say nothing.

"And the man still hasn't come for the car," she says, moving her sunbed so it's entirely in the shade.

Unbelievable! And it's still there when we go back 90 minutes later and the Githeads are still playing their "music" and no one else has complained, apparently. Thank God for the back door where we can't hear it and have our apéritifs in peace. The problem is we can't see the man coming for the car, so I have to get up and check from time to time, not trusting entirely to my note. Surely he must be coming soon! And of course, when I return to the back door, that would be the very moment when he comes and spirits it away. But no, each time I go back, it's still there.

It's a very pleasant evening now with just enough cloud to make a good sunset, so I suggest that on the way to the restaurant, we make a slight detour to the end of the street, where, I reckon, if we're lucky, we might be able to see it set over Mallorca.

And we can. Away in the distance, though I believe it's only about twenty-five miles, as the seagull flies, Mallorca looms indistinctly out of the sea, looking incredibly ragged and mountainous. Behind the jagged peaks, the sky is barred with deep red, yellow and orange. It would have been nice to have sat on a bench to watch it, but unfortunately, there's nowhere to sit here. In any case, what's this? It looks as if it's beginning to rain, just a few light droplets that I never would have noticed if I had not been wearing my short-sleeved shirt. I'd chosen this one because if I hadn't worn it tonight, it would have been a passenger, taking up space in the case. Now it is usefully turned into a sensitive rain detector.

It is my lucky day after all, for Iona, dressed entirely in black, as if prematurely mourning my access to heaven, must now return to the apartment and get her raincoat, a nice bright red and it's just as well that it started now before we were any further away. After all the rain we've had this week, it was an act of folly to leave without a brolly.

We've decided to go back to *Es Choix* where we had a good meal and the waiter was friendly, though not so friendly that he had dished out the free Glenmorangies. I hadn't particularly noticed before, but as we go in, there are some paintings to which I now devote some attention, in particular, one of a figure of a man, seen from the back. I recognise that style. I'd seen it before, today, at the Torrent museum. Unless I am much mistaken, this is an early Torrent, before he learned how to do faces apparently.

It's not the same waiter unfortunately, (not much chance of getting a free Glenmorangie for loyalty then) and as he brings the menu I ask: "Is that a Torrent, just as we came in?" And just in case he thinks the heavens have opened again, I add, "The painting of the back view of the peasant."

It's a bit hard to make out his English, but I gather that the waiter's girlfriend, (possibly the one we had when we here the first time?) is Torrent's grand daughter and on his decease, was allowed to pick any two of his paintings. Incredible! Imagine choosing this one, when she could have had one of the Van Gogh's! Even if she did pick one of those as her other choice, why on earth pick this faceless painting as nondescript as the couple on the bus and which looks like something I could have done? Naturally, I don't say this of course, but the waiter goes on to say (I think) that that is typical of Torrent's style, preferring to paint people from the back. Ah, yes. I see, like film directors who film actors from the back when they're not up to expressing the emotions in close up.

Still on the related matter of torrents, he tells us that there was no rain from April to September. Well there is now – with a vengeance, well not at the present moment, but how remarkable it should retain it all, just for release, to coincide with my visit. I call that very considerate. But when I consider how it was nearly responsible for us ending up in the ditch, but we didn't, I reckon it could have been a whole lot worse.

We end up having the fish again. There's a surprise! You would think there was nothing else to eat in Menorca. We've eaten nothing but fish this holiday, not that we're complaining about that, not like Marilyn Monroe whom, you felt, was a bit disgruntled when she announced, at the in-laws, at the Arthur Miller household in fact, on being served matzo balls again: *Isn't there any other part of a matzo you can eat?* I don't know which to me is the most astonishing: that she could, in all seriousness, have dropped a clanger of such outrageous proportions; or that our Marilyn had a wit greater than her dumb blonde image; or that she was married to Arthur Miller in the first place, which seems to me one of the most unlikely pairings you are ever likely to come across. But maybe people think that about Iona and me.

Anyway, the fish was entirely our choice. That means white wine again. Being the last night, the last evening, I choose the Nuviana 2004 for no particular reason other than it's not too expensive, but hopefully better than the *vino del casa*.

I watch as the waiter goes away to a cabinet and selects a bottle which he brings over for my inspection. He tilts it so I can read the label. Yes, that says Nuviana all right, but wait a minute, that date isn't 2004, it's 2001, isn't it? I haven't dedicated my life to drinking wine to know that this could make a crucial difference as far as price is concerned, never mind taste. I need to check it at closer hand.

"Can I have a look at that please?" I ask the waiter.

He looks puzzled but I am the customer and the customer is always right. Besides, there are not many of us and he must cling on to those he's got.

I thought so. 2001. It's 13% and it's warm. He must have got it out of the warm cabinet, especially for us.

"Very good, wine," says the waiter and then, after a slight pause, he adds, "Very expensive."

That puts it beyond any doubt. I would never have ordered *that*.

"I asked for the 2004," I point out.

His face falls. He has probably not sold one of these all year and realises he's not going to now either. Actually when I ordered it, I had just pointed to it. Maybe I had pointed to the 2001 by mistake. Thank God I had spotted the mistake in time. Imagine the shock I would have got when the bill came only to find that the wine cost more than the meal! It's enough to give you indigestion, even ruin your holiday. No wine, in my opinion, is worth that, though I know there are some people who pay even more than that for a bottle, more than a bottle of malt for God's sake! I'm glad I haven't got a palate for anything more expensive than £4 a bottle (reduced from £5 or £6 though) and I hope I never do. And I hate the mark-up on wine in restaurants, where £14 gets you a very mediocre bottle indeed. I'd really rather not have it. That's what I like about the continent – you can get a reasonable bottle for less than a king's ransom. I may be many things, but one thing I am not is a wine snob. Wine snobbery is a kind of daylight robbery in my book.

The waiter takes the wine, returns it to its cabinet and brings me the 2004. This one is nicely chilled. There you go, you see. The expensive one, not expected to be sold, is kept nice and warm, while this one is kept chilled. It tastes fine.

I'd like to try the other one, just for the sake of comparison, but I bet I couldn't tell the difference and if I did, I bet I wouldn't think it was worth the price difference.

He is just about to leave. "Could you light the candle please?" I ask.

I may not splash out on the wine, but I know how to make a splash in other ways. I may have been brought up in the boondocks of Banff, but I know how to create a romantic atmosphere with this our last evening, and Menorca yet to consummate. There are no people near us requiring spelling lessons this time, and even the din from Danny's Bar is muted. The omens look good. Then I drop my knife.

I'm not superstitious, at least not about the one that says that if you drop a knife on the floor, it means a death, but maybe I should. La-Belle-Dame-Sans-Merci gives me one of her Frau Ning looks. It's not because I dropped the knife, but what I said immediately afterwards that's the problem.

"Oooh...er!" I say, stooping to pick it up.

"Look, will you stop mocking my mother!"

It's true, I just have. That's what she says. She also says Lawks! And so do I. That's the worst of not having a good imagination, I have to copy other people's idiosyncrasies. I used to say defin*ate*ly and it took years to expunge it from my vocabulary. I have been saying *ooh...er* and *lawks* for some time now and it looks as if it's finally got on La-Belle-Dame-Sans-Merci's nerves. And, Oooh...er! I'm in trouble.

Actually, I think it's got less to do with insulting her mother and more to do with appearing an idiot, especially when I'm in her company. I remember the incident in the leather shop and instantly feel humble and the need to apologise.

"Sorry."

"You just don't realise you're doing it do you?"

"No," I have to admit contritely. What had started out as mere mockery of my mother-in-law, has now become an ingrained and automatic reaction to events which come as a sudden surprise or shock and are more likely than not to happen in the hearing of the general public. Mind you, she should be grateful, I suppose, that I don't say what I imagine Mr Githead says when he gets a sudden fright, like catching a glimpse of himself in a mirror. Just like I bet the lady next to me at the concert I was at was very glad that she was accustomed to using refined and restrained language, when the percussion, just in front of us, who up till now had been doing nothing, (probably because the conductor wasn't looking at them and they were taking the chance to do a bit of skiving) unexpectedly and very loudly, began to play. Quite involuntarily, she clutched her chest and shouted out: *Jeeso!* I jumped myself, and jumped again at her reaction, but managed to avoid saying Lawks! or fortunately, the name of the Lord, both of them, together, or even more fortunately, anything stronger. In vain the audience tried to control its mirth at her reaction and the percussionists bravely played on like the musicians on the *Titanic*, though their shoulders were heaving massively. After that, she kept her eye firmly on the percussionists, especially that lunatic with the drums. She wasn't going to let them do that to her again, especially *him* with that bloody big drum.

When we get back to the apartment, unbelievably, the car is *still* there. Annoying to think we could have used it and gone into Ciutadella and the *Café Balear.* Annoying also to find the Githeads still up and their "music" pumping out into what is now a warm, sticky evening. We keep our eyes down to avoid eye-contact and having to indulge in any platitudes such as: *Lovely evening now isn't it? (Or it would be if you weren't blasting our brains out with that infernal noise. But then you wouldn't know what that feels like, would you?)*

It'll have to be round the back again, for the *apérabeds*, but it doesn't really make much difference at this time of day. It's quiet round there and private and a lot more roomy. I get Iona a gin and go back in to get myself a Drambuie, but before I go out again, I strip down to my copulating rabbits boxer shorts.

"What do you think you are doing?" She sounds panicky as if I had every intention of consummating Menorca, right there and then on the patio.

"It's all right, nobody can see anything. And I'll keep the little button buttoned up so there are not any accidents. Besides, nobody comes round this way anyway."

She may not approve but it's nice and cool, to be underdressed like this, this humid evening and cool too to drink the wine of one's country in these warm climes. In fact, it is so ambient, I think I'll just have another.

"That's all you're having, right!" By the tone, there is no question that it is not a question but a suggestion that I disregard at my peril. "I'm tired and I want to get to bed soon."

Ah, yes, it's been a strenuous day. I don't know why she just doesn't come straight out with it and tell me what she really means is that she wants to add Menorca to her list of consummated places. I'm practically undressed for the part already. The things, apart from driving, one has to do when one is on holiday.

"Serpently, my love. Would you like me to freshen up your gin?" She's not a very fast drinker.

"No thanks."

If this has to be the last one, then let it be a big one but the trouble with Drambuie, unlike gin, is it looks as big as it is, whereas you can hide a pretty big gin with a little tonic.

"That's a big one."

"Oh, the drink!" I say in mock surprise after a moment. "I thought for a minute you meant my little button had come undone!" Naturally, I thought nothing of the kind, but I thought any sort of diversionary tactic advisable under the circumstances and she might even find it amusing.

"Don't be disgusting."

The sound of approaching footprints breaks what has been an uncomfortable silence. That's strange. What an odd occurrence! There is the click-click of women's stilettos and the slap-slap of flip-flops, by the sound of it, more than one. Who could it possibly be? We're not going to have long to find out. They are coming closer.

"Good evening."

" 'Evenin'."

It's the longest conversation I've ever had with her. Ghetto Blaster Woman, accompanied by The Wild Bunch. I would scarcely have recognised her, all dolled up like this, would never have guessed that she has what looks like an old fashioned toilet chain dangling from her navel. She's been out on the town, possibly celebrating her last night too or else out trying to trap a father-figure for her brats. Love me, love my brats. Some hope. Pity really, as in the fleeting glimpse of her, she looked quite attractive actually, with her war paint on.

"I'm going to bed," says Iona, a few minutes later, pushing her chair back. "Don't be long."

I suppose it is a bit boring for her sitting out here, too dark for her to do any sewing or reading and not drinking anything and the conversation is hardly scintillating. I suppose that's the good thing about having drinking as a hobby. You don't need to be able to see in the dark to do that.

The nightingales are in what Keats called *full-throated ease* but it's really just the cicadas rubbing their hind legs together in glee at another warm evening. I love that sound, I love being able to sit outside at 10 30 in the evening, just in my underpants. This is the last night. God knows when

I'll get the chance to do this again. I think I'll just have a tad more Drambuie, just to make sure that the remainder will fit into the lemonade bottle. The trick is going to be getting it. Through the bedroom is the only way in and out of the apartment from the back door.

As soon as I hear the bathroom door close, I am like a greyhound out of trap and tiptoeing through the bedroom to the kitchen as quiet as a mouse. It's the work of a moment to tip some Drambuie into my glass. Now I need some ice. I turn round to face the fridge and – bloody hell, there's La-Belle-Dame-Sans-Merci. How did she do it? How did she know? Was it just instinct or does she just know me too well?

"Uh, huh! I knew it! I saw you pass the door."

So that's how she did it, and I didn't even have to ask. The bathroom door has a dirty big panel of opaque glass in it. You can't see anything but a vague shape but as I twinkle toed past, it was enough. Had she been a moment or two earlier I could have pretended that I was just tidying up, but she had probably timed it to catch me red-handed.

"I was just making sure that the Drambuie would fit in the lemonade bottle."

"I'm sure you were and I'm sure it will, considering how much you've got in your glass."

I look at it as if stunned that so much could have ended up in the glass after such a small pour. I am opening my mouth to say something but whatever it is I haven't time to say it to her face for she's already turned on her heel, leaving me speechless and feeling like a heel. I pour the Drambuie back into the bottle, an action a lot harder than pouring it down my throat. It may have a wide neck but it's not nearly as big as my mouth.

When I get to the bedroom, there is a white shape in the other bed, like a piece of furniture in storage, or more sinisterly, like a corpse under a sheet. I am accustomed to Iona having her head sandwiched between a couple of pillows – it's just the funny way she sleeps, but for her to be completely under the sheet (it's all we need in this temperature) is a new departure. The body language from the body under the sheet could not be more obvious: *You definitely do not have the body even if it is the last night.* I have really overstepped the mark tonight. She must be really, really mad at me. But then, spookily, from beneath the sheet, comes a voice.

"There's a mosquito in here."

So I am not the only form of low life in this apartment. And to think I had thought it was from me she was hiding! It's funny how you can get a hold of some really ridiculous ideas sometimes.

15. Bean or Boomerang?

Because of the mosquito, it's been a sleepless night again, although I had another dream. It wasn't a very good dream, like the one I had before, though it was a bit embarrassing. I was having a party for some reason (does one need a reason, even in a dream?) and for another obscure reason, had invited one of my two Alistair friends, but not the other, and guess what, at the party, the other Alistair turned up! It took me by surprise, I can tell you and I don't know how he found out about it, but it was very kind of the other Alistair to turn up since the other hadn't, especially when he hadn't been invited. But that's dreams for you. They don't make any sense.

At least the Githeads weren't playing furniture removers on manoeuvres but it would have been something else to listen to apart from that irritating buzz from the mosquito. In the end I got fed up of trying to kill it or swishing it away and just let her bite me, then I could get some peace. Apparently the ones who bite you are females. I read that somewhere. I'm not sure if there are any parallels with the human condition or not from which we might derive some lessons, but I'm sure it must be of some significance, somehow. It was after she had her tea on me that I must have slept. I just hope there was so much alcohol in my blood that she took off and immediately crashed and broke her bloody neck.

If I had a dream in the Martin Luther King sense of the word, it would be death to all female mosquitoes - not that I'm sexist. I don't know why Noah bothered with them.

I expect he knew God was watching and counting, and frightened not to obey. But why He ever invented them in the first place was the real mistake in my opinion and if you are reading this, I hope you don't mind me saying so, your Lordship.

I have a theory about this in fact. The only logical explanation is the illogical, which leads me to believe You are a woman, aren't You? (Go on, admit it!) And I'll tell You another thing – You were born in Italy weren't You? Ah, hah! You're amazed I've blown Your cover, aren't You! I didn't spend that holiday in Italy and not learn a thing or two about logic – or rather the lack of it. I know You would not like this spread abroad, because I'm sure, You have Your reasons – but perhaps, if it's not too much trouble, Your Lordship, if You could just confirm that I am right and reveal it to me in a dream – I've been having quite a few of them lately and I believe this is the way You normally communicate with people.

After breakfast, it's time to pack. Funnily enough, the Drambuie fits into the lemonade bottle with room to spare. Isn't it amazing how it evaporates during the night! In my haste and shame, I had forgotten to cork the bottle last night. In the distilleries it's a well-known phenomenon which they call the angel's share, but I have a devil of a job explaining this to La-Belle-Dame-Sans-Merci, who seems to think I drank it.

My suitcase weighs a ton. It's all those plastic bottles. If in the original glass containers, I would certainly have been over my weight allowance. In fact, I'm not so sure that I'm not, even now. But that's a good sign – it shows that I have saved an enormous amount of money by importing all this booze, enough hopefully, until I come back to Spanish shores again. This is why Iona doesn't want us to have a pied-à-terre in Spain. She's quite firm about that and she's probably right - I'd be afloat at these prices most of the time and my feet hardly ever on terra firma, or that is to say, without it going round and round, like Glasgow on a Saturday night as the music hall song puts it so eloquently.

As all package travellers know, the worst thing about being on holiday is having to be out of your apartment by 10 am and spending the rest of the day homeless. Not too bad in our case, since we are being picked up at 1pm. Not like the time in Corfu when we went with a well-known airline, one of the leaders in the field whom I'd love to expose, but daren't although it's absolutely true, that we were chucked out of our apartment at 10, all toilets locked because the proprietrix was attending a meeting somewhere (though I don't see what that had to do with anything) and our luggage was deposited *outside* a *kafenion,* at a crossroads, for twelve hours from noon to midnight.

I met the company rep by accident in the town and voiced my criticism of these arrangements. It wasn't good timing. It was the end of the second last week of the season and he was chatting up a female colleague and made no secret in displaying his resentment at the interruption. I suppose it was his lunch hour after all, and he's got only one week left to make an impression, get her telephone number back home, and here he's being interrupted by some stupid, ignorant customer wanting to know what he'll say when he's asked at the airport: *Did you pack your luggage yourself? Has your luggage been out of your sight? Could anyone have interfered with your luggage?*

But I've got his number all right. I know exactly what he's thinking: *Look sod off you little runt. Can't you see I'm trying to get into this lady's knickers? (Not that I haven't already of course, as I am so dazzlingly handsome and irresistible but I want to get this onto a more permanent basis). And are you totally thick or what? Since you seem to be incapable of working out the answers for yourself, the answers to the questions are: Yes. No. And No. Now sod off!*

Well, after that and a letter of complaint which got me nowhere, we never took another tour with that company, though we did, and still do, take to the air with them. After all, if they offer the cheapest flight to my preferred destination, I'm not one to cut my nose off to spite my face. And they don't know I have my hip flask with me, so that's another one in the eye for them.

But this is different, we're all packed up, our luggage trundled up to the little cubby hole which serves as reception and which is closed as usual but it's within eyesight (if you sit out on the pavement) and in any case, it's hardly the hub and epicentre of Menorca, so like me, it's very unlikely to be interfered with.

Having done that, we can stay in our apartment, go to the pabby as often as we like, lie down on the beds if we feel inclined to recline. In short, although we are officially out, we might just as well be in residence, just like, although we had officially given the car back, there it is *still* there with the keys and my sunglasses and specs - and my phone inside.

I could go and open my case, get out my swimming trunks (wherever they are) and sit by the pool and get all hot and sweaty and have a shower again and put my swimming trunks back and get dressed again, but it seems a lot of effort for just a couple of hours in the sun, though God knows I should take advantage of it while I still can. Instead, I decide I may as well walk round to the car rental office. I could phone but after my last experience, I'm not confident about using this Spanish phone and anyway it will take up some time and avoid the Githeads. It must be close to Miss Githead's getting up time. Besides, time is running out if I want to get my phone back – and I do.

I leave Iona to her cross-stitching in the shade and set off on the sunny side of the street. I take the route past the bakery which she takes each morning whilst I lie in my scratcher, or as my father used to put it, annoyed by my terminal laziness, where I *lay stinking in my bed all day*. No heavenly scent of fresh bread at this time of course, but the scent intermittently wafting from the orange hedges as the breeze rises and falls is just as delicious. It's actually quite a way. I'm lucky she volunteers for this service every morning. She may be the drinks police whom some rude people call the pigs, but I am grateful that she does bring home the baking.

It's quite a bit further to the car rental office and when I get there, I can't believe it. It's definitely the right place, next to the Chinese restaurant with the big red lanterns and the name is still over the door but the big plate-glass window is whitewashed from side to side, from top to bottom and someone has written in the wet paint, with his finger, in mirror writing: **OFFICE CLOSED. PHONE** followed by a string of numbers.

I look at it dumfounded. I had not expected this. How can I possibly remember all these numbers? I'm hopeless with figures at the best of times. I stare at it and try to commit it to memory, then close my eyes and repeat it to myself. Was that right? I'm not sure and even if it were right, would it still be right by the time I got back to the apartment? I know. I have a solution. Are there any dates, any birthdays that I could use as a mnemonic?

Right, let's see. The Battle of Bannockburn less three, my age plus six, the year I was born back to front, the number of offers I've had from nymphomaniacs multiplied by three (I'll remember that. 00 is still zero, no matter how often you multiply it). It's no good. I'll never remember even how I am to remember the mnemonic. I need to write it down but I have neither pen nor paper.

Hmm! There's a wastepaper bin nearby. You never know and beggars can't be choosers. Doesn't look like there's anything in there and I don't want to put my hand in particularly and rummage about. Mind you, there might be a bit of white space on this leaflet. Let me see. It's for an "escort" agency. Not much white space, but I could write the number down on the acres of brown flesh which these comely ladies are displaying - if only I had a pen.

I look up and see some people coming down the street. Have they seen me taking this out of the bin, I wonder? The only thing to do is brass it. I stand in the middle of the pavement so they can't avoid me.

"Erm…excuse me. But you wouldn't happen to have a pen would you?"

It's a man and a woman, in their forties, I should say, with a teenage son. They look at me in much the sort of way you would if someone you had seen raking in a bin just a minute ago, is now engaging you in conversation.

"It's just you see, the car rental office is closed and I need to phone that number because I've left my sunglasses in the car and the sun cream, not to mention my phone and we're leaving in a couple of hours and I've locked the keys in the car and …"

I let my voice trail off. Too much information and I've been flapping my hand with the escort agency flyer in it. They've probably noticed what it is and think I'm a patron - or intending to be one. Or maybe the father is thinking: *Where did you get that?* -even if all he wants to do is look at the pictures.

"Wie bitte?"

Ah, so they are German. Out of all the people, in the entire world, it would have to be Germans that came strolling along, walking into my net. Mind you, it would have been worse if they had been Spanish of which there is a statistically higher chance. I have never been exposed to any Spanish apart from the accented English of Spanish waiters.

I hope that's why the Germans were looking at me in that strange way. I haven't done German since school. What the hell is the German for *pen*? The mind is racing, galloping back the decades. It's no good. It just won't come. *Stilo*? No. That's French. Wait a minute, though, isn't that *plume*? *La plume de ma tante* and all that. But that's probably the sort of pen you get from a goose. A *stilo* is probably the sort of pen you get in France when you borrow it to sign your name at the check-out or something and absently happen to put it in your pocket.

Then, out of nowhere, the word *Bleistift* comes into my head. That's a pencil isn't it? But maybe it isn't? What if it's a swearword or an insult? Why, oh why, did I not pay more attention in German classes? A simple word like *pen*. You would think that I could remember that for God's sake, wouldn't you? But I can't, as it happens.

"Bitte, haben Sie ein Bleistift?" I make a writing sign, just in case. *"Ich brauche das Nummer,"* and I indicate the digits scrawled with someone's digit on the whitewashed pane. That's exactly what the writer of the moving finger probably thought when he writ that back to front before he moved on... But to where? Where is the office now? Have they gone bankrupt, unable to compete with their giant international competitors? I knew I should have waited to hire a car when I arrived.

And when it comes to sex in German, I haven't a clue, though I believe they make a number of films about it apparently, but I don't know anything about that of course. And if I did, La-Belle-Dame-Sans-Merci would kill me. No, I just have no idea what sex a pencil is, or a number either. All I can remember is that a girl is neuter. And I don't know what the feminists make of that either which just goes to show you that when it comes to German, the extent of my ignorance is overwhelming, but there is one thing I do know: it's no wonder English caught on and German didn't as a lingua franca. It's even worse than French which at least has the sense to realise that two sexes are quite enough in anybody's language.

Whatever I've said, it seems to be good enough, or maybe it was the sign language which did it. The lady is raking in her handbag and produces a pen. I don't think it is a *Bleistift* but it *is* a writer. Self-consciously, as they watch, I copy the numbers across the bulging brown bosoms and although my figures are quite large, her figure is bigger and there is room to spare at least for a couple more.

"Danke schön." I hand back the pen. It would be a bit much to steal it, whatever it's called, even although it's only a cheap biro.

"Bitte."

Back at the apartment, I tell Iona what's happened, though I skip the bit about the figures and head off to the bar to phone. Just my luck, Prunella is there at the bar with her cigarette, her nicotine-stained fingers and, as usual, her pages of figures. They're a bit different from the figures I've got in front of me which I smooth out, trying as best as I can, not to let her see, but there is a stiffening of her body which I catch out of the corner of my eye which tells me she *has* seen and is not impressed. My God, I realise with horror, she thinks I'm actually phoning *them.* She won't be able to see the actual number I'm phoning. I feel myself blushing.

The phone makes an intermittent buzzing sort of noise. Is that it ringing or is it an engaged tone? No point in asking Prunella, she'll not help me make an extra-marital appointment. She's got quite enough of that in her own marriage, thank you very much. If it is the ringing tone, please God let the person who answers speak English.

"Hola!"

"Is that the Carefree Car Rental Company?" This loudly, for the benefit of Prunella, who is apparently engrossed in her addition, but she probably thinks it is a prearranged code.

The voice at the other end testifies that it is and I explain my problem. They say that they'll send someone for the car.

"Well, thank you but can you send someone soon? I'm leaving in a couple of hours. I don't have much time."

Prunella looks up and meets my eye. She doesn't look amused, but then she doesn't look the type who, if you were to come up behind her and give her a tickle, (as if you ever would) that she'd be tickled in the slightest. She looks down at her papers again, hurriedly. I feel myself blushing more than ever, my face, already red, turning an even deeper shade. Prunella obviously thinks I am desperate. (If only I were sending an e-mail instead of phoning since, unlike the woman in the restaurant, I do know how to spell *soon*).

The company say they'll send someone just as soon as they can. I don't even know where they are coming from, unlike Prunella who thinks she definitely knows where *I* am coming from, so I've no idea how long that is going to take.

I go back to the apartment. The Githeads' "music" is in full flow but of course I expected no less. Iona is inside out of the blast, though you can still hear the thump thump thump through the wall. She looks cross but that's maybe just because of the cross stitching she's doing.

There's no sun out the back and I resent having to miss it because of the Githeads so I tell her I am going to take my book (one of those Iona had the foresight to buy at the airport as I had finished mine yesterday) and sit in the sun on the suitcase at reception. There are no other cases there. If anyone else had been leaving, their cases would have been here by now. It looks like the Githeads are staying on and in all probability will have new neighbours next week.

Lucky them. They are probably on the plane now, imagining a week of peace and relaxation and what have they got waiting for them when they get here after spending all that money on their great escape - The Githeads - and, by the looks of the sky, which is starting to cloud over - rain. Yes, the gods will be having a jolly good laugh at their expense I have no doubt.

Oh God, here comes Mr Githead waddling up the street like an obese duck with haemorrhoids. He's probably on his way to the bar to buy more cancer sticks. If I stay here he's going to have to pass within a foot of me. I'll have to purposefully ignore him or acknowledge his presence. What to do? I suppose it would be a way of expressing my distaste of him and his execrable taste in music to stare fixedly ahead and pretend I am deaf to the flap flap of his duck feet in the flip flops and blind to his bowlegs, biceps and beer belly but as I sit there with him approaching inexorably closer by the second, I realise I just haven't the courage or the bad breeding to do that. Equally, I think the words would stick in my craw if I had to as much as give him a Cro-Magnon grunt in acknowledgement. How am I going to handle this dilemma?

Of course, that's the answer. La-Belle-Dame-Sans-Merci quite often says that I am sitting on my brains as, if I have any at all, that is where she supposes I keep them. It's hardly the most comfortable of seats this suitcase, especially with that handle sticking up as an awkward protuberance, necessary for its purpose as a suitcase, but definitely a design fault as far as a seat is concerned. I get up, as if I hadn't seen him, and presenting my back, and bending over slightly, rub both cheeks of my bum as if restoring the circulation but which I hope he will interpret as a salutation, from one arse to another.

I wander off in a leisurely fashion to the pool area. As I thought, he has gone into the bar. I stop and gaze at the pool, apparently fascinated by the play of light on the water, but really watching him out of the corner of my eye. I can't see what he's doing precisely at the moment but shortly he leaves and he appears to have a small package in his beefy paw. I was right then.

I wait a couple of minutes, judging it safe to go. I can't hang about here looking like an idiot, looking at nothing. Not that there is anyone to see me apart from whoever is serving in the bar. Since I got up, the pale blue sky has turned a darker shade of grey and no one has come to the pool area. Mr Githead is waddling down the street as if he'd wet his pants, unaware that I am looking at his retreating back. I hope I have seen the back of him now.

"It looks like reindeer," I report to Iona, apropos of nothing since there's been no evidence of any such animals, but which she rightly hears as a meteorological forecast, and I go back to my post.

Each time a car comes along the street, which is seldom, my spirits rise, hope fills my heart, only to be dashed as it turns out not to be the one I want. I know what I'm looking for. It'll probably be like the car I was picked up in and there will be two people in it and there will be a sticker with *Carefree Car Rentals* on the back window.

With an hour to go, there is still no sign of the car rep, and I am beginning to give up all hope. I realise that it was a mistake to have said we were leaving in a couple of hours. I wish I had been more specific and, if I'd had any sense, I should have put the time forward by an hour as an insurance policy. I'm not going back in to phone again though. But then, just when I think all hope is lost, here comes a car, very slowly, as if it is looking for something - except there's only one person in it. Just the gods playing their little joke again, raising your hopes, just to dash them.

But wait a minute! He's stopping behind my car! I jog down the street towards it. It's him all right. He opens my car for me and I retrieve my belongings. I thank him and he locks the car again and drives off. It's only taken a couple of minutes and he's probably come all the way from Ciutadella. Well, that was nice of him to go to the trouble. I mean, if he hadn't, what could I have done about it? I wonder how long the car will stay there. Another day perhaps? No wonder they have had to close the office.

Before I go back to tell Iona he has been and gone, I check my messages. None. Missed calls. None. Well, there's a surprise. The chances of winning the lottery are pretty small. And if you do win a prize, it's usually peanuts. The only boat I'm likely to be sailing off into the sunset in, is Ghetto Blaster Woman's inflatable.

The rain, which had been promising, finally plummets down. Imagine the Githeads' neighbours, very possibly off this very plane. Fifteen degrees and chucking it down. Just like Scotland. They may be disappointed at that but they don't yet know the trouble ahead, that they have yet to face the "music". Still, you never know – maybe they'll have their own ghetto blaster and will blast their own brand back. The battle of the ghetto blasters. I'd love to see that, just as long as I didn't hear it.

As it turns out, that *was* the last I saw of the Githeads, for our bus turns up on time and whisks us away to the airport, the only ones to leave, to exchange the rain of Spain for the delightful climate of Scotland. It wouldn't surprise me if it *had* been good weather whilst we were away. And it wouldn't surprise me if it *stopped* being good, just as we get back.

Incredible! As we queue up to check in, there's the non-descript couple we saw on the bus! And there's the woman with the buck teeth. I've never thought of her since I saw her a week ago and the instant I see her, I recognise her. Some people have unforgettable faces I presume. I wonder if some people, seeing me now are saying: *There's that red-faced git who looks like George W Bush. Thank God I managed to put him to the back of my mind all this week.*

It's always an anxious moment, the weigh-in, when I've been to Spain. No point in having saved all that money just to pay excess baggage. I'd take the bottle out first and drink it before I'd let that happen, except La-Belle-Dame-Sans-Merci would never let that happen. She's quite right of course, I don't want to be like my cousin who has been refused permission to board the aircraft on account of being under the influence. But it's all right; as usual I have judged it just about right. Just as well I was not allowed to go back to the *hipermercado* then.

It's not always a good idea, once you've bought something to check the price somewhere else. It can of course give you a sense of elation, but on the other hand, it can throw you into the depths of depression and Iona never does it. But hanging about airports is one of the most tedious activities devised by man and when they tell you it is, say a four hour flight to somewhere, they should also say plus two hours before the flight and at least half an hour to get out the other end, even if all your luggage does make it back with you. So shopping in the duty free is one way at least of relieving the tedium. It is a relief to see that in the duty free, the price of the booze is a lot dearer than I paid, but I felt certain it would be, otherwise I would never have imported so much.

Ah, here's the perfume department. I'm only following Iona. I've no interest in such things. God knows, I've no sense of smell, or at least a very poor one as I have already said, and in any case, I regard fragrances for men as well, something only certain types of men have a need for. I don't see the point in putting obstacles in the way of your natural pheromones, though God knows mine didn't seem to have much effect when I was young. Maybe I should have tried a bit of the *Old Spice* after all, but it's a bit late for that now.

Iona likes such things though, perfumes I mean, not pheromones. She's got her favourites, but I have no idea what they are. In fact, there's only one perfume I've heard of – Chanel No 5. There is a tester. I wonder what it smells like? I have a good spray on my wrists. I don't know much about perfume, but I know that's where ladies put it as well as behind their ears which is where I normally park my *Bleistift*. In the great lottery of plane seat distribution, if I am unlucky enough to be next to the man with sweaty oxters who was next to Iona on the way out, I could always have a sniff of my wrists. Actually it will be Iona who will be sitting next to him as I need to sit near the window to do my trick with the hip flask. It would be a rather cruel joke of the gods to make Iona sit next to him on the way back as well as on the way out, but that's just the sort of thing which appeals to the gods' sense of humour.

Curiously enough, the man in question is just ahead of us in the queue for boarding. That doesn't mean anything. I try to read his ticket which is poking out of the passport he's got in his hand but I can't make it out. Anyway, we'll find out our fate soon enough.

We're in luck. He's sitting down in a seat a few rows before us. We carry on, looking for row 16. I don't believe it! Here it is, the seat by the emergency exit, the one with the extra legroom. Sometimes you have to pay extra to sit in these seats. Incredible! I must remember this for the next time I fly. No flies on me. A Boeing 737–400. Row 16. Just as long as the girl in the check-in desk knows what kind of plane we're using and you're allowed to make requests like that. But she's more likely to look at me and think: *You've got short legs, squirt. I only give those seats out to tall, dark and handsome men, along with my telephone number. And you fail on all three accounts.* It's true. I do have short thighs and am built for aeroplane and theatre seats. I'm not saying anything about the other two, though I used to be dark.

When we are airborne, I do what I always, do – slip my feet out of my shoes. Because of the extra room, I can see the reason for our good fortune. I am wearing odd socks. If you do that all day and don't notice, it's a sign of good luck. So far it's been working very well. I just hope that now I've noticed, my luck doesn't run out. More space means more chance of detection of using the hip flask and because we are in the middle, we are last to be served with the drinks – in our case, ice and tonic which Iona thinks is a peculiar sort of drink to order. She might be right but I'm sure the airline is used to odd people, not to mention people who wear odd socks.

That's what the woman across the aisle seems to think as she catches me slipping my hip flask from my camcorder bag and pouring out generous libations. Her eyes are popping out of her head. I give her what I hope is a charming smile which says: *Please don't tell.*

In fact, an instant later, I no longer think that her popping eyes are anything to do with me but due more to some sort of thyroid trouble. The expression *eyes like organ stops* never seemed more apposite and I cannot stop stealing a look at her from time to time. She reminds me of the bulging trout eyes on the tower of the Museu Diocesà in Ciutadella. There is something magnetic about it, something hypnotic, which although you don't really want to look, draws your gaze back inexorably, just to make sure that what you have seen really is true.

It reminds me of years ago, when, at mealtimes, in spite of my best efforts, my eyes kept wandering back to my old landlady, in both senses of the word, Miss Thomas, with a face that only a mother could love, to where she sat in a corner next to the fire with a tray upon her lap, legs apart to balance the tray apparently, rather than any attempt to seduce her lodgers, showing an expanse of pink bloomers and at which I just *had* to look as if the brain were in denial at anything so awful and the eyes were saying: *No, no! It's true. Look! Look!*

It wasn't all that was awful about living with Miss Thomas. So was the food and so was the hygiene. Whilst she sat unseductively in her corner, we lodgers sat at the table, eating our meat loaf lovingly kneaded by her own fair hand with black fingernails (in mourning presumably for her inability to attract a suitor) and stale bread and the half tomato which had been dropped on the floor and according to Sod's Law, fell cut side down, thus having, amongst other things, added ingredients such as cat hairs and coal dust, but predominantly hairs freely donated by Peter, the aged, half-blind and fully-flatulent Boxer. Peter actually belonged next door but was a refugee escaping the boisterousness of the three sub-teenagers in his actual household and whom Miss Thomas periodically used to kick as he lay, incontinently and completely unaware of his offence in front of the fire, at the same time spraying him with a mouthful of meatloaf as she spluttered incomprehensibly: *Stop that, Peter! Ye dirty beast!*

At least the aeroplane food has to be better than that and it's bound to be a whole lot more hygienic. I wonder what can it be! Being last to be served, I can let my imagination soar and let my gastric juices anticipate the delights in store. Ah, chicken nugget. Delicious! And a slice of Edam cheese! Too much happiness! And what's this hiding underneath? A lettuce leaf smothered in mayonnaise and Dijon mustard! Stop! Stop! This is too much! Munch! Munch! It's finished after two mouthfuls.

"Hey, where did you come from? Buzz off!" I am speaking to a fly which is trying to share my meal when it can see perfectly well that there's not enough for one, let alone two. I flap at it and it goes off to dine somewhere else. Is it a Spanish flea hitching a lift to visit relations or a Scottish fly returning from its holiday like me? Maybe it's a frequent flier and gets a discount.

Well, the meal has been cleared away and there's an hour and a quarter to landing. It's been cloudy all the way and according to the pilot, the weather in Edinburgh is even worse than that we left in Menorca. Well, there's a surprise! At least the rain there was warmer.

But I'm not going to let that get me down. I've had a good holiday in spite of the weather and the Githeads but despite that, I don't know if we will ever come back. Menorca is shaped like a boomerang after all, so I might, but it's also shaped like a kidney bean and I've been there and done it, seen the island I mean. And there are so many other places in the world I have never been to, so many other places which have to be consummated.

I'm not going to let it worry me. I close my eyes. I don't expect I'll sleep, but I may nod off and, you never know, the answer may be revealed in a dream.

Born in Banff, Scotland (the original and best) David Addison was schooled at the academies of Fordyce and Banff. Having enjoyed his education there so much, he took a teaching degree from Aberdeen University and subsequently taught English in various locations in Scotland as well as Montana and Poland before retiring early from the chalk face to indulge his unquenchable thirst for travel (and his wife would say, for Cabernet Sauvignon and malt whisky) and thus ensuring that his two children, or at least the two he admits to, are left without a bean.

This is his second book about places he has been.

Printed in the United States
45598LVS00001B

9 781420 896152